# Ferry to Tasmania

## A Short History

*Australian Trader* (Devonport Maritime Museum)

# Ferry to Tasmania

## A Short History

Peter Plowman

ROSENBERG

First published in Australia in 2004
by Rosenberg Publishing Pty Ltd
PO Box 6125, Dural Delivery Centre NSW 2158
Phone: 612 9654 1502  Fax: 612 9654 1338
Email: rosenbergpub@smartchat.net.au
Web: www.rosenbergpub.com.au

*The National Library of Australia Cataloguing-in-Publication*

Plowman, Peter.
Ferry to Tasmania : a short history.

Bibliography.
Includes index.
ISBN 1 877058 27 0.

1. Ferries - Tasmania - History.  2. Shipping - Tasmania - History.  I. Title.

386.609946

Cover design by Highway 51 using the author's photograph of *Empress of Australia* on the front
and a photograph of *Spirit of Tasmania* by Lindsay Rex on the back

Set in 11 on 13 pt Warnock Pro
Printed in China through Colorcraft Ltd., Hong Kong

# Contents

Currie

Lady Barron

Stanley
SMITHTON
Port Latta
BURNIE
DEVONPORT
Port Sorell
GEORGE TOWN
Beauty Point
Bridport
ST HELENS
LAUNCESTON

STRAHAN

Swansea
Coles Bay

Triabunna

HOBART
Margate
HUONVILLE
Kettering
Port Huon
Cygnet
Dunalley
Nubeena
Port Arthur

Port Davey
Dover
Southport

Map of Tasmania courtesy of Geodata Services, Information and Land Services, Department of Primary Industries Water & Environment, Tasmania

# Introduction

On the afternoon of Tuesday, 10 February 2004, I boarded the ferry *Spirit of Tasmania III* in Sydney for the overnight voyage to Tasmania. For me this was the culmination of a long delayed ambition to visit the island state, and also travel there by ship from Sydney.

Back in the 1970s, I had the good fortune to join the Sydney office Union Travel, the travel section of the Union Steam Ship Company of New Zealand, who were the agents for the Australian National Line ferry service to Tasmania, then being operated from Sydney by *Empress* of Australia. My first job in Union Travel was in the 'Searoad' section, dealing directly with the Tasmanian service. Part of my job involved going to Mort Bay whenever the *Empress of Australia* arrived or departed, and I got to know the ship very well. Several times I hoped to make the journey to Tasmania and back on that ship, but each time circumstances prevented me going—either unavailability of accommodation, or in a couple of instances, strikes causing the departure to be cancelled. In the end I never made that trip to Tasmania, and I moved on to other sections of the travel industry, but I never lost my interest in the ferry services and the ships that operated them. The island state of Tasmania has been dependent on ferry services to the mainland almost from the time of first settlement. Over the past two centuries the size and number of the vessels employed on this vital trade has steadily increased. Over the years there have been a few books published that provided some information on these ships, most notably the two written by Tasmanian maritime historian G W Cox, and published about twenty

across Bass Strait right up to the introduction of *Spirit of Tasmania III* in January 2004 on the service from Sydney to Devonport.

It is truly quite amazing how much the ferry service from the mainland to Tasmania has developed in a very short time. As recently as 2002 there was but one ferry making three return trips a week between Melbourne and Devonport, capable of transporting some 8,500 passenger a week. Today there is a nightly departure from both these terminals, providing up to 2,000 passages a day. During peak periods, when both night and day trips are being operated, almost 20,000 passengers can be carried in each direction in a week. In addition, the recently opened service between Sydney and Devonport has the capacity to transport about 150,000 passengers in each direction during the year.

There is no doubt that Tasmania is now enjoying the best ferry service ever provided between the mainland and the island state. I have had the pleasure of travelling on both the ferry service from Sydney to Devonport on *Spirit of Tasmania III*, and from Devonport to Melbourne on *Spirit of Tasmania II.*

The comfort and facilities provided by these ships is almost what one would expect on a modern luxury cruise liner, and for many passengers, including myself, the voyages are too short to really enjoy everything these ships have to offer. When this is added to the many delights to be enjoyed while touring around Tasmania, the entire experience is truly unforgettable.

I hope that you, the reader, will find the ships described in the following pages as fascinating and full of life as any great ocean liner. To all those who have been generous in their assistance in the preparation of this book I extend my grateful thanks. Wherever possible I have tried to credit the actual photographer regardless of the source of the picture, but if there are any that have been overlooked I express my regrets. Any errors, omissions or misinterpretations included in the manuscript are entirely my own responsibility.

# Acknowledgments

A book of this nature cannot be written without the assistance of others, and in this case I have been greatly helped by several people. When I decided to start writing this book, I already had a considerable amount of historical material and a reasonable collection of photographs, much of which had been provided to me over a number of years by Robert W Brookes, of Launceston.

Although I never met him, Bobby Brookes and I developed a regular correspondence some years ago, and he provided me with a huge amount of information about his experiences when working on the Nairana in the 1930s and during the war. I have incorporated all this into the text, which has added an extra dimension to the story, especially the personal reminiscences, and some quite amusing tales. Bobby Brookes also sent me many photographs from his personal collection, which he allowed me to retain.

Sadly, Bobby Brookes passed away several years ago, and thus will not be able to see the culmination of my efforts, but I hope he would have been pleased with the result.

It will be noted that the photographs in this book have come from a wide variety of sources, all of whom were more than generous in allowing me access to their own photos and their collections. In this regard I must express my warmest thanks to my friend Lindsay Rex, without whose generous assistance I would not have been able to compile this book. Grateful thanks are also due to Rex Cox, who provided me free access to the extensive photo collection held by the Maritime Museum of Tasmania, in Hobart, as well as some of his own pictures. In addition, both Lindsay and Rex were very helpful in answering my numerous Emails seeking further information on various ships as I strove to complete the book by the end of May 2004.

Warm thanks are also extended to Bob Vellacott at the Devonport Maritime Museum, who also gave me free access to their extensive photo collection, and allowed me to copy the pictures I wanted to use in this book. I was also given similar assistance by Glen Stuart at the Polly Woodside Museum in Melbourne. While in Hobart I was taken on a very interesting tour of the International Catamarans building yard by Justin Merrigan, who also kindly provided me with considerable background material and several excellent photographs of the various Incat fast catamarans to have operated across Bass Strait.

Special thanks are extended to Jim Freeman, Dale Crisp, Ian Edwards, Andrew Mackinnon, David Robinson, John Beckhaus, Rhod Jones and Mel Gatehouse, whose photographs have added greatly to the book, particularly in the final chapter.

## Chapter One

# Early Days

In 1642, the Dutch explorer *Abel Tasman* discovered the island now known as Tasmania, which he named Van Diemen's Land, after Anthony Van Diemen, who was the Dutch Governor General at Batavia and had commissioned Tasman's voyage.

For the next thirty years no more vessels visited the island, but between 1772 and 1803 it was explored by ten different parties. The most notable of these were those led by du Fresne, a Frenchman, in 1772, Captain James Cook in 1777, and Captain William Bligh, of *Mutiny on the Bounty* fame, who visited the island twice, in 1788 and 1792, while serving a term as Governor of New South Wales.

All these expeditions explored only the east coast of Van Diemen's Land. Matthew *Flinders* and George Bass were the first people to actually sail around Van Diemen's Land, in 1798, and prove it was an island. However, no attempts had been made to establish any settlements by the end of the eighteenth century.

In 1802 another Frenchman, Nicholas Baudin, explored the island, prompting rumours that the French intended to establish a settlement. As a result, the Secretary of State for the Colonies, Lord Hobart, ordered an expedition be sent to establish British control of the island.

In 1803 naval Lieutenant John Bowen was sent from Sydney by Governor King to establish a Van Diemen's Land Settlement at Risdon Cove, near the mouth of the Derwent River. In 1804 this was moved to the opposite shore at Sullivan's Cove, where there was a better water supply. The new settlement was then named Hobart Town.

Various attempts were made to establish settlements in the north of the island, and in 1806 a suitable site was found, but it was not until 1808 that it was named Launceston, after the birthplace of Governor King, and the island was included in the colony of New South Wales. Almost from the start the original name of Van Diemen's Land was discontinued in favour of Tasmania, though this was unofficial.

The settlements in and around Hobart Town and Launceston flourished, but the rest of the island remained uninhabited. In 1815, Captain James Kelly discovered Macquarie Harbour on the west coast of the island, and it was here in 1822 that the first of Tasmania's infamous penal colonies was founded for the most hardened convict offenders transported from Britain and the mainland colonies.

In 1825 Maria Island, located north of Hobart Town, also became a penal colony, and in 1830 the most famous penal colony in Australia, Port Arthur, was built seventy miles north of Hobart Town. Macquarie Harbour ceased to be a penal colony in 1833, and Maria Island closed in 1851, but Port Arthur remained in use until 1877.

Hobart Town soon became a thriving centre, second only to Sydney in importance, while Launceston also grew steadily in size and importance. In 1825 the island colony separated from New South Wales. By then a trade had developed between the mainland and the island. The regular traders were sailing vessels, mostly sloops and schooners in the range of 12 to 25 metres in length. They carried everything from sheep, cattle and timber to shell grit and general cargo, as well as passengers and the mail, and provided the sole link between the colonies.

During the 1830s and 1840s the passenger, mail and higher grade cargo services were taken over by steamers, and the sailing craft became known as the 'mosquito fleet', handling timber and other low-value bulk goods across Bass Strait

It was not until 1831 that the first steamship appeared in Australian waters, this being the paddleboat *Surprise*, built at the shipyard of Mr Millard at Neutral Bay, in Sydney Harbour. Launched on 31 March 1831, the *Surprise* was fitted with a 10-horsepower high-pressure steam engine, and made its first trip on Sydney Harbour on Wednesday, 25 May 1831. The *Surprise* was then placed on a ferry service along the Parramatta River between Sydney Town and Parramatta.

Unfortunately, the *Surprise* was not a success, in spite of taking only three and a half hours for the journey. In January 1832, the *Surprise* was sold to Dr Alexander Thomson, of Hobart Town, but made the journey south under sail. In Tasmania, the paddlewheels were fitted again, and the vessel was mainly used on a ferry service between Hobart and Kangaroo Point, with some trips up to New Norfolk.

Dr Thomson had previously placed an order in Britain for a paddlesteamer to be built and sent out to Hobart in sections, arriving on the barque *Platina* early in 1832. The vessel was assembled on the banks of the Derwent, being named *Governor Arthur*, after the Governor of the colony at that time. She joined the *Surprise* in ferry services on the Derwent, but in October 1833 *Governor Arthur* was sent on a voyage to Launceston, becoming the first steam vessel to make a voyage along the coast of Tasmania.

Encountering heavy seas, *Governor Arthur* was forced to put into Georges River, now St Helens, for repairs. When the voyage continued, the vessel steamed past the mouth of the Tamar and reached Circular Head before the mistake was realised, and she turned back to reach Launceston. Here the vessel was offered for sale, but no buyer was forthcoming.

Dr Thomson was able to secure a cargo of flour, and returned to Hobart with the vessel. Shortly afterwards, Dr Thomson sold both his vessels, and in 1835 took his family to the mainland to live in a new settlement on the banks of the River Yarra, which became Melbourne. He later moved to Geelong, and became its first mayor in 1850.

It was in 1835 that John Batman led a group of Tasmanian settlers on a voyage to the mainland, seeking land on the shores of Port Phillip Bay on which to settle. Batman 'purchased' 600,000 acres of land from the local Aborigines for some trade goods, but when he returned with the Port Phillip Association, comprising business and professional men and pastoralists, they found another group camped on the site, under the leadership of John Fawkner. Then Sir Richard Bourke, Governor of New South Wales, refused to accept the land purchase Batman had organised. In 1836 Bourke sent Captain William Lonsdale to Port Phillip as resident magistrate, with surveyors to map out streets and subdivisions. Governor Bourke himself visited the site in 1837, at which time the settlement was named Melbourne, after the then Prime Minister of Great Britain.

In June 1837 came the first attempt to establish a steam connection between the mainland and Tasmania, using the paddlesteamer *James Watt*. Built in Britain in 1824, it had operated a service between Glasgow and Dublin until being sold in 1836 to two Sydney merchants, Joseph Grose and Thomas Street.

*James Watt* arrived in Sydney from Britain on 18 February 1837, only the second steamer to make the long voyage, and was then placed in service between Sydney and the Hunter River. However, in April 1837 it was advertised in Sydney that the *James Watt* would make a voyage to Hobart via Twofold Bay, the one-way fare being £10 in a private cabin, £7 in the fore-cabin, and for anyone prepared to remain on deck throughout the voyage, £5. This voyage departed Sydney on 4 May, but proved to be unsuccessful, and was not repeated.

On 19 June 1837, the *James Watt* departed Sydney bound for Launceston via Twofold Bay. The arrival of the vessel on 26 June was reported in the Launceston *Advertiser* three days later:

The steam-ship *James Watt* arrived in this port on Monday, having put in to Twofold Bay for coals. Seven days were occupied (this stoppage included) in the passage from Sydney. She leaves this morning for Port Phillip, returning hither in about a week or ten days, when she will start again for Sydney. We most heartily wish the proprietor success.

The *James Watt* anchored in Hobson's Bay on 4 July 1837, becoming the first steamer to enter Port Phillip Bay, and carrying the first mail to be delivered to Melbourne by a steamship. *James Watt* made a second voyage from Sydney to Launceston in September 1837, and returned for a third time in January 1838, but that was the final visit to Tasmania by this vessel.

It was another three years before a second steamer, *Clonmel*, was placed in service from the mainland to Tasmania. Built at Birkenhead in Britain in 1836, *Clonmel* was a wooden-hulled paddlesteamer of 598 gross tons designed to operate across the Irish Sea between Liverpool and Waterford. Purchased in 1840 by prominent Sydney businessman Edye Manning, the vessel made the long voyage to Australia under sail, taking nearly five months, ending in Sydney on 5 October 1840.

*Clonmel*, which provided comfortable cabin accommodation for thirty-six passengers, was by far the largest and finest steamer yet seen in Australian waters, being 47.5 metres (156 feet) long, and powered by a 220-horsepower engine. Manning had bought the *Clonmel* to operate a service from Sydney to Melbourne and Launceston. The fare charged was quite high, from Sydney to Melbourne being 15 guineas (£15 15s 0d) for a cabin, or £9 for deck accommodation.

The first voyage on the coastal trade by *Clonmel* did not depart Sydney until early in December, and after calling at Melbourne, the vessel arrived in Launceston for the first time on 10 December. The return trip went first to Melbourne, then back to Sydney.

In the last days of December, *Clonmel* departed Sydney on her second voyage, but had the misfortune to run aground on a reef close to Wilson's Promontory at 3 am on 2 January 1841, and was totally wrecked. The seventy-five passengers and crew were able to reach the shore safely, and had to camp under sails recovered from the wreck, while the ship's whaleboat set off for Melbourne.

It took three days sailing to reach Port Phillip Heads, and then they had to cross Port Phillip Bay to Williamstown, where the alarm was raised. Ten days after being wrecked the stranded survivors were rescued by a sailing ship. In this way a brave attempt to establish an intercolonial trade came to a premature end.

For some months there was no further steam ship service between the mainland and Van Diemen's Land. Then in October 1841 the paddlesteamer *Corsair* was chartered by the Port Phillip Steam Navigation Co. *Corsair* had been built in Scotland in 1827, and originally operated in the Irish Sea.

On 10 October 1840 the vessel departed London for Australia, arriving in Adelaide on 3 March 1841. It was announced that *Corsair* was to be placed on a service from Adelaide to Melbourne and Launceston, but this never commenced, and the vessel remained idle until it began operating between Melbourne and Launceston.

The distance between the two ports was 277 miles, and it took the vessel up to two days to make a one-way voyage, depending on wind and sea conditions. Unfortunately, *Corsair*'s engine gave a lot of trouble, and the vessel was often under repair, losing £1,000 for her operators in the first four months of the service.

At that time, the large paddlesteamer *Seahorse*, owned by Benjamin Boyd, was running a service between Sydney and Melbourne, and the timetables of the two ships were arranged to provide a through connection to Launceston. However, in April 1842 the *Seahorse* was taken out of service, and in August 1842 the *Corsair* was taken off the Launceston trade, and placed in service between Melbourne and Geelong. At the same time the *Seahorse* returned to service, but now operated from Sydney to Melbourne, then George Town, at the mouth of the Tamar River, and Hobart.

*Seahorse* was a 439 gross ton wooden-hulled steamer built at Dundee in Scotland in 1837 for service on the Irish Sea. Purchased by Benjamin Boyd in 1840, *Seahorse* left London under sail on 3 October, carrying passengers and cargo as well as some livestock. Off Cape Finisterre *Seahorse* came into collision with another vessel, and had to put in to Lisbon for repairs. She finally arrived on 17 April 1841 in Hobart Town, where she was refitted as a steamer, then set off for Sydney, making the trip in five days, arriving on 1 June. The next day the *Sydney Morning Herald* reported:

We have to congratulate the colonists on the safe

arrival yesterday of the *Seahorse*, intended as a packet between Sydney and the southern ports. She is a very fine boat. She has two engines of 125 hp each. Her cabins are very roomy and her accommodation altogether of a very superior description. She makes up 70 beds. At Hobart Town she made a trial trip ... and we are informed that she ran 50 miles in four hours and ten minutes which is at the rate of 12 miles per hour. She left Hobart Town at 2 o'clock on Tuesday and was five days on her passage, but for the first day or two she had very heavy headwinds to encounter. Her destination is not yet fully determined upon, but we presume it will be to Port Phillip.

On 27 July 1841 *Seahorse* departed Sydney to commence a fortnightly service to Melbourne. The vessel's owner, Benjamin Boyd, had established his own settlement at Twofold Bay, on the opposite side to Eden, which he called Boydtown. *Seahorse* stopped there to take on coal, which extended the time of the journey between Sydney and Melbourne.

Due to rising costs and lack of patronage *Seahorse* was withdrawn from the trade in April 1842, and laid up in Sydney. When *Seahorse* returned to service in August 1842, it became the first steamship in Australia to be awarded a mail contract, receiving £200 for every trip between Sydney and Melbourne on which mail was carried. The vessel then continued on to George Town and Hobart Town, and for a short while was the only steamer operating between Sydney, Melbourne and Tasmania, though still stopping at Boydtown for coal. Then, in September 1842 a competitor appeared. This was another paddlesteamer, *Shamrock*, owned by the Hunter's River Steam Navigation Co.

*Shamrock* was the last of three new steamers

built in Britain for the Hunter's River company, and had arrived in Sydney for the first time on 18 October 1841. *Shamrock* was smaller than the *Seahorse* at 294 gross tons, but had an iron hull. After a short spell on the Hunter River trade, *Shamrock* began operating between Sydney and *Moreton* Bay in Queensland, early in 1842, but later the same year was transferred to a service from Sydney to Melbourne and Launceston, providing serious competition to the *Seahorse*. The *Seahorse* was a veritable coal-eater, while the *Shamrock* was an economical vessel to run, enabling her owners to charge a much lower fare, just £10, but the competition between the two was intense.

Although the *Seahorse* was the only steamer offering a service from Hobart to the mainland, it was not well patronised, and really was too large and expensive to operate to be a commercial success. Of one departure by the *Seahorse* from Hobart Town in October 1842, the Hobart *Town Courier* reported that the vessel had left carrying 'stock and sundries; 3 women, 3 children, 1 man'.

On the afternoon of 4 June 1843, the *Seahorse* left George Town bound for Melbourne, under the control of a licensed pilot for the trip down the Tamar River. As night fell the vessel dropped anchor in George Town Cove, where it remained overnight.

At seven the following morning, just past high tide, the crew raised the anchor, but before the *Seahorse* could get under way, it was caught in a current and ran aground on a sandbar. As the tide dropped the vessel heeled over to one side, but at the next high tide it was able to float free.

*Seahorse* continued its voyage, arriving back in Sydney on 11 June, but the hull had been badly strained in the grounding, and it was also claimed by Benjamin Boyd that the engines had been damaged trying to refloat the ship when it first went aground. However, the *Sydney Morning Herald* shipping report stated that 'having taken the mud in the Launceston River'. the vessel had 'completed the passage in 73 hours (allowing for her detention in Twofold Bay)'.

The damage to the hull could have been repaired, but at that time there was no dry dock in Australia large enough to hold the *Seahorse*. The closest facility of suitable size was at Calcutta in India, and the engine could only be repaired in Britain.

The paddle steamer *Shamrock* began running to Tasmania in 1852 (Author's collection)

As a result the vessel was withdrawn from service and laid up in Sydney, while Benjamin Boyd claimed it on insurance as a total loss. The insurers refused to pay on the claim, and lengthy court litigation followed, which Boyd lost.

The *Seahorse* remained idle in Sydney for six years until, in November 1849, the vessel was sold at auction for just £850 and converted into a wharf hulk. By that time all of Benjamin Boyd's enterprises in Australia had failed. These included the Royal Bank of Australia and his Boydtown settlement and whaling station on Twofold Bay. Boyd fled Australia, and was eventually killed by natives in the Pacific, though the exact circumstances are unknown.

Following the withdrawal of the *Seahorse*, the *Shamrock* was the only steamer engaged in the trade from Sydney and Melbourne to Van Diemen's Land, and operated to a fortnightly schedule for many years.

On 30 June 1851 the Hunter's River Steam Navigation Co was wound up, and the next day the Australasian Steam Navigation Co, usually known as the ASN, came into existence, taking over the business of the former company as a going concern. This change had no immediate effect on the ships formerly operated by the Hunter's River company, which all remained on their trades.

In January 1852 the *Shamrock* completed her hundredth round voyage between Sydney and Melbourne, and an article in the Melbourne *Argus* of 7 June 1852 stated 'this favourite steamer, now advancing in years, still keeps up her character for regularity and despatch. Her last trip to Sydney occupied only 72 hours, during five of which she was detained at Twofold Bay'.

The region around Melbourne was known as the Port Phillip District of New South Wales until 1851, when it became the separate colony of Victoria. The same year the discovery of gold in Victoria started a gold rush to Melbourne, which resulted in an upsurge in the number of steamers operating to Melbourne. The ASN placed several of their ships on services to Melbourne, including the *Shamrock*, which remained on the service from Sydney to Melbourne and Launceston until 1857, when she was sold to overseas buyers.

In May 1851 what can be described as the first regular steam ferry service across Bass Strait was commenced between Melbourne and Launceston. It was operated by the *City of Melbourne*, owned by Melbourne shipowner George Ward Cole, and built on the banks of the Yarra River at the shipyard of J Kruse, a German immigrant.

This wooden-hulled, 138 gross ton vessel was the first propeller-driven vessel to be built in Australia, but was underpowered. The *Launceston Examiner* of 4 June 1851 commented on the new type of propulsion thus:

> In smooth water the screw has less power than the paddle, but in rough weather it has a decided advantage, as, unlike the paddle, it is always under water and the vessel is not encumbered with those unseemly appendages – the paddle boxes.

On 6 August 1852 the *City of Melbourne* encountered strong winds while on a voyage from Launceston to Melbourne, and the captain realised his ship was being blown in a westerly direction out of Bass Strait instead of crossing it. To save his ship and the lives of those on board, the vessel had to be run ashore on King Island to prevent it being swept out into the open ocean.

The *City of Melbourne* was subsequently refloated and brought back to Melbourne for repairs, but never returned to the Bass Strait trade. As a result of this misfortune to the *City of Melbourne*, the ASN took the opportunity to place another of their vessels, *Yarra Yarra*, on a regular service between Melbourne and Launceston.

*Yarra Yarra* was an iron-hulled paddlesteamer of 337 gross tons, built in Scotland, being completed in October 1851. The vessel arrived in Sydney on its delivery voyage on 5 April 1852, and entered service between Sydney and Melbourne.

In September 1852 *Yarra Yarra* was transferred to the Bass Strait trade. It was much larger than *City of Melbourne*, with accommodation for 51 cabin class and 350 steerage passengers.

Also during 1852 another new ASN steamer, the *Waratah*, was placed in service between Melbourne and Hobart. Built in Britain, the 256 gross ton *Waratah* arrived in Sydney for the first time on 26 March 1852, and was almost immediately placed on the trade to Hobart, but was withdrawn from the route before the end of that year.

However, 1852 was most notable for the establishment of two new shipping companies in Tasmania, of which one would soon come to dominate the Bass Strait trade.

## Chapter Two

# Two Tasmanian Shipping Companies

From the time of the establishment of the first settlement in 1804 until 1825, Van Diemen's Land was part of New South Wales, but it was not until 1856 that the island was granted self-government.

At the same time the name of the island was officially changed to Tasmania, which had been in general use for many years, islanders referring to themselves as Tasmanians long before the name was officially adopted.

Over the years there had been a number of attempts at forming shipping companies in Tasmania, but none had succeeded. One of the first was the Derwent Steam Navigation Company, which operated ferries across the river at Hobart, while the Tamar Steam Navigation Co was very short-lived, as was the grandiosely titled Hobart Town, Launceston and Port Phillip Company.

The first Tasmanian Steam Navigation Company was formed in Hobart in 1845, and operated a variety of services from Hobart to the mainland. A combination of unsuitable ships and poor management compelled the company to cease trading in 1851.

The merchants of Hobart realised the value of having their own steamer service, and during 1852 several public meetings were held with regard to forming a steamship company. The first steps to form a new company were taken following a meeting in the Hobart Town Hall in June 1852, when £10 shares were offered to the public and capital of £18,620 was raised. A second firm to be called the Tasmanian Steam Navigation Company was subsequently formed in 1852, Mr Charles Toby being appointed general manager at an annual salary £500.

*Tasmania* was the first ship to be built for the TSN (Maritime Museum of Tasmania)

Immediately a ship was ordered to be built in England, which was named *Tasmania*, and arrived in Hobart on 3 February 1853. The new vessel could carry about 200 passengers, had an iron hull and was propeller driven.

At 526 gross tons *Tasmania* was the largest vessel registered in Hobart, and also one of the largest vessels operating on the Australian coastal trades at that time. The *Tasmania* began operating a regular service between Hobart and Melbourne. The new Tasmanian Steam Navigation Co quickly gained a strong hold on the trade to the mainland with their propeller-driven steamer, with the result that the major competitor, the ASN paddler *Waratah*, was soon withdrawn from the Hobart route. For many years after, almost all services from the mainland to Hobart were operated by ships owned by the Tasmanian Steam Navigation Co.

The merchants of Hobart were not the only ones keen to have a company of their own, as similar sentiments were found in Launceston. In October 1852, following a public meeting there, the Launceston Steam Navigation Company was formed. A local merchant who also owned several vessels, George Fisher, was appointed manager of the new concern. They soon arranged the purchase of a brand-new vessel, the *Clarence*, for £40,000. The *Clarence* was a 346 gross ton iron-hulled paddlesteamer that had been built at Birkenhead in England in 1851, and was intended to operate a service between Sydney and Grafton, on the Clarence River. However, soon after the vessel arrived in Sydney on its delivery voyage it was inspected by representatives of the Launceston company, and sold to them for a large profit, reportedly twice the amount she had cost to build.

*Clarence* was placed in service between Launceston and Melbourne, in direct competition with the larger *Yarra Yarra* of the ASN, although the *Clarence* offered better passenger facilities. From the start there was an intense rivalry between the two paddlers, commencing with the very first voyage made by the *Clarence*. The ASN scheduled *Yarra Yarra* to depart Melbourne at the same time as its new rival, and the pair crossed Port Phillip Bay together, and stayed close all the way across Bass Strait. Next morning they entered the Tamar River at 7 am, and began a race up the river for the honour of being the first to berth.

Reaching a section of the river where the channel narrowed, *Clarence* closed in on *Yarra Yarra*, which made no effort to get out of the way, and a collision resulted, with the Clarence losing its figurehead while *Yarra Yarra* lost a portion of her bulwarks.

Although this type of incident was not repeated, the two ships competed fiercely for the available trade until April 1854, when the *Yarra Yarra* was withdrawn from the Bass Strait trade. This also ended the ASN interest in the Tasmanian trade in general.

The Launceston company also had some competition from three smaller propeller steamships operated by private owners, the *Pirate, Queen of the Netherlands* and *Lady Bird*. By 1854 the first two had been driven off the route, while the *Lady Bird* was purchased by the Launceston Steam Navigation Co, which in 1853 had added two propeller driven steamers to their fleet, the *Royal Shepherd* and *Black Swan*.

Both vessels were built in Scotland, by different builders and to different designs. *Royal Shepherd* was the larger of the two at 331 gross tons, as against 309 gross tons for *Black Swan*, but it was the longer of the pair at 174 feet.

The demise of their competition left the Launceston Steam Navigation Co as the only major operator on the route between Melbourne and Launceston. Their four ships were scheduled to make eighteen crossings to Melbourne and back per month, but this timetable could be easily maintained by three ships, so the *Clarence* spent considerable periods laid up, it being considered that propeller ships were better suited to the Bass Strait conditions than the paddler.

Meanwhile, the Tasmanian Steam Navigation Co had ordered a second ship, which was named *City of Hobart*. At 613 gross tons it was larger than the *Tasmania*, had two funnels, and a service speed of 13 knots, making her very fast for that time. On arrival in Hobart in July 1854, *City of Hobart* was described as 'a fine looking vessel, with a clipper stem and three masts, square-rigged on the foremast, and painted gun ports along her side'.

For her first trip from Hobart, *City of Hobart* went to Melbourne, but on her return to Hobart was placed in the trade to Sydney, on which it ran until 1860, when it began making voyages across the Tasman Sea to New Zealand.

A few months after *City of Hobart* entered service, the *Tasmania* came close to being wrecked, in an incident that could have destroyed the fledgling company. Leaving Hobart in October 1854, with about 200 passengers on board, *Tasmania* ran into a thunderstorm in Storm Bay, which reduced visibility to almost nil. As was usual in those days, the vessel was carrying sail fore and aft, as well as using the steam engine, but in the bad weather speed was reduced to about three knots. About 8.30 pm, as the storm reached its climax, the ship was felt to strike an object under water. Captain Clinch, thinking he was clear of land, decided the ship had struck floating debris, but as a precaution he ordered that the ship's lifeboats be swung out anyway.

Subsequently a series of vivid flashes of lightning revealed that the *Tasmania* was almost alongside very high sheer cliffs at Cape Pillar, and had in fact grazed a rocky ledge.

The ship was backed away from the cliffs, but

*City of Hobart* was a fine looking vessel (Maritime Museum of Tasmania)

an inspection revealed water leaking slowly into the forward hold. All available hands were put to the pumps, and the *Tasmania* limped back to Hobart. Fortunately the damage to the hull was only slight, and quickly repaired, while a fault in the compass, which had misled the captain, was also fixed.

The Tasmanian Steam Navigation Co had the trade from Hobart to themselves, but from time to time competitors challenged the Launceston Steam Navigation Co's domination of the trade between Melbourne and Launceston. One of these was the paddlesteamer *Fenella*, of 261 gross tons, which had been built for the Irish Sea trade, then sent to Australia in 1856 in the hope of finding a buyer. *Fenella* ran to Launceston for only a short time before seeking a new area of operation.

In 1857 another paddlesteamer, the 453 gross ton *North Star* joined the trade. Built in Britain in 1843, North Star had been sent to Australia in 1854 and offered for sale on arrival. After three years lying idle off Sandridge Pier in Port Phillip Bay, *North Star* was bought by a Captain Lawrence, who placed the ship in service between Melbourne and Launceston. However, after only a few months the ship was withdrawn and sent to Shanghai, being offered for sale there.

To counter such opposition, the Launceston

Steam Navigation Co engaged in a price-cutting war. While this effectively defeated the competition and forced them out of the trade, it also had disastrous economic results for the Launceston company.

In 1856 the *Clarence* was offered for sale, being purchased by the ASN, who used the vessel on the route for which it had originally been built. *Clarence* was eventually wrecked on 1 June 1872 on Diamond Head, south of Port Macquarie.

Despite selling the *Clarence,* the Launceston Steam Navigation Co went into liquidation in 1857, and a new firm, the Launceston & Melbourne Steam Navigation Co, also headed by George Fisher, took over their ships on the Bass Strait trade.

The new firm almost got off to a disastrous start, as in 1858 the *Royal Shepherd* collided with the sailing ship *Formose* in Port Phillip Bay. Fortunately the damage was minor, the rigging being damaged and several hull plates dented, and after repairs in Melbourne *Royal Shepherd* was soon back in service again.

In 1861 the Launceston & Melbourne Steam Navigation Co purchased the 301 gross ton *Havilah* from McMeckan, Blackwood & Co. This vessel had been built in Britain in 1853, and been captained by Hugh McMeckan himself

*City of Launceston* on the slip (Maritime Museum of Tasmania)

on the trade between Melbourne and Adelaide. She was primarily a cargo carrier, with some passenger accommodation.

A far more impressive addition to the Launceston & Melbourne Steam Navigation Co fleet was *City of Launceston*, a 176-foot long, 368 gross ton steamer built in Glasgow in 1863. She had excellent passenger accommodation, and was a fine looking vessel, with three island deckhouses, a sharp clipper bow and bowsprit, and square-rigged on the foremast.

*City of Launceston* joined *Havilah*, *Royal Shepherd* and *Black Swan* on the service between Launceston and Melbourne, and appeared set for a long and successful career

In 1864 the Tasmanian Steam Navigation Co added two vessels to their fleet. The first was the *Southern Cross*, an iron-hulled steamship of 779 gross tons, with three masts, a single funnel and a clipper bow. It had been under construction in Scotland for use as a blockade-runner in the American Civil War when it was purchased by the Tasmanian company.

Instead of operating out of Hobart, *Southern Cross* was placed on the trade between Launceston and Melbourne, and provided stiff competition for the vessels owned by the Launceston & Melbourne Steam Navigation Co.

Later in 1864 the Tasmanian Steam Navigation Co took delivery of a fourth vessel, also built in Scotland. Named *Derwent*, the 478 gross ton vessel joined *Tasmania* on the service between Hobart and Melbourne, which enabled the pair to provide the first regular weekly service between the two ports.

It was also in 1864 that the Tasmanian Steam Navigation Co commenced a regular service across the Tasman Sea to New Zealand, using

*City of Hobart*. This vessel had been operating between Hobart and Sydney, but in 1860 made a special trip from Sydney to New Zealand, carrying troops to New Plymouth for the Maori War. Over the next three years *City of Hobart* made several more trips to New Zealand, mostly carrying cargo from Hobart and Melbourne, returning with prospectors seeking their fortunes on the Victorian goldfields.

*City of Hobart* operated regularly across the Tasman during 1864 and 1865, then resumed her former trade between Hobart and Sydney.

On the service between Launceston and Melbourne, the only vessel the Launceston & Melbourne Steam Navigation Co had that was comparable to *Southern Cross* was *City of Launceston*, but her career was tragically short. On 19 November 1865 *City of Launceston* was coming down the west channel in Port Phillip Bay when it was rammed by the steamer *Penola*, which caused *City of Launceston* to sink.

This disaster brought about the financial collapse of the Launceston & Melbourne Steam Navigation Co, and by the end of 1865 a takeover offer from the Tasmanian Steam Navigation Co had been accepted.

As a result of the takeover, the Tasmanian Steam Navigation Co now had a fleet of eight ships, and was the dominant operator on all the major Bass Strait trades. The three surviving Launceston company ships, *Havilah*, *Royal Shepherd* and *Black Swan*, were added to the Tasmanian company fleet, but they were all taken off the main Bass Strait trade from Launceston. To replace them, *Derwent* was transferred from the Hobart service to join *Southern Cross* and soon became very popular.

The three former Launceston company ships were used for services to the mainland from ports along the north coast of Tasmania. West of Launceston, fertile farming land well suited to growing potatoes and apples and grazing dairy cattle had also been discovered along the lower valley of the Mersey River. Two settlements grew up on either side of the river estuary, Formby and Torquay, which in 1890 were joined into one city, named Devonport.

The largest populated area along that coast at that time was around Emu Bay, where the town of Burnie developed. Further west again was Stanley, established in 1825 by the Van Diemen's

Land Company, which bred merino sheep on the surrounding lands. At one time Stanley was a busy port, but its importance quickly waned. Stanley was the birthplace in 1879 of the only Tasmanian to become Prime Minister of Australia, Joseph Lyons.

One misfortune for the Tasmanian company occurred on 16 July 1867. On that morning the *Black Swan* left the company wharf on the Yarra River, with passengers and cargo, including sheep, but off Gellibrand Point at Williamstown she collided with the paddle steamer *Luna*, which was arriving from Geelong. The bow of *Luna* struck *Black Swan* on her starboard side forward, and for some time the two vessels remained locked together. When they separated, *Black Swan* rapidly filled with water and sank, fortunately without loss of life.

However, being in shallow water it was possible to raise the vessel, which was repaired and then sold, leaving the company with seven ships. This was back to eight in 1869, when a new ship was built for the Launceston trade, being named *Tamar*. Although smaller than the *Derwent* at 453 gross tons, *Tamar* proved to be an excellent sea boat, with well appointed cabins and public rooms, which quickly made her a favourite with travellers. When *Tamar* entered service, *Southern Cross* was transferred to the service between Hobart and Melbourne to partner Tasmania.

In 1870 the Tasmanian Steam Navigation Co was operating four separate passenger services. The two major routes were from Launceston to Melbourne, providing two departures a week in each direction, and Hobart to Melbourne, with a departure every ten days. There was also an occasional sailing from Hobart to Launceston and Melbourne. The fourth route was between Hobart and Sydney, usually made direct, but on occasions there would also be a call at Eden.

The 1870s saw considerable changes to the fleet of the Tasmanian Steam Navigation Co, with most of the older ships being sold and replaced. In 1871 *Tasmania* was sold, but not replaced until 1873, when a new, 721 gross ton vessel was built and named *Tasman*.

It is often said that *Tasman* was the best looking vessel ever owned by the TSN. Following the existing fashion for steamers, the vessel

*Tasman*, the last TSN ship built with a clipper bow (Maritime Museum of Tasmania)

was square-rigged on the foremast, and had a bowsprit with a figurehead of *Abel Tasman*, but she was the last of the company's ships to be built with a clipper bow. *Tasman* was placed in service between Hobart and Sydney, on which it served for the next ten years.

*City of Hobart* had been serving on the route between Hobart and Sydney, but was now twenty years old. In March 1875 it was sold and converted to transport coal between Newcastle and Melbourne. Her new career was short, as in July 1877 the tail shaft broke and punctured the hull when the vessel was in Bass Strait. After drifting for several hours, *City of Hobart* sank off Cape Schank, but her crew was saved.

The replacement for *City of Hobart* was the first ship to be built for the TSN with a straight bow, *Mangana*, of 752 gross tons. Completed in Glasgow in 1876, it joined *Tasman* on the trade between Hobart and Sydney. In 1877 *Royal Shepherd* was sold, her place on the trade from ports in north-west Tasmania to Melbourne being taken by *Southern Cross*.

In 1877 this vessel went to Sydney for rebuilding. It was cut in two and lengthened by 30 feet, and rerigged with just two masts instead of three. Extensive alterations were also made to the accommodation, which was greatly improved. Also during 1877 the TSN added two cargo steamers, *Esk* and *Truganini*.

One of the major problems with Launceston as a port was the lack of water in sections of the Tamar River at low tide. A particular problem was a bar at the mouth of the North *Esk* River, which disrupted sailing schedules as it forced vessels to wait until the tide rose before they were able to cross it and proceed down the river. As the ships being built became larger, the lack of water in the River Tamar became an increasing problem.

In 1877 a small steamer, *Corio,* arrived to operate a regular service along the Tamar between Launceston and George Town, joined in 1878 by another steamer, *Empress of India.*

With the advent of these two vessels the TSN arranged that, when the tide was low, their vessels would leave Launceston before their scheduled departure time, and move down the river as far as Rosevears. There they would wait, while one of the small steamers would leave Launceston at the scheduled time with passengers who would join the ship waiting at Rosevears. It would then depart for Melbourne. However, the transfer from tender to ship was not an easy process, and many passengers expressed their dismay at the procedure.

Another passenger vessel was added to the TSN fleet in 1878, the *Flinders*, an iron-hulled steamer built in Glasgow. At 948 gross tons, *Flinders* was the largest vessel yet owned by the TSN, and was placed in service between Launceston and Melbourne.

*Flinders* proved a most successful ship, as she could navigate the tricky channel along the Tamar River with ease, and also rode the sea well even in the roughest of weather.

With the arrival of *Flinders*, in 1879 two older Tasmanian Steam Navigation Co vessels, *Havilah* and *Derwent*, were sold, along with *Truganini*, which only had two years with the company.

The Tasmanian Steam Navigation Co was left with a fleet of just five passenger steamers. *Flinders* and *Mangana* now operated the service between Launceston and Melbourne, while *Southern Cross* and *Tamar* were placed on the route from Hobart to Melbourne, and Tasman ran from Hobart to Sydney.

Although the Tasmanian Steam Navigation Co had added a number of new ships, they were not being used to their best advantage, and the company was not prospering as it should. The first signs of dissatisfaction with the company arose in Launceston, but soon Hobart merchants were also voicing concerns.

# Chapter Three

# Bitter Rivalry

During 1878, the Melbourne based firm of McMeckan, Blackwood & Co, and their fleet of four vessels, *Albion*, *Arawata*, *Ringarooma* and *Tararua*, was bought by the Union Steam Ship Company of New Zealand Ltd.

The Melbourne company had been involved in the Australian coastal and trans-Tasman trades for many years, and had their first association with Tasmania in 1863, when *Otago* inaugurated a service from Melbourne to Hobart and on to New Zealand. The Union Steam Ship Company had not entered the trans-Tasman service until 1876, the year after it was founded, but soon became a major operator on that trade.

With their acquisition of McMeckan, Blackwood the Union Company also gained access to services on the Australian coast, which they soon sought to expand. Within a year the first Union Steam Ship Company vessel appeared in Hobart, and soon they would become major rivals for the Tasmanian Steam Navigation Co on all their routes.

If the Tasmanian Steam Navigation Co was not immediately aware of how much competition they would be facing from the Union Steam Ship Company of New Zealand, it did not take them long to find out. The purchase of McMeckan, Blackwood & Co enabled them to commence what became known as the 'horseshoe service'. This ran from Sydney to various ports in New Zealand, then back across the Tasman Sea to Hobart and on to Melbourne, from where the the reverse route was followed.

While the Tasmanian Steam Navigation Co continues to operate without major opposition on the service between Launceston and Melbourne, they faced stiff competition on their service from Hobart to Melbourne, as the ships of the Union Company were larger and faster. Both companies offered a departure in each direction every ten days, those of the Union company scheduled to depart between the TSN sailings, rather than in direct competition. The directors of the TSN realised that they had to improve their fleet quickly, so orders were placed in Britain for the construction of two ships, to be delivered in 1882 and 1883.

The first of the new ships to arrive was the *Corinna*, of 1,271 gross tons, a considerable increase in size on the *Flinders* built four years earlier. She was placed on a new service from Launceston to Sydney, and only occasionally was used on other routes.

Also during 1882 the Tamar was sold, her place on the Bass Strait trade being taken by the second new vessel, *Pateena*, delivered in 1883. The arrival of this ship in Launceston for the first time, on the morning of Sunday, 23 December

*Flora* at Port Arthur (Maritime Museum of Tasmania)

1883, was greeted by a large crowd. *Pateena* joined *Flinders* on the regular service between Launceston and Melbourne.

In 1884 the TSN fleet was further enlarged by the purchase of *Flora*, slightly larger at 1,283 gross tons. Built in 1882 for the service between Hull and Hamburg, she ran from Launceston to Melbourne, and sometimes between Hobart and Sydney.

Paddler *Natone* was built for service as a tender on the Tamar (Author's collection)

It was also during 1883 that the Tasmanian Steam Navigation Company ordered another vessel, though this one was built at Mort's Dock in Sydney as a double-ended paddlesteamer for use on the Tamar River as a tender. Launched in June 1884 and named *Natone*, the vessel could carry up to 800 passengers, and left Sydney on 23 October. Going down the New South Wales coast the vessel encountered very heavy seas, and sought shelter in Jervis Bay and Twofold Bay. *Natone* arrived in Launceston on 29 October.

*Natone* spent several months operating as a tender between Launceston and Rosevears, where *Pateena*, *Mangana* and *Corinna* would anchor at low tide. The use of this anchorage instead of the Launceston wharves provoked widespread protests from travellers, as well as the Launceston Chamber of Commerce.

However, work was then under way to remove the notorious bar at the mouth of the North *Esk*, and when this was achieved, *Natone* was no longer needed. In October 1885 *Natone* was sold, and left Tasmania for Sydney. She later went to Queensland, then operated on Port Phillip Bay as the excursion steamer Queen, before being converted into a lighter in 1911.

Up to this time the ships engaged in the trade between Launceston and Melbourne had taken ten days to complete a single round trip. This included a day and night steaming time in each direction, and several days in port for unloading one cargo and taking on another.

*Pateena* was designed to reduce this schedule to seven days, to enable a regular weekly schedule to be maintained, and for this purpose was fitted with powerful engines which gave her a service speed of 14 knots. *Pateena* was also fitted with better accommodation, but still in the old sailing ship configuration, first class at the stern and second class midships.

*Pateena* soon broke all the existing records for the Bass Strait crossing, but her high speed also caused excessive vibration, especially in the stern areas. The new vessel also proved to be a veritable coal-eater when operating at her regular service speed. As a result she was only used during the peak passenger months on a regular basis, and in the slack season was either laid up, or operated at a reduced speed.

It was also in 1883 that the Tasmanian Steam Navigation Co suffered a major loss, when *Tasman* was sunk. The vessel left Sydney on 27 November 1883, carrying 29 passengers, including 6 children, as well as mail and cargo, including 71 head of cattle in pens. *Tasman* called at Eden, then headed off for Hobart.

At dawn on 30 November, *Tasman* was steaming down the east coast of Tasmania towards Hobart, while about five miles ahead was another TSN vessel, *Corinna*, also bound for Hobart. As the ships passed Tasman's Peninsula, Captain J W Evans was still in his cabin when the chief officer, who was in charge on the bridge of the *Tasman*, decided to try and overtake the *Corinna*. He ordered a change of course that would take the ship between the Hippolyte Rocks, which was not a safe channel.

Travelling at speed, *Tasman* struck a rocky outcrop hard, almost tearing the bottom out of the ship before it drifted into deeper water, and within fifteen minutes had sunk. Fortunately all the passengers and crew were able to escape the sinking ship, and were rescued by the *Corinna*.

The loss of *Tasman* caused some upset to the TSN operation for a short period, but services were soon re-arranged to make better use of existing ships, and no replacement was built. The chief officer was dismissed by the TSN, while Captain Evans was reduced to the rank of Chief Officer for two years.

A further disaster befell the Tasmanian Steam Navigation Co on 24 April 1886, when the small cargo ship *Esk* struck Hebe Reef, at the mouth of

*Oonah* quickly became popular with passengers (Maritime Museum of Tasmania)

the Tamar River, and sank in ten minutes, though all the crew got away in lifeboats. Unfortunately, the master of the *Esk* at the time was none other than Captain J W Evans, who had been given command of the ship in October 1885, when the TSN restored him to his former rank. Following the loss of the *Esk*, Captain Evans had his master's certificate cancelled. To replace *Esk*, the TSN purchased the *Moreton*, though it was a smaller vessel.

It was not until 1888 that another new passenger vessel was added to the TSN fleet, which would also become their most famous ship. *Oonah* was built in Glasgow for the service between Hobart and Sydney, and soon gained a reputation for her speed and comfort, quickly becoming popular with travellers. Completed in February 1888, *Oonah* was the first TSN steamer to have all passenger accommodation and public rooms located midships.

Once in service, *Oonah* broke all existing records for the journey between Sydney and Hobart, and although slightly faster than *Pateena*, did not suffer from the same vibration problems. At first *Oonah* carried yards on her foremast on which sails could be set in favourable wind conditions, but these were soon dispensed with.

The addition of *Oonah* to the TSN fleet was unfortunately offset within a year by the loss of yet another vessel. In February 1889 the veteran steamer *Southern Cross*, after giving the company twenty-five years of good service, struck an uncharted rock off Table Cape, on the north-west coast of Tasmania, while on a voyage from Burnie to Stanley.

The vessel remained stuck on the rock, which enabled all the passengers and their baggage to be transferred to a passing steamer, while many cabin fittings and other items were also removed and sent ashore by the crew. Twelve hours after the ship ran aground, the wind changed to an easterly, and the seas rose rapidly. Soon after the *Southern Cross* slid sideways off the rock, and sank in deep water.

Bad as the loss of *Southern Cross* was, worse was to follow for the Tasmanian Steam Navigation Co, as it was also during 1889 that they found themselves facing a competitor, Huddart Parker Limited, on the trade between Launceston and Melbourne. In fact, the entry of this Melbourne-based company was caused by dissatisfaction among residents in Tasmania, especially those in Launceston, with the service being offered by the TSN to Melbourne.

In August 1889 the Tasmanian Woolgrower

This poster depicted the main Tasmanian Steam Navigation Company fleet as it stood in 1888 (Maritime Museum of Tasmania)

*Burrumbeet* was the first Huddart Parker ship to visit Tasmania (Author's collection)

Agency Company asked Huddart Parker Limited to provide a ship to carry a cargo of valuable stud sheep from Launceston to Melbourne. Huddart Parker agreed, providing one of their newest vessels, *Burrumbeet*.

James Huddart himself travelled on the vessel, and during the trip to Melbourne the representatives of the Tasmanian Woolgrower Agency Company expressed regret to him that they would have to return to Launceston on a Tasmanian Steam Navigation Company vessel. Mr Huddart offered to arrange for them to be transported home on another of his vessels, the *Coogee*, and this was agreed. *Coogee* left Melbourne on 23 August, arriving at Launceston the following day, her first visit to Tasmania.

This encounter resulted in Huddart Parker Limited entering the passenger trade between Melbourne and Launceston, placing two ships on the route. These vessels were the *Burrumbeet*, of 2,420 gross tons and built in 1885, and the slightly larger *Elingamite*, 2,585 gross tons, which had been built in 1887. Both these vessels were primarily colliers, intended to carry coal from Newcastle to Melbourne.

However, they were also fitted with accommodation for 150 first class passengers in cabins, and steerage quarters for another 80, so on the return trip they could carry passengers from Melbourne to Sydney. *Burrumbeet* made the first regular voyage across Bass Strait for Huddart Parker in September 1889, being joined by *Elingamite* the next month.

The accommodation on *Burrumbeet* was similar to that offered by passenger ships operating on the Australian coast at the time, with one or two berths, a small chest of drawers and wardrobe, and a washbasin. Toilet and shower facilities were shared by the passengers.

The steerage quarters, however, were extremely basic, being located in a 'forecabin' under the forecastle head, near the bow. The single large room was fitted along either side with rows of lower and upper berths, fitted with curtains for privacy. Each bunk had a mattress filled with straw, but no blankets, these having to be supplied by the passengers themselves.

Male berths were on the port side, with females and children on the starboard side. Along the midship bulkhead there was a long table for meals, with a bench seat on each side. For washing there were two large enamel basins on a benchtop at one end of the cabin. However, *Burrumbeet* did have one luxury, electric lighting, which was fitted to very few steamers of that period.

Neither of these vessels was really suited to such a trade, but they were intended to be used only as a temporary measure until the vessel Huddart Parker had decided to place on the route permanently, *Coogee*, underwent extensive alterations. However, it soon became apparent that a better vessel was required if Huddart Parker was to make any impact on the trade, so in October 1889 they arranged to charter the Newcastle from the Newcastle Steamship Co, and operate it across Bass Strait until the *Coogee* was ready.

*Newcastle* was a paddlesteamer built in Britain in 1884 for the short coastal trade between Sydney and Newcastle. *Newcastle* could carry about 300 passengers, and proved to be very fast, with a top speed of over 16 knots, but her usual service speed was 12 knots.

The vessel was notable for having three funnels in an unusual arrangement, with closely spaced twin stacks forward of the paddleboxes,

Paddlesteamer *Newcastle* (Author's collection)

and a single stack further aft. At the time the *Newcastle* was built a railway line was under construction between Sydney and Newcastle. This was completed in 1887, except for a bridge across the Hawkesbury River, which was completed in 1889. Following this the number of passengers opting to travel by ship between Sydney and Newcastle declined sharply, so it was a great relief to the Newcastle Steamship Co to be able to charter their vessel, with an option to buy, to Huddart Parker.

At 1,251 gross tons, the *Newcastle* was larger and also faster than the vessels being operated on the route by the TSN. The paddler was scheduled to operate three return trips a week across Bass Strait, carrying passengers and only a small amount of cargo. Initially *Newcastle* was commanded by Captain H C White, who had previously been with the TSN.

In order to gain a foothold in the Bass Strait trade, Huddart Parker started a price war. They reduced their one-way fare to just £1, forcing the TSN to do the same, though they had previously been charging £3 5s 0d. The *Newcastle* was advertised as 'the fastest steamer in the colonies, with accommodation for 400 passengers, and engines of 4,000 hp'. Her main TSN competition was the *Pateena*.

*Newcastle* departed Melbourne for her first crossing of Bass Strait on the afternoon of Saturday, 26 October 1889, arriving in Launceston the following morning. In order to maintain her schedule, *Newcastle* would only spend about nine hours in Launceston, then depart for Melbourne the same evening.

Initially *Newcastle* operated jointly with *Burrumbeet* and *Elingamite*, which both extended their voyages to Sydney, but they were withdrawn in November 1889. It was also in November 1889 that Captain Frederick Carrington took over command of the *Newcastle*, which subsequently also made a fortnightly trip from Melbourne to Burnie and Devonport on the north-west coast. Sometimes *Newcastle* and *Pateena* would engage in a race across Bass Strait when their schedules coincided, but the pair was very evenly matched.

The Newcastle Steamship Co had hoped Huddart Parker would buy their ship, but the *Newcastle* proved to be very expensive to operate across Bass Strait, with an enormous appetite

*Coogee* entered the Bass Strait trade in April 1890. (Author's collection)

for coal to enable a speed of about 16 knots to be maintained. So *Newcastle* was returned to its owners when *Coogee* entered the Bass Strait service in April 1890.

*Coogee* had quite an interesting background, having been built in England in 1887 as *Lancashire Witch* for the Isle of Man Steam Navigation Co, formed in 1886 to compete with the long-established Isle of Man Steam Packet Co on the service across the Irish Sea between Liverpool and Douglas. During the summer of 1887 the *Lancashire Witch* proved herself the fastest vessel on the route, but was unable to compete on an equal basis with the numerous ships owned by the other firm.

Early in 1888 the new company went bankrupt, and *Lancashire Witch* was offered for sale. It so happened that James Huddart was in England at that time to order new ships for Huddart Parker. He inspected the *Lancashire Witch*, and purchased the vessel in May 1888.

Renamed *Coogee*, the vessel was prepared for the long voyage to Australia, which would be made under sail, rigged from the foremast, mainmast and funnel. However, the propeller was not removed, but fixed in place, which caused considerable drag and slowed the progress of the vessel considerably, so the *Coogee* did not reach Melbourne until 25 January 1889.

When James Huddart purchased the vessel, it was his intention to operate it on Port Phillip Bay between Melbourne and Geelong. Following a quick refit, the *Coogee* duly entered this trade on 8 February 1889.

When Huddart Parker entered the Bass Strait trade later the same year, it was decided that *Coogee* would be an ideal ship for this service. So the vessel was refitted, including the installation of cabins for passengers.

The work was completed in April 1890, and *Coogee* then began operating between Melbourne and Launceston, replacing the *Newcastle*. Captain Carrington transferred to the *Coogee*, and would remain in command of the vessel for the next thirteen years.

At just 762 gross tons the *Coogee* was smaller than the *Newcastle*, and also much slower, with a service speed of just 12 knots, so could manage only two return trips per week.

Despite being smaller and slower than the newer vessels operated on the route by the Tasmanian Steam Navigation Co, *Coogee* soon proved quite popular with travellers, and Huddart Parker decided to obtain a second ship for the trade. In 1890 they purchased the 649 gross ton steamer *Nelson* from the Western Steam Navigation Co, for whom she had been built in 1896.

Without change of name, the vessel was placed on the Bass Strait trade at the end of June. On her very first voyage for Huddart Parker, the *Nelson* was wrecked on 27 June at the mouth of

The Huddart Parker vessel *Elingamite* (Author's collection)

the Tamar River.

To replace her, a new vessel was ordered from builders in Britain, and in the interim a variety of Huddart Parker steamers were used to partner the *Coogee* until the new vessel arrived in 1892. It was named *Tambo*, of similar size to the *Coogee* at 732 gross tons.

When *Burrumbeet* and *Elingamite* were withdrawn from the Bass Strait service in November 1889, they did not immediately leave the Tasmanian trade. *Burrumbeet* was sent to Hobart to commence a service for Huddart Parker to Sydney, again in direct competition with the Tasmanian Steam Navigation Co, though their latest vessel, the *Oonah*, was far superior to *Burrumbeet*. Again this was a mere temporary measure for Huddart Parker, as it was their intention to place *Elingamite* on this route.

*Elingamite* had cost £50,000 to build less than three years previously, but now Huddart Parker spent a further £20,000 improving and enlarging the accommodation. When the work was completed, *Elingamite* replaced *Burrumbeet*, which went back to its original service between

Newcastle and Melbourne. *Elingamite* was much larger than the *Oonah*, and offered a similar standard of accommodation, providing the Tasmanian Steam Navigation Co with major competition.

In 1890 Huddart Parker increased their presence on the Hobart to Sydney route when they added *Wendouree* to the trade. Smaller than *Elingamite* at 1,640 gross tons, *Wendouree* was the third vessel to be built for Huddart Parker, and the first with a steel hull, being completed in 1882. Designed for the coal trade between Newcastle and Melbourne, in 1883 rather basic accommodation had been installed in the vessel, so it could carry passengers between Melbourne and Sydney on the return voyage to Newcastle.

*Wendouree* was primarily used as a cargo carrier between Hobart and Sydney, but also carried passengers, though not in any great comfort. However, the combined service of *Elingamite* and *Wendouree* was major competition for the Tasmanian Steam Navigation Co, which was now struggling to stay afloat financially.

The situation in 1890 saw the Tasmanian Steam Navigation Co facing strong competition on all their major routes. They had to contend with Huddart Parker Limited on the service between Melbourne and Launceston and that between Hobart and Sydney, while the Union Steam Ship Company of New Zealand was their competitor on the trade between Hobart and Melbourne.

It was inevitable that a 'rate war' would break out, and by 1890 fares had been reduced to an absurd level. The first class fare between Sydney and Hobart came down to only ten shillings, while to ship a case of fruit cost as little as three pence. With all three companies suffering financial losses, they realised the situation could not continue. A truce was called, and fixed rates agreed between the three companies, with a rationalisation of services.

While both Huddart Parker and the Union Company lost money on their Tasmanian services, they could recoup this from profits on other trades. The Tasmanian Steam Navigation Co, however, suffered very badly financially, as it had no other source of income.

Also creating problems for all shipping companies in 1890 was a strike that affected both Australia and New Zealand. Such a confrontation between the employers, who comprised the Steamship Owners Association, and labour in the shipping industry had been brewing for some time, but it came to a head in August 1890, when the Mercantile Marine Officer's Association went on strike. Soon they were joined by seamen, stewards, cooks and wharf labourers, all of who lodged claims for better working conditions and wages.

*Flinders* with Union Steam Ship Co funnel colours (Author's collection)

*Talune* was the last vessel to be built for the TSN (Maritime Museum of Tasmania)

The strike effectively crippled the entire shipping industry, and for several weeks almost all shipping movements stopped, though some vessels continued to operate using non-union labour. Even when the men went back to work the problems continued over the next four years. Just to compound the situation further, in 1891 a depression started in Australia that would last until 1894, during which time many companies in all trades and industries were forced out of business, and even banks collapsed.

Not anticipating any of these catastrophic occurrences, during 1890 the Tasmanian Steam Navigation Co took delivery of another new vessel, *Talune*, which, at 2,087 gross tons, would be the largest ship they would ever own, and was also destined to be the last to join their fleet.

*Talune* was built to a design that was considered out of date, and did not compare favourably with other recent additions, such as *Oonah* and *Pateena*. *Talune* also proved a very costly ship to build, and the TSN coffers, already severely drained by the 'rate war' and the strike, were all but emptied to pay for the vessel. *Talune* was placed in service between Hobart and Sydney, but by that time the future of the TSN was extremely bleak.

Early in 1891 the Union Steam Ship Company of New Zealand made a takeover bid for the Tasmanian

Steam Navigation Co, which the TSN had no real alternative but to accept. The New Zealand company was backed by a nominal capital of £1 million, while the TSN had a nominal capital of just £6,000. The total price paid by the New Zealand company for the TSN on 1 April 1891 was £185,000, partly in cash, the rest in shares.

The Union Line took over the eight vessels in the Tasmanian Steam Navigation Co fleet, these being the passenger carriers *Talune*, *Oonah*, *Pateena*, *Flora*, *Corinna* and *Flinders*, and the cargo ships *Mangana* and *Moreton*. Also included in the deal were all the buildings and wharves owned by the TSN in Hobart, Launceston, Melbourne and Sydney, which the Union Line subsequently used.

Within a short time of the takeover, the Union Line transferred four of the former TSN vessels to New Zealand coastal trades, these being *Corinna*, *Flora*, *Pateena* and *Oonah*. This move brought an outpouring of protests from residents of Tasmania, who were furious that two of their best ships, *Pateena* and *Oonah*, had been taken away from them. Within weeks both these vessels had been brought back to their original trades from Tasmania, and the fury subsided, but it was not a promising start for the new operation.

At first the Union Line seemed quite content to operate former TSN ships on the service between Launceston and Melbourne, but during October 1891 they withdrew the *Flinders* from the Bass Strait trade, and the vessel was sold in 1894. As a replacement, the Union Line brought over from New Zealand one of their most famous ships, *Rotomahana*, which spent several months crossing Bass Strait.

Built in Scotland in 1879, *Rotomahana* had made history in being the first vessel constructed of mild steel, and also the first to be fitted with

*Rotomahana* at Hobart early in her career. (Maritime Museum of Tasmania)

bilge keels. In design she was totally unlike any other vessel ever owned by the Union Line, but this is said to have been because the vessel was originally ordered as the private yacht of a wealthy prince, who died before it was completed. Subsequently it was sold while still on the stocks to the Union Line, and launched on 5 June 1879.

*Rotomahana* was quite small by today's standards, being just 1,727 gross tons and 298 feet /90.8 m long. Her appearance was enhanced by a clipper bow and jib boom, complete with figurehead and decorative scroll work.

The single compound engine installed was quite large for a ship of that size, comprising a high-pressure cylinder with a diameter of 42 inches/1.2 m, while the low-pressure cylinder had an 82-inch/2m diameter. Steam was supplied by six boilers, each with a working pressure of 70 pounds per square inch.

The single propeller was also quite large, with a diameter of 14 feet 6 inches/4.4 m. On trials *Rotomahana* reached a top speed of 15.5 knots, very fast for the times.

For her delivery voyage, *Rotomahana* left London on 5 August 1879, boarded 100 passengers at Plymouth, and under the command of Captain T Underwood, voyaged by way of South Africa to reach Melbourne on 22 September.

After several days in port, she crossed the Tasman Sea in just 3 days 16 hours, arriving in Port Chalmers on 1 October 1879.

*Rotomahana* was placed on the trans-Tasman trade, and caused enormous interest due to her yacht-like lines and internal fittings, with accommodation for 140 first class, 80 second class and 80 steerage class passengers.

The first and second class staterooms and public rooms were panelled in fine woods, such as mahogany, polished bird's-eye maple, rosewood, satinwood and teak, while the lounges featured elaborate carvings, beautiful mirrors and quality furnishings.

On her maiden trans-Tasman voyage from New Zealand, *Rotomahana* arrived in Hobart for the first time on the morning of 9 December 1879, berthing alongside the Argyle Street Pier. Her arrival in Hobart caused great interest in the town, and an article in the *Mercury* newspaper the next day stated *Rotomahana* 'far eclipses any steamer that has before visited Hobart Town'.

The vessel's stay in Hobart was very short, as she departed at 12.30 pm for Melbourne. On her return trip to New Zealand, *Rotomahana* called back at Hobart on 19 December, and subsequently became a regular visitor to the port.

Unfortunately, a limited cargo capacity combined with excessive coal consumption at high speed made *Rotomahana* a very expensive

*Pateena* in Union Steam Ship Company colours (Maritime Museum of Tasmania)

ship to operate, and she was often laid up during off-peak periods.

By 1891 the Union Line had taken delivery of a number of larger and more economical vessels, so *Rotomahana* was transferred to the Bass Strait trade, on which she could maintain a lower service speed. *Rotomahana* made her first departure from Melbourne on 15 October 1891, completing the voyage from Williamstown to Town Point in 17 hours 10 minutes.

At the same time, *Pateena* was put on a secondary service, Melbourne to Launceston, then on to Devonport, Burnie and Stanley before returning directly to Melbourne. *Rotomahana* was left to operate the service to Launceston on her own.

However, the smaller *Coogee* was also capable of a good turn of speed, and the opportunity to show this came on 28 October, when both vessels left the Tamar for Melbourne.

*Rotomahana* was the first to depart Launceston, with *Coogee* leaving nineteen minutes later, but by the time they reached the mouth of the Tamar, *Coogee* was only thirteen minutes behind.

The two ships stayed close together as they crossed Bass Strait, and when they passed through Port Phillip Heads, *Rotomahana* was only some five minutes ahead.

A keen race ensued across Port Phillip Bay, with both ships berthing at the same time, resulting in a moral victory to *Coogee*. A few weeks later another race resulted in a narrow victory to *Rotomahana*, but the pair was very evenly matched for speed.

The arrival of *Rotomahana* had caused a great deal of interest in both Melbourne and Launceston, but her time on the trade lasted only a few months, as in May 1892 *Rotomahana* went back to New Zealand.

After several years on various coastal trades, *Rotomahana* joined the major ferry service between Wellington and Lyttelton in October 1897.

With *Rotomahana* gone, the Bass Strait trade was maintained by *Pateena* and *Coogee*, and for the first time the Union Line and Huddart Parker worked in unison instead of competing. A schedule was arranged that provided a better service, with the ships departing on different days, and passage tickets interchangeable between the two companies.

The new arrangement also brought an end to the financially ruinous fare wars that had beset the trade in previous years, and was a foretaste of the harmonious relations that would in future years result in the formation of a joint company.

With the demise of the Tasmanian Steam

# Chapter Four

# Consolidation

Navigation Company, Huddart Parker and the Union Line had the Tasmanian trades between them, and the final years of the nineteenth century were a period of consolidation for both companies.

By the end of 1891 Australia was sliding into the depths of a major depression, which would slow the economic activity in the country for the next four years. As businesses began to collapse and more and more men lost their jobs, the shipping companies were affected by a reduction in both passenger and cargo traffic.

Rather than engage in more cut-throat competition on their services to Tasmania, Huddart Parker and the Union Line came to an agreement on new passenger and freight rates and combined schedules, which came into effect on 1 July 1892. At that time, *Pateena*, and *Coogee* were operating the service between Launceston and Melbourne, while *Elingamite*, *Wendouree*, *Oonah* and *Talune* were on the service between Hobart and Sydney, though later in 1892 both *Wendouree* and *Talune* were withdrawn, the latter vessel being sent to New Zealand.

The route between Hobart and Melbourne was only operated by various ships of the Union Line, being included in their trans-Tasman 'horseshoe service', on which the vessels voyaged between Sydney and Melbourne via various New Zealand ports and Hobart.

As an indication of their intention to become a major force in the Tasmanian trade, Huddart Parker had ordered a new vessel to built in England, which was launched by Mrs Huddart in February 1892 and named Tasmania. The new vessel arrived in Australia in July 1892, and replaced *Wendouree* on the service between

*Tasmania*, built for Huddart Parker in 1892 (Author's collection)

Sydney and Hobart.

Instead of being registered in Melbourne as was usual with Huddart Parker vessels, Tasmania was registered at Hobart. Her first voyage departed Sydney on 2 August. Although smaller than *Elingamite*, Tasmania offered equally good accommodation, but remained on the Tasmanian trade just under a year. Following the discovery of gold in Western Australia, in July 1893 Tasmania was transferred to the booming trade between east coast ports and Fremantle.

In November 1893, Huddart Parker entered the trans-Tasman trade, with Tasmania making their first sailing from Sydney, to Auckland, Gisborne, Napier and Wellington in North Island, then across Cook Strait to Lyttelton and Dunedin. This brought Huddart Parker into more direct competition with the Union Steam Ship Company.

Initially this created another 'rate war' on that trade, but in 1894 the two companies negotiated an agreement under which they shared that route too, including the provision of reciprocal booking and ticketing arrangements.

In 1896 the Union Line removed *Oonah* from the trade between Hobart and Sydney, on which the vessel had operated constantly since 1888, apart from a short period in 1891. *Oonah* was put into dock for a major refit, which included the addition of a raised forecastle and a new deckhouse. When the work was completed, *Oonah* was placed on the Bass Strait service between Launceston and Melbourne, on which it partnered *Pateena*.

In 1897, Huddart Parker removed *Elingamite* from the service between Hobart and Sydney as well, and this trade was subsequently continued only by cargo ships for a number of years. The service across Bass Strait from Melbourne was maintained for the next several years by *Coogee*, *Oonah* and *Pateena*.

The Union Steam Ship Company also entered the passenger and cargo trade between Sydney and Launceston. This was always operated on a smaller scale than the Sydney to Hobart and Melbourne to Launceston services, but still provided an important link between the mainland and northern Tasmania.

In 1899 the Union Line placed one of their earliest vessels, *Wakatipu*, on the trade between Sydney and Launceston, on which it would operate for the next twenty-two years.

Built in 1876, *Wakatipu* was a 1,944 gross ton steamer with a large cargo capacity that

*Wakatipu* spent over twenty years operating to Tasmania (Author's collection)

was originally owned by Captain Angus Cameron, of Dunedin, whose shipping company was amalgamated with the Union Steam Ship Company in 1878. For some years *Wakatipu* operated across the Tasman Sea, until superseded by larger and better tonnage. It was then transferred to the Tasmanian service.

The accommodation provided for about 40 passengers on *Wakatipu* was quite basic, with berths located in separate male and female saloons. The only public room was a lounge that also served as the dining room. For many years *Wakatipu* was the only vessel providing a direct

passenger connection between Sydney and Launceston, but its primary role was as a cargo carrier.

The vast majority of passengers travelling to and from Launceston were carried on the vessels operating from Melbourne. Between them they offered four or more departures each week, the schedule only being upset by bad weather and the occasional mishap.

Usually the problems affecting the vessels were not of a major nature, but in December 1903 there occurred the worst accident to befall any passenger vessel operating across Bass Strait.

At 7.15 pm on Christmas Eve 1903, the *Coogee* departed Launceston on a regular voyage to Melbourne, with only thirty passengers on board. Some time earlier the Union Line steamer *Pateena* had also left Launceston for its trip to Melbourne.

After leaving the mouth of the Tamar River, Captain Frederick Carrington, in command of the *Coogee*, set a course for Port Phillip Heads, and within a short time the *Coogee* had overtaken the slower *Pateena*.

As the *Coogee* moved further into Bass Strait, it ran into a thick fog, and Captain Carrington ordered a reduction of speed. As far as he was aware, the only other vessel near him was the *Pateena*, which was somewhere astern, and no doubt had reduced speed too when it encountered the fog bank.

Believing there were no other ships in his vicinity, Captain Carrington decided not to sound the ship's whistle at regular intervals, which was standard procedure when a vessel entered fog.

What Captain Carrington did not know was that a large square-rigged Italian flag sailing ship, the *Fortunato Figari*, was drifting in Bass Strait in close proximity to the *Coogee*. The *Fortunato Figari* had left Melbourne almost a week earlier, on a voyage to Newcastle, but had been unable to make any headway in Bass Strait due to headwinds, and was now drifting aimlessly in light air.

Meanwhile, the *Coogee* continued on its way at a slower speed than normal, while Captain Carrington remained vigilant on the bridge. As midnight passed, and the ship steamed into Christmas Day, the fog showed no sign of lifting, with visibility almost nil.

Over three hours later the *Coogee* was some 70 miles from Port Phillip Heads and still steaming steadily through the fog when, at 3.45 am, the steamer collided with the *Fortunato Figari*, there having been no time for the steamer to take evasive action.

The starboard bow of the *Coogee* smashed into the bow of the sailing ship, whose massive bow sprit, held firm by strong iron stays, raked along the deck of the steamer, smashing the bridge structure to pieces, along with the lifeboats on the starboard side. The foremast, funnel and mainmast of the *Coogee* all collapsed as their starboard stays were torn away, and the deckhouses were also badly damaged on one side.

On the bridge, Captain Carrington was killed instantly. The helmsman, Frank Golly, was severely injured and died soon after. The only other man on the bridge at the time, second mate Arthur Durant, was badly injured.

The *Coogee* had suffered enormous damage to its upperworks, but the hull had remained intact, and the ship was not taking on water. However, the bow of the *Coogee* had split open the side of the *Fortunato Figari* from the deck to the waterline, leaving a hole ten feet high and four feet wide.

Following the collision, the mess of fallen ropes and wires locked the two ships together, causing the *Coogee* to swing around until the vessels were lying side by side. As they lay there, many crew members from the *Coogee*, who had been roused from their sleep by the collision, and all the firemen from the engine room, believing their vessel was sinking, raced up on deck and swarmed over the side onto the deck of the sailing ship. Some frightened passengers who watched this sudden exodus also managed to climb on board the *Fortunato Figari* before the two vessels managed to disentangle themselves, and drifted apart.

Soon after a lifeboat appeared out of the fog rowing towards the *Coogee*. It contained the chief mate and some crew members, and was soon followed by a second boat containing the remaining crew members, who reboarded the *Coogee*. The women passengers on the *Coogee* were then transferred in one lifeboat to the *Fortunato Figari*.

By that time an inspection of both ships had shown that neither was in immediate danger of sinking, but the engineers on the *Coogee* could not restart the engine, and the vessel was drifting

helplessly. The master of the *Fortunato Figari*, Captain G B Schiaffino, discussed the situation with the coastal pilot he had taken on board in Melbourne, and they decided that the sailing ship would take the *Coogee* in tow for Melbourne. After a line was passed between the two vessels, the *Fortunato Figari* set full sail, and the strange tow began moving very slowly westwards.

During the day the cable-ship *Restorer* happened to come upon the two ships, and after stopping to offer assistance, hurried off to report the incident to the pilot mother vessel which was stationed at Port Phillip Heads. From there a message was sent to Melbourne, on receipt of which a tug was dispatched to take over the tow.

By the time the tug reached the stricken vessels the engineers on the *Coogee* had managed to get the engine going again, and the steamer was able to drop the towline and continue at slow speed under her own power, while the tug attached a tow line to the *Fortunato Figari*.

It was not until late in the afternoon of Boxing Day, 26 December, that the *Coogee* finally reached Melbourne, berthing as usual at No 4 Wharf in the Yarra River. The bodies of Captain Carrington and Frank Golly were carried ashore, while Arthur Durant was rushed off to hospital.

The collision and its aftermath were the talk of Melbourne and Launceston for some time. The action of many crew members in abandoning the *Coogee* and clambering on board the *Fortunato Figari* was the subject of many interpretations. These included an official announcement by Huddart Parker that the men had boarded the sailing ship in response to a definite order to bring back boats from it in case the *Coogee* sank.

As always after such an incident at sea, a Court of Marine Inquiry was convened to investigate how and why the accident occurred, and apportion blame. The Court decided that no blame could be attached to Captain Schiaffino, but found that Captain Carrington was partially to blame.

The Court declared that, by failing to sound the ship's whistle in fog, Captain Carrington had contravened article No 15 of the regulations, and also article No 16 by allowing his vessel to travel at too great a speed in a thick fog.

The Court was also quite scathing in its criticism of the crew members who deserted the ship, finding 'That all the seamen and firemen of the *Coogee*, except one of the latter, appear

The enormous amount of damage suffered by *Coogee* in the collision with the *Fortunato Figari* (Author's collection)

to have been panic-stricken and deserted the *Coogee* in a body'.

However, the Court cleared the chief mate of desertion, stating he was dazed by the collision and could not be held responsible for his actions. The *Coogee* was out of service for several months while repairs were effected, but once they were completed the vessel resumed its place on the Bass Strait trade.

During 1904, *Oonah* was taken off the Bass Strait trade and once again began operating between Sydney and Hobart, offering a departure every ten days. This service was also operated by Huddart Parker, who in 1904 was using *Anglian* on the route.

Up to the end of October 1904, *Coogee* maintained the Launceston service with *Pateena*, but then the Union Line vessel was replaced by a new steamer that would totally transform passenger travel across Bass Strait.

# Chapter Five

# Loongana

In 1903 the Union Steam Ship Company of New Zealand won the contract to operate a mail and passenger service across Bass Strait between Melbourne and Launceston. The conditions of the contract included providing a ship with a service speed of 17 knots, so the company had to have a superior vessel to those then operating the service.

The Union Line immediately ordered a new vessel to be built in shipyard of Wm Denny & Bros at Dumbarton in Scotland. This firm already had a long record of building fine ships for the New Zealand company, and they had also built most of the vessels then operating ferry services from Britain to Europe and Ireland. The new vessel for Bass Strait was designed along the lines of the latest ferries built by Denny Bros for the English Channel services.

Launched on 2 June 1904, the new vessel was named *Loongana*, and three months later was ready to leave the builders' yard for Australia. In appearance *Loongana* was unlike any passenger vessel then in service on the Australian coast.

Another notable feature of *Loongana* was the machinery, as she had been fitted with three direct-drive turbine engines. Although the turbine machinery occupied the same amount of floor space as the machinery then in common use, it required only half the same height in the engine room.

There were 18 furnaces altogether, with two double-ended and two single-ended boilers. Each engine was connected to a rather small propeller, which turned at up to 450 revolutions per minute. This type of machinery was quite new, and originally had only been installed in small excursion craft operating on the River Clyde.

On her delivery trip to Australia, *Loongana* became the first vessel fitted with turbines to make a long ocean voyage. Departing the Clyde on 1 September, under the command of Captain Malcolm Livingstone, no attempt was made to push the vessel along at top speed, with only two of the four boilers being used. *Loongana* passed through the Mediterranean, stopping first at Port Said and then Perim for bunkers. The passage down the Red Sea was particularly trying for the crew, with temperatures in the engine room reaching 134 degrees F. The voyage continued across the Indian Ocean to Colombo, where more bunkers were taken on, with *Loongana* reaching Fremantle on 3 October, and arriving in Melbourne for the first time on the evening of 7 October. The geared turbine machinery performed faultlessly throughout the long voyage.

On arriving in Melbourne, *Loongana* created enormous interest with her modern design, new machinery, and also being the first Australian coastal vessel to be fitted with three propellers. *Loongana* lay at South Wharf in the Yarra while final internal fitting out was completed, and then went into Duke's dry dock for a final hull cleaning. Here the clean lines of the lower sections of her hull were visible for the first time. Captain Livingstone was justifiably proud of his new command, which he described as a magnificent seaboat. Standing on the bridge, he also commented to visitors that when the vessel was moving at speed, 'There is no noise, no vibration. As a matter of fact I have had to

The fine lines of *Loongana* are shown to advantage in this photo showing the vessel moving at speed (David Robinson collection)

leave here and go to the side to make sure she was moving.'

The standard of accommodation was particularly noteworthy. A report in the *Launceston Examiner* on 13 October 1904 stated:

Within, the vessel has been fitted up with absolutely no regard for expense. Every aid to navigation has been provided. Above the navigating bridge is a smaller one, designed especially for river use, and giving the eye a commanding range. Telephones run everywhere from the bridge. The steam steering gear with which we are familiar, if only by the ceaseless rattle of its chains, is replaced by hydraulic power - an apparatus that is next door to noiseless. In short, the vessel is fitted with everything that is latest and best.

Another striking feature are the vessel's magnificent decks, delightful promenades. There is nothing mean or contemptible in their dimensions.

And what applies to the decks applies to the state rooms. They are spacious and luxuriously appointed. The captain's quarters are fit for a king. The officers are comfortably housed in his vicinity. The accommodation for passengers is characterised by its liberality and luxury.

The fittings are lavish, but in excellent taste. Every berth has its spring mattress and its eider down quilt. The accessories are of the newest and best.

The first class dining saloon is a charming room. Its embellishment is thoroughly artistic. In fact, all through the ship luxury hasn't once violated a single canon of good taste.

The music room is another delightful resort. The saloon accommodation is forward, and the second class aft. Practically the only difference between the first and second saloons, excepting cuisine, of course, is in what appeals to the eye.

Aft is everything that makes for comfort, but naturally simplicity is the dominant note. The cabins are roomy, nicely fitted, and, like everything else in connection with the vessel, a vast improvement on anything we have known in the trade.

Indeed, put a stranger in a second class cabin aboard *Loongana* and he would be a long time before he 'dropped' that he wasn't first. The second class accommodation will be a revelation to those who hitherto have travelled 'steerage'. That word doesn't apply to anything on the *Loongana*.

Captain Livingston is very proud of the *Loongana*. 'She simply glides along. There is no noise, no vibration...I never want a better sea boat than this. She's a beauty. I'm proud of her, I can tell you.'

On 13 October, Pateena left Melbourne on her final voyage to Launceston. At 4.20 pm on Tuesday, 18 October, *Loongana* departed Queen's Wharf on her first commercial voyage, travelling overnight across Bass Strait to Launceston, where she berthed at 7.50 am, and received a rapturous reception.

On 30 October a party of 500 invited guests, including the Prime Minister of Australia, Mr G H Reid, boarded *Loongana*, and were taken on a special cruise around Port Phillip Bay, during which the vessel steamed at up to 21 knots.

*Loongana* was a huge improvement on the two vessels the Union Line had been using on the service in recent years, *Oonah* and *Pateena*, both of which were withdrawn and transferred to other routes. *Oonah* went back to her original trade between Sydney and Hobart, while *Pateena* was sent to New Zealand.

On 15 October 1904, *Pateena* departed Launceston for the last time, bound for Wellington, but unlike the events of 1891, her departure this time brought no public outcry. *Pateena* was placed on the Cook Strait service from Wellington to *Nelson* and Picton, then on 7 October 1905 she joined *Rotomahana* as the second ship on the service between Wellington and Lyttelton, which up to then had been operated by only one vessel. *Pateena* was soon replaced by the larger *Mararoa*, then spent the next fifteen years plying across Cook Strait.

*Loongana* was by far the largest vessel yet used on the Bass Strait trade, being 300 feet/91.4 m long, with a beam of 43 feet/13.1 m. *Loongana* provided comfortable cabin accommodation for 200 first class and 100 second class passengers, each class having the use of several lounges and separate dining rooms. In peak periods, the vessel would also carry some unberthed passengers, who slept in shakedowns set up in the lounges.

Departures from Melbourne were scheduled for Monday, Wednesday and Friday evenings, returning from Launceston overnight on Tuesday, Thursday and Saturday, with Sunday night spent alongside in Melbourne. The Union Line was so proud of their new vessel, it was described in newspaper advertisements as a 'turbine yacht'.

The fact that *Loongana* was very fast had been proved on her first crossing of Bass Strait, when she travelled from wharf to wharf in the record time of fifteen and a half hours. However, on the overnight crossing that departed Melbourne on 23 December 1904, *Loongana* cut a further four minutes off her previous record, with an average speed of 20.2 knots. This was achieved with 370

saloon and 80 steerage passengers on board, and the vessel also ran into fog in Bass Strait.

Just how fast *Loongana* could go was indicated in October 1912, when the vessel was called upon to make a fast emergency voyage from Melbourne to Burnie carrying rescue teams and equipment following a mine disaster. On Friday, 11 October, 93 men working in the Mount Lyell copper mine, near Queenstown, were trapped underground by pungent smoke and poisonous gases when a fire broke out in a pumphouse located some seven hundred feet underground.

Local fire and rescue service were overwhelmed by the magnitude of the disaster, and after two days of fruitless efforts to rescue the trapped miners asked for help from the mainland. *Loongana* was in Melbourne, and her departure for Launceston was cancelled. Instead the vessel took on board a contingent of firemen along with fire fighting equipment and a large number of extra smoke helmets.

With all her boilers fired up, *Loongana* left her berth about 5pm on Monday, 14 October, passing through Port Phillip Heads at 6.40 pm, and heading for Burnie. During the crossing the vessel reached in excess of 22 knots, in spite of very stormy conditions in Bass Strait, arriving in Burnie at 5.30 am the next day.

The firemen and their equipment were quickly transferred to a train, and rushed to Queenstown. With the extra men and equipment, air pipes were lowered one thousand feet down to a group of 51 trapped miners, who were eventually all brought safely to the surface. Sadly the other 42 trapped men lost their lives.

Despite the introduction of *Loongana*, Huddart Parker retained the much smaller *Coogee* as their representative on the Launceston service. As had been the case previously, the two vessels operated to a joint schedule, providing up to five trips in each direction per week, of which *Loongana* made three, though in winter this was reduced to two.

A new berth was built in Launceston for *Loongana*, being completed in 1906 as the Alexandra Wharf, and on the ends and roof of the shed was painted, 'Turbine Steamer *Loongana* Melbourne and Launceston Express'.

With both *Oonah* and *Pateena* removed from the Bass Strait trade, there was the need for a ship to operate the secondary service from Melbourne to Burnie and Devonport. In December 1904 the Union Line brought *Flora* back from New Zealand to operate on the Tasmanian trades once again.

Built in 1882 for the Tasmanian Steam Navigation Co, *Flora* joined the Union Line fleet in 1891, and spent the next thirteen years in New Zealand waters. On returning to Australia, *Flora* began operating two departures a week from Melbourne, on Tuesday and Friday, to Burnie and Devonport.

In May 1907 the Union Line took *Rotomahana* off the service between Wellington and Lyttelton, and brought her back across the Tasman Sea to partner *Loongana* on the service between Launceston and Melbourne.

*Rotomahana* had operated briefly on this route in 1891/92, and in 1901 had undergone a major refit. The accommodation had been upgraded, and various external changes made, though the vessel still retained her graceful lines and clipper bow, complete with bowsprit.

At the same time the original boilers had been

*Rotomahana* after being rebuilt in 1901 (Author's collection)

removed, and six new boilers installed, and on returning to service *Rotomahana* had been able to maintain an average speed of 16 knots. While this was not as fast as *Loongana*, it was more than a match for the *Coogee*, which was by now totally outclassed by the two Union Line vessels.

With two fast vessels operating, the Union Line was able to offer a departure from both Launceston and Melbourne six nights a week, with Sunday being spent in port. Even though *Coogee* was now much too small and slow to be competitive with the Union Line vessels, Huddart Parker retained her on the Launceston trade for almost three years after *Loongana* entered service.

It was not until June 1910 that the *Coogee*

Appearance of *Coogee* after being rebuilt in 1910. (Author's collection)

was finally withdrawn from the Bass Strait trade, following which the vessel was extensively rebuilt, and subsequently spent many years operating as an excursion boat on Port Phillip Bay, mostly operating between Melbourne and Geelong.

Considerably changed in appearance, *Coogee* made her first trip from Melbourne to Geelong on 10 December 1910, but on 25 February 1914 the little vessel was again involved in a major accident. Returning from an excursion to Geelong, *Coogee* was proceeding up the Yarra River as the Howard Smith Limited coastal liner *Bombala* was being towed by the tug *James Patterson* to the swinging basin, prior to setting off for north Queensland ports. Captain W A Croft on the *Coogee* tried to squeeze his boat through a narrow gap between the stern of *Bombala* and the wharf, but failed.

The overhanging counter stern of *Bombala* came into collision with the upperworks of *Coogee*, smashing the bridge and shearing off the promenade deck. The debris came crashing down on passengers standing below, waiting to disembark, but amazingly there were no serious injuries.

*Coogee* was able to make her way to 2 Queen's Wharf, while *Bombala*, having suffered no damage, continued on her voyage. Later Captain Croft was found guilty of 'a gross act of misconduct' in trying to pass *Bombala* instead of bringing his vessel to a stop, and had his master's certificate suspended for one month.

Meanwhile, *Coogee* was repaired, and returned to service until being requisitioned for duty as a mine-sweeper on 20 May 1918. Returned to Huddart Parker in February 1919, *Coogee* resumed her place on the excursion trade to Geelong until 1927, when the old vessel was finally withdrawn. After being stripped of all worthwhile parts, the hulk of the vessel was towed outside Port Phillip Heads on 27 February 1928, and scuttled.

Huddart Parker did not replace *Coogee* on the Bass Strait service, instead opting to withdraw from the trade altogether, which thus became the preserve of the Union Line. They continued to operate *Loongana* and *Rotomahana* on the Launceston route for the next ten years.

In December 1907 the veteran *Oonah* was taken off the trade between Sydney and Hobart, and replaced *Flora* on the service from Melbourne to Devonport and Burnie, with two round trips a week.

The winter weather experienced in Bass Strait gave all these ships a hard time from time to time. The little *Oonah* came close to being overwhelmed on several occasions during her Bass Strait career, one particularly bad voyage occurring in June 1911.

The vessel left Burnie on the evening of 7 June, and during the night suffered a terrible pounding from huge seas whipped up by a westerly gale. The seas were so strong that the vessel was seven hours late arriving in Melbourne on the evening of 8 June.

The following day the *Argus* newspaper published this description of the voyage, which was made even more graphic by the vernacular of the day:

Varying between north-west and west, the wind blew in fierce squalls, bringing up exceptionally dangerous seas in which steamers traversing the coast sustained a buffeting, the like of which some of them had never previously undergone.

The Union liner *Oonah*, especially, experienced a stirring adventure on her passage across the Straits from Burnie. She was flung about and swept by seas in an alarming manner, while considerable damage was done about the decks.

It being unsafe for passengers to expose themselves to the storm, they all remained below, but even in their seclusion consternation was caused among them by a huge billow smashing in the saloon skylight and partly flooding that apartment.

This volume of water thundering on board caused the vessel to heel to a startling angle, while it bent the port iron rail for a distance of about fifteen feet as if it had been so much wire. Stanchions were broken, awnings carried away, and sundry other damage done, but no one was injured.

*Oonah* in Union Line colours. (Author's collection)

Captain Madden states that he has never known a more severe storm, and considers the *Oonah* was lucky to come through it without greater ill-effects. The vessel, which should have reached Melbourne at 1 o'clock yesterday afternoon, did not berth until 8 o'clock last night.

*Oonah* had another brush with disaster late the following year. Sailors are well known to be superstitious creatures, and no doubt there were those on board *Oonah* who felt apprehensive when the vessel was scheduled to leave Melbourne for Burnie on the afternoon of Friday, 13 December 1912.

The vessel left South Wharf in the Yarra River on time, having on board 62 passengers in saloon class and 11 in steerage. As *Oonah* was proceeding down the river a fireman fell down the stokehold, and was so badly injured the master, Captain W Madden, diverted to land him at Williamstown for treatment.

About 5.20 the next morning *Oonah* was approaching Burnie when it ran into a thick bank of fog. Captain Madden ordered speed reduced to dead slow, but continued on his way, with a lead line being used at the bow to check the water depths.

One throw of the line showed five fathoms, but the next throw revealed only two fathoms, and as the ship was drawing more than this, about 14 feet, at the stern, Captain Madden ordered the engines be put into reverse.

However, at the same moment *Oonah* ran aground amidships on a small bank of mud, clay and gravel at 6.10 am, and remained held firm. The sea was very calm, and the impact so slight some passengers who were having breakfast did not know the ship had run aground.

Shortly afterwards the fog suddenly lifted, and Captain Madden discovered that his ship was aground some 300 feet off the shore at Cooee Creek, about one and a half miles west of Burnie. A crowd quickly gathered on the shore, and a message sent to Burnie brought the small local steamer *Taroa* to the scene.

As the sea was reasonably calm, and the passengers were not in any immediate danger, they remained on board as Captain Madden waited for high tide shortly after 1 pm. With the *Taroa* standing by, the engines of *Oonah* were put full astern, and at 1.10 pm the vessel glided serenely free, and then proceeded to Burnie.

An inspection by a diver indicated one plate was dented, but otherwise the vessel was

*Oonah* aground near Burnie in December 1912 (Polly Woodside Museum)

undamaged. Despite this, *Loongana* was diverted to call at Burnie the same evening to take on the mails and passengers booked on *Oonah*, and carry them to Melbourne.

Meanwhile *Oonah* left Burnie at 8.30 pm for Devonport, arriving there at 11 pm, and after cargo for that port had been unloaded, *Oonah* left Devonport at 2 am on Sunday to return to Melbourne.

It was also during December 1912 another company entered the Tasmanian passenger trade, though on quite a small scale. Since 1892 The Melbourne Steamship Company had been operating a few small cargo ships with limited passenger accommodation on the trade from Sydney and Melbourne to Fremantle.

In 1908 two of their smaller ships, *Brisbane* and *Melbourne*, were transferred to operate a cargo service from Sydney and Melbourne to ports in northern Tasmania.

During 1912 The Melbourne Steamship Company took delivery of a new vessel named *Dimboola*. This enabled them to transfer another of their older ships, *Sydney*, of 1,989 gross tons, to the trade operating to northern Tasmania, replacing the original two cargo steamers.

*Sydney* berthed at Burnie (Author's collection)

Built in 1902, *Sydney* was fitted with rather basic accommodation for 50 first class and 60 third class passengers, and had a large cargo capacity.

Commencing in December 1912, *Sydney* operated a fortnightly triangular service from Sydney to Eden and Melbourne, then across Bass Strait to Stanley, Burnie and Devonport before returning to Sydney with another stop at Eden.

This service did not pose any major competition to either the Huddart Parker or Union Line services from the mainland to Tasmania, but *Sydney* continued to operate to Tasmania until

1916, when boiler problems caused the ship to be laid up.

The Tasmanian services across Bass Strait were not affected by the outbreak of war in August 1914. The Union Line retained *Loongana* and *Rotomahana* on the main route between Melbourne and Launceston throughout the conflict, while *Oonah* operated from Melbourne to Devonport and Burnie.

Huddart Parker had hoped they would be able to return to the Bass Strait trade in 1915 with a new vessel being built in Britain, but the war intervened, and the new vessel would not enter service until six years later than planned.

Early in 1914 the Marine Board of Launceston had plans drawn up for the construction of a new wharf to be used by the Bass Strait ferries. The wharf was scheduled to be completed in 1915, in readiness for the new Huddart Parker vessel.

This construction was also delayed by the war, and the new berth was not opened until 1917, being named King's Wharf. At that time a new bridge over the North *Esk* River, the Charles Street Bridge, which would provide easy access to King's Wharf, was not finished.

In spite of this, the new wharf was brought into use. The first vessel to dock there, on 12 July 1917, was *Rotomahana*, under the command of Captain F Maitland, which was maintaining the service between Melbourne and Launceston on her own, as *Loongana* was out undergoing extensive engine repairs in Sydney.

During the war years the vessels on the service across Bass Strait were operated at full capacity with very little maintenance, and eventually this caused problems with the turbine engines installed in *Loongana*.

During a crossing from Melbourne to Launceston in stormy weather on the night of 9 April 1917, one of the blades on the middle propeller broke off, and the centre engine had to be stopped. *Loongana* completed the voyage at reduced speed on two engines, and also returned to Melbourne on two propellers.

However, the Union Line decided they would send the vessel on another return trip to Launceston at reduced speed before having the vessel drydocked for repairs.

*Loongana* left her berth on the evening of 11 April, but was still in the Yarra River when

*Sydney* loading potatoes at Devonport about 1912 (Devonport Maritime Museum)

the starboard turbine broke down under the extra load. With *Loongana* unable to manoeuvre on just the port engine and propeller alone, the hopper barge *Batman*, which happened to be in close proximity, was quickly called upon to tow the disabled vessel back to its wharf.

An inspection showed that the blades of the rotor drum on the starboard engine had become weakened by corrosion, and would have to be replaced. This would be an expensive and lengthy procedure, which could only be carried out in Sydney.

In the meantime temporary repairs were effected to enable *Loongana* to resume service until it was able to go to Sydney. On 15 May 1917 *Loongana* arrived at the Cockatoo Island dockyard in Sydney Harbour for the work to be done.

Over a seven month period the three turbine engines were all removed and new rotors and blades made for them in the dockyard, to replace the original parts that were worn out.

It was not until 29 December that *Loongana* left Cockatoo Island and returned to Melbourne

to resume her place on the Launceston trade, which, during the time *Loongana* was away, had been maintained by *Rotomahana* on her own, making two departures a week from Melbourne, on Wednesday and Saturday.

It was also reported that when *Loongana* went to Sydney she had on board a spare tail-shaft, which weighed two and a half tons, in case it was needed as a replacement. This did not happen, and *Loongana* carried the shaft back to Melbourne when she returned.

Once *Loongana* was alongside her wharf, a crane was brought in to offload the shaft, but as it was being lifted off the ship a malfunction caused the load to drop. It fell back into the open hatch, then went on down to tear through the hull plates, leaving a gaping hole below the waterline.

*Loongana* had been scheduled to return to the Bass Strait trade with a departure from Melbourne on 4 January 1918, but the accident put her out of action for a further three days while repairs were completed, and *Rotomahana* continued the service on her own.

The Union Line veteran *Oonah* had also

*Loongana* at speed (Author's collection)

continued to operate a regular service throughout the war years from Melbourne to Burnie and Devonport. All the vessels on the Bass Strait trade were amazingly reliable, and managed to plough their way through the worst the weather and sea could throw at them, but sometimes they came very close to disaster.

In his book *The Vanished Fleet*, T K Fitchett recounted an incident involving *Oonah* that he witnessed himself from Point Lonsdale on a windy winter afternoon in 1918, which is told best in his own words:

> She left Melbourne at 1.00 pm for Burnie in the teeth of a roaring southerly gale. Upon reaching the Heads, she rashly attempted to continue her voyage through the treacherous Rip, despite the fact that ships twice her size were discreetly sheltering off Portsea.
>
> As she headed for the ocean, watchers on the clifftops at Queenscliff and Point Lonsdale were horrified to see what can only be described as a tidal wave advancing on the hapless *Oonah*. It was a terrifying sight. A wall of water, stretching across the entire width of the Heads, rolled in from the ocean, every moment gaining height as it squeezed in through the narrow Rip.
>
> *Oonah* met it head-on fairly between Point Lonsdale and Point Nepean. There came a report like gunfire as she drove her bow deep into the mountainous wave. *Oonah* almost disappeared from sight under hundreds of tons of water and flying spray. For one dread second it seemed to the watchers that the game little ship had been overwhelmed. Then as the giant wave passed on, up she came like a surfacing whale, still in one piece and steaming forward.
>
> When she finally reached the less chaotic water of the open ocean, and it seemed the worst was over, she began to circle about in an erratic fashion, uncomfortably close to the projecting reefs lining the shore.
>
> It became obvious that something had gone amiss. As night fell, however, *Oonah* straightened her course, and it was with relief that the onlookers on the cliffs saw her disappear in the distance on her way to Burnie.
>
> It was later revealed that while battling her way out of the Heads her steering mechanism had suffered damage, rendering her out of control until, under great difficulties, repairs were made,

and she was able to continue her journey.

In the spring of 1918 *Oonah* was taken off the Bass Strait service and returned to her previous route between Sydney and Hobart. *Rotomahana* replaced *Oonah* on the trade from Melbourne to Burnie and Devonport, but was taken out of service for two weeks during October 1918.

As a replacement, the Union Line chartered the 1,122 gross ton *Merimbula* from the Illawarra & South Coast Steam Navigation Co. Built in 1909, *Merimbula* usually operated two round trips a week from Sydney to Merimbula and Eden, on the New South Wales south coast. The vessel provided accommodation for 96 first class and 10 second class passengers.

*Merimbula* departed Melbourne on Tuesday, 15 October on her first voyage to Burnie and Devonport, followed by another round trip commencing on the Friday. The same pattern was followed during the next week, then Merimbula went back to her regular trade when *Rotomahana* returned to service.

The end of the First World War in November 1918 brought about an unexpected series of disruptions to the Bass Strait ferry service. Although the war was now over, a very serious

*Merimbula* operated across Bass Strait for two weeks in October 1918 (Author's collection)

medical problem arose, when a deadly strain of pneumonic influenza swept through Europe in epidemic proportions at the end of 1918.

This influenza was contracted by many Australian troops returning home from Europe. When the ships carrying these men arrived at their Australian destination, they were placed in quarantine, usually at anchor with the troops forced to remain on board.

Troops destined for a port other than that in which the ship was quarantined were sometimes allowed to disembark and be taken on to their home port by another vessel, but on arrival

*Rotomahana* berthed in Burnie. (Devonport Maritime Museum)

there they were then placed in quarantine. Unfortunately, despite these safeguards, the influenza epidemic began to spread within Australia, and eventually restrictions were placed on interstate travel by passenger ships.

At the end of January 1919, *Loongana* was taken off the Bass Strait trade. *Rotomahana* took the departure from Melbourne to Launceston on 3 February, but was then also taken out of service, and for a while the Bass Strait passenger trade came to a halt.

In their place the Union Line placed one of their older cargo ships, *Wainui*, to maintain an irregular service between the mainland and Tasmania carrying necessary cargo, but no passengers.

*Loongana* left Melbourne for Hobart on Saturday, 8 February 1919, carrying 400 troops who had arrived in Melbourne from Europe and needed to be taken to their home state. When *Loongana* arrived in Hobart, the troops were immediately transferred to local excursion boats and taken to Barnes Bay on North Bruny Island, where they were placed in quarantine until being cleared medically and allowed to go home.

It was reported in the papers that *Loongana* would be allowed to carry passengers on the return trip from Hobart to Melbourne, but whether this was actually done is not recorded.

At a later date *Loongana* was also called upon to transport a contingent of troops from Melbourne to Queensland.

Meanwhile the only vessel operating a service from Melbourne to Tasmania was *Wainui*, which made its first departure on Monday, 10 February.

Built in 1886, *Wainui* was just 640 gross tons, and had been operating a cargo service from Melbourne to Strahan, on the west coast of Tasmania, for many years.

*Wainui* left Melbourne once or twice a week until the end of March, when the restrictions on trade caused by the influenza epidemic were lifted, and normal services resumed as quickly as possible.

*Loongana* made her first departure from Melbourne to Launceston on Tuesday, 1 April, while *Rotomahana* left Melbourne on 4 April for Burnie and Devonport. The vessels each operated two return trips a week, as the trade did not warrant any extra sailings at that time.

All shipping services to Tasmania were again totally disrupted by the start of a strike by members of the Federated Seaman's Union on 20 May 1919. Both *Loongana* and *Rotomahana* were left idle in Melbourne when their crews walked off, and even the cargo services across Bass Strait came to a stop.

At first it was hoped the strike would be shortlived, but weeks dragged into months as the dispute continued. It was not until 25 August that mass meetings of seamen around the country agreed to return to work immediately.

By the end of the month both *Loongana* and *Rotomahana* were back in service, but they only operated a limited service, as passenger numbers remained low for some time.

By the end of 1919, *Loongana* was again regularly making three round trips a week to Launceston, while *Rotomahana* maintained the service to Burnie and Devonport twice a week.

Early in 1920 *Oonah* was taken off the route between Sydney and Hobart, and returned to Bass Strait, initially making some voyages between Melbourne and Hobart. Over the rest of the year *Oonah* spent some time laid up, and at other times replaced *Rotomahana* on the service to Burnie and Devonport.

On the afternoon of 13 April 1920, *Loongana* left Launceston on a regular trip to Melbourne. During the night the radio office on *Loongana* picked up a distress message from the Huddart Parker steamer *Westralia*, which had run aground while passing through Banks Strait, which separates the northern tip of Tasmania from the Furneaux Group of islands.

*Westralia* was on a voyage from Wellington to Melbourne, and had attempted to pass through Banks Strait in bad weather with very poor visibility. The passengers were being entertained by a concert when the ship suddenly came to a grinding halt.

As waves began to pound the stranded vessel, passengers quickly put on their life jackets, and lifeboats were swung out, but not lowered.

On receiving the distress message, *Loongana* immediately turned around and headed east towards Banks Strait, arriving at first light. Passengers on board *Loongana*, who had woken up expecting to see the shoreline of Port Phillip Bay, were shocked to find themselves further away from Melbourne than when the voyage began.

Meanwhile it had been determined that *Westralia* was stuck on a sandbar off Clarke Island, and soon after dawn the vessel was able to refloat itself as the tide rose. Apart from water entering one hold, *Westralia* was undamaged, and, escorted by *Loongana*, continued its voyage to Melbourne, where both vessels docked later the same day.

In December 1920 there was another in the series of major maritime strikes that caused enormous disruption in Australia during the inter-war period. At a meeting held in Sydney on Wednesday, 15 December, members of the Marine Stewards & Pantrymen Union decided to start an immediate strike, affecting interstate shipping only.

As a result the three Bass Strait passenger steamers, *Oonah*, *Loongana* and *Rotomahana*, were all tied up, which eventually lasted eleven weeks.

*Oonah* was not being used when the strike began, but when *Rotomahana* arrived in Melbourne on Thursday, 16 December 1920, on what would prove to be her final crossing of Bass Strait, the stewards and pantrymen all walked off, and the vessel had to be laid up.

The same thing happened when *Loongana* arrived from Launceston on Sunday, 19 December. In place of the regular vessels, three small steamers, *Marrawah*, *Kooringa* and *Awaroa*, attempted to maintain a skeleton passenger service, but were not able to come close to meeting the demand for passages.

In desperation some travellers resorted to making the trip across Bass Strait in sailing ships, some voyages taking as long as four days. Despite intensive negotiations, the strike continued into January 1921, by which time hundreds of coastal vessels were sitting idle in ports around the country.

Going into February there were hopeful signs that a resolution was about to be reached, but it was not until mass meetings held around the country on Friday, 25 February, that the strikers decided to return to work.

It took a while to prepare the idle ships for a return to service, so it was not until Wednesday, 2 March 1921 that *Loongana* finally left Melbourne for Launceston once again, and subsequently departed every Monday, Wednesday and Friday.

On 3 March, *Oonah* left Melbourne to reopen the service to Burnie and Devonport, and subsequently departed each Tuesday and Friday. However, there would be no return to service for *Rotomahana*, which finally came to the end of a long and illustrious career.

The old vessel was laid up in Melbourne, and remained idle there for the next four years before being sold at auction on 3 April 1925 to a firm of Melbourne shipbreakers, Power & Davis.

Over the next three years they slowly dismantled *Rotomahana*, along the way discovering some interesting items, including a large sign that read:

STEERAGE PASSENGERS ARE
REQUESTED TO REMOVE THEIR
BOOTS BEFORE RETIRING TO BED

Eventually only the empty hulk was left, and on 29 May 1928 what remained of this once fine vessel was towed through Port Phillip Heads and scuttled in the ship's graveyard three miles out to sea.

Just three months earlier another veteran of the Bass Strait trade, *Coogee*, had made the same trip at the end of a towline, so the two ships rested together on the ocean floor.

# Chapter Six

# Hobart Services

While the services across Bass Strait from Melbourne to ports in northern Tasmania were the prime connections between the mainland and the island state, there were also passenger services linking Hobart directly to Sydney and Melbourne.

The major operator on these routes was the Union Steam Ship Company of New Zealand, which had bought out the Tasmanian Steam Ship Company in 1892, and retained most of their services. Their only competition came from Huddart Parker Limited, whose ships tended to be smaller and less well appointed.

The service between Sydney and Hobart had not been operated by passenger vessels from the late 1890s until 1904, when *Oonah* was taken off the Bass Strait trade and once again began operating between Sydney and Hobart, offering a departure every ten days. At that time Huddart Parker was using one of their older steamers,

*Anglian*, on the route, but in December 1905 *Anglian* was replaced by *Westralia*.

*Westralia* was built in 1897 for the service from Sydney and Melbourne to Fremantle, having accommodation for 180 first class and 200 steerage passengers. On entering service in April 1897, *Westralia* was the largest vessel then operating around the Australian coast, at 2,884 gross tons, but was soon surpassed by newer ships.

In July 1897, *Westralia* was transferred to the service from Sydney to New Zealand, remaining there until the middle of 1899, when she reverted to the Australian coastal trade again.

When the new *Riverina* arrived in Australia in December 1905, it took over from *Westralia*, which was then transferred to the Tasmanian service. *Westralia* would be associated with the service between Sydney and Hobart for most of the next fifteen years.

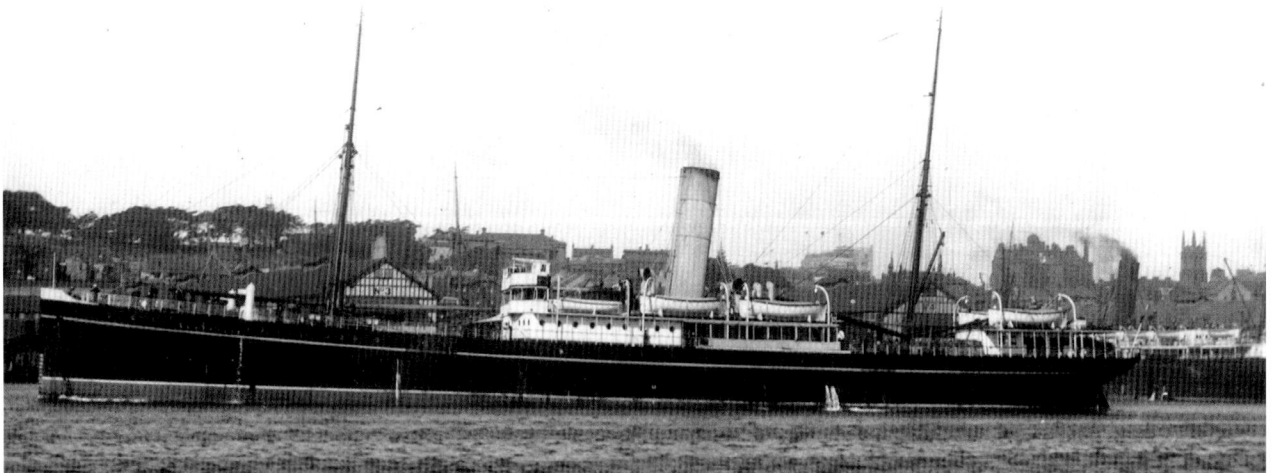

*Westralia* spent many years trading to Hobart (Author's collection)

The design of *Westralia* proved so successful that it became the basis for the next three ships to be built for Huddart Parker Limited. The first of these vessels, built in 1899, was named *Zealandia*, and intended for the service between Sydney and New Zealand. In 1902 *Zealandia* was joined by the *Victoria*, and in 1904 the slightly larger *Wimmera* was completed, and these three vessels maintained the Huddart Parker presence on the trans-Tasman trade.

While *Zealandia* and *Victoria* only operated between Sydney and New Zealand, *Wimmera* became the first Huddart Parker vessel to compete against the Union Line steamers on the 'horseshoe service', which enabled Huddart Parker to enter the trade between Hobart and Melbourne in 1904.

During these years the Union Line also built a series of vessels of increasing size for the 'horseshoe service', commencing in 1897 with the *Waikare*, of 3,071 gross tons, which was joined the following year by the 3,502 gross ton *Mokoia*.

This pair initially operated alongside the older *Monowai*, built in 1890, but in 1902 they were joined by the much larger *Moeraki*, of 4,392 gross tons. *Moeraki* was notable in being the first vessel built for the Union Line to be fitted with twin propellers, and in 1903 she was joined by a slightly larger sister, *Manuka*. These two liners could accommodate 230 passengers

*Mokoia* joined the horseshoe service in 1898 (Author's collection)

in first class and 135 in second class. *Manuka* was transferred to the trans-Pacific route from Sydney to Vancouver in 1904, and did not return to the 'horseshoe service' until 1906.

In 1905 the Union Line took delivery of one of their most famous and beautiful liners, *Maheno*. She was the first trans-Tasman liner to have two funnels, and also the first with three propellers, which were powered by direct drive turbines, another innovation on the trade.

At 5,282 gross tons, *Maheno* was by far the largest vessel yet to have operated across the Tasman Sea, entering the 'horseshoe service' with her departure from Sydney on 18 November 1905. *Maheno* was also the fastest ship on the trade, and soon broke every record between ports.

*Maheno* was the first Union Line ship to have two funnels (Author's collection)

*Maheno* had beautifully appointed accommodation for 234 first class passengers and 116 in second class, and also rather basic quarters for 60 third class passengers. *Maheno* created as big a sensation in Hobart as she had in every other port on her maiden voyage, and then continued to Melbourne.

Despite her size and elegance, *Maheno* had one major failing, an enormous appetite for coal, which made her expensive to operate. *Maheno* had only made a few voyages on the 'horseshoe service' when in April 1906 she was transferred to the longer route from Sydney to Vancouver. After two round trips across the Pacific, *Maheno* returned to the 'horseshoe service', on which she remained extremely popular for many years.

The Union Line then brought out an even larger liner, the *Marama* of 6,437 gross tons, which entered the 'horseshoe service' in November 1907. *Marama* lacked the beautiful lines, elegance and speed of *Maheno*, having only one funnel and being fitted with old-fashioned triple expansion machinery, but was much more economical to operate.

Accommodation was provided for 229 first class, 79 second class and 153 third class passengers, but the accent was on comfort rather than luxury. However, after only three months on the 'horseshoe service', *Marama* was transferred to the Vancouver route.

Faced with this major competition on the Tasman services, Huddart Parker had little option but to order a larger liner for themselves. As a stopgap measure, in January 1907 they placed their largest coastal liner, *Riverina*, on the 'horseshoe service' for several voyages.

Built in 1905, *Riverina* was smaller than the *Maheno* at 4,758 gross tons, but offered better accommodation than the ships Huddart Parker were regularly using on the trade. During this period *Riverina* made several voyages between Hobart and Melbourne, but then returned to the Australian coastal trade.

In 1908 Huddart Parker took delivery of their largest liner to date, the 5,777 gross ton *Ulimaroa*, a name derived from an old Maori term for Australia, which translated as 'blue and distant'.

Launched on 20 July 1907, *Ulimaroa* arrived in Sydney on 26 February 1908 at the end of her delivery voyage, departing on 29 February for her maiden trip across the Tasman Sea, to New Zealand ports, then to Hobart and on to Melbourne.

Comfortable cabin accommodation was providing a departure from Sydney and Hobart every Tuesday. However, on 26 November 1907 *Oonah* left Sydney on her final round trip to Hobart, departing there on 3 December.

*Oonah* was then transferred back to the Bass Strait trades, being replaced in Sydney by *Mararoa*, which was a larger vessel at 2,465 gross tons, but of the same vintage as *Oonah*. Built in 1885, *Mararoa* was the largest vessel in the Union Line fleet at that time, and was initially placed on a service from Australia and New Zealand to San Francisco.

Subsequently *Mararoa* was used on services across the Tasman Sea until 1903, by which time newer and larger vessels were available. For the next few years *Mararoa* was used on New Zealand domestic routes, including that between Wellington and Lyttelton. *Mararoa* could carry about 200 passengers in two classes, and also had a large cargo capacity.

*Mararoa* was always a difficult ship to handle, as she was fitted with a tiller instead of a conventional wheel, and the rudder was moved by hydraulic power, which required a full head of steam being maintained at all times.

On 10 December 1907, *Mararoa* departed

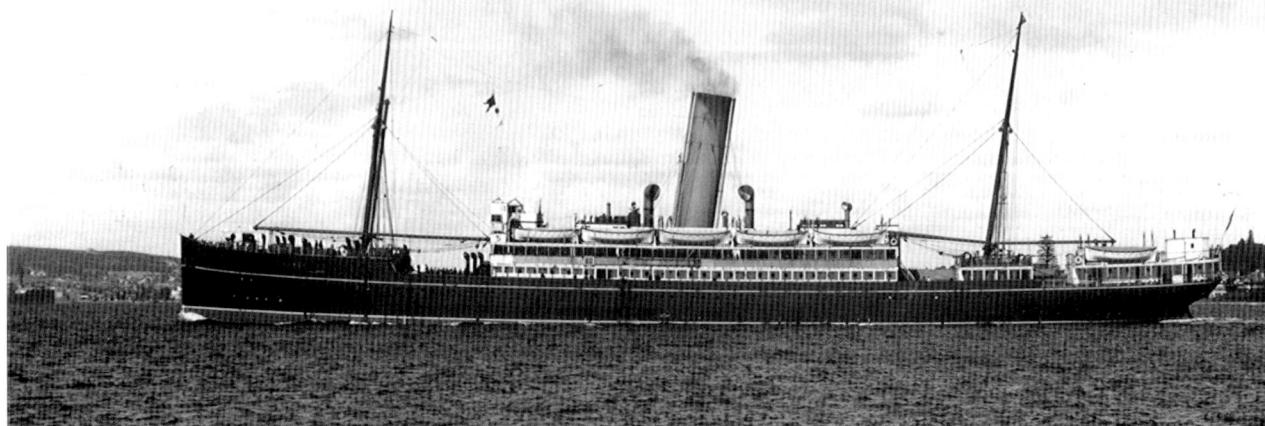

*Ulimaroa* entered service in February 1908 (Author's collection)

provided for 292 first class and 121 second class passengers, and *Ulimaroa* soon became popular with travellers. With the withdrawal of *Marama* from the 'horseshoe service' in March 1908, *Ulimaroa* became the largest ship on the route, though not as fast as *Maheno*.

The trade between Sydney and Hobart was still being maintained by *Oonah* and *Westralia*. Each vessel made one round trip a fortnight, thus Sydney on her first voyage to Hobart, making the round trip in just over a week, to provide extra departures during the peak Christmas/New Year travel period.

Through February and March of 1908, *Mararoa* departed Sydney every second Tuesday in conjunction with *Westralia*, and continued this pattern into April, but was then replaced by *Zealandia*.

Mararoa operated between Sydney and Hobart for several months (Author's collection)

Maunganui was a fine addition to the horseshoe service in 1912 (Author's collection)

Following the entry into service of *Ulimaroa*, Huddart Parker Limited had transferred *Wimmera* to their shorter services from Sydney to New Zealand, which made *Zealandia* redundant on the Tasman trade.

As Huddart Parker had no alternative use for this vessel, in April 1908 *Zealandia* was chartered by the Union Line, and placed on a regular service between Hobart and Sydney.

*Zealandia* departed Sydney on her first trip to Hobart on 21 April, replacing *Mararoa*, which then returned to New Zealand. *Mararoa* was used on various New Zealand domestic routes until being withdrawn in 1927, and dismantled in 1931.

In September 1909 the Union Line bought *Zealandia* outright, and she was renamed *Paloona*. The vessel was then given an extensive refit, which included the heightening of the funnel. *Paloona* returned to service on 13 December 1909 on the trade between Hobart and Sydney, offering a departure from each port once a week.

It was not until 1912 that another new vessel

Paloona was easily recognised by its very tall funnel (Author's collection)

was completed for the 'horseshoe service', this being the 7,527 gross ton *Maunganui* of the Union Line. Larger and faster than both *Maheno* and *Ulimaroa*, *Maunganui* provided accommodation for 244 first class, 175 second class and 80 third class passengers, and entered service in February 1912. *Maunganui* remained the largest vessel on the 'horseshoe service' until war broke out in Europe in August 1914.

In 1913 the veteran *Mokoia* was taken off the 'horseshoe service' and joined *Paloona* operating between Sydney and Hobart. Towards the end of 1913, Huddart Parker took *Wimmera* off their trans-Tasman service, and she was also placed on the service between Sydney and Hobart alongside *Westralia*. However, *Wimmera* only remained on the Tasmanian trade until the autumn of 1914, then returned to the trans-Tasman service again.

Going into 1914, the Union Line was operating *Moeraki*, *Manuka*, *Maunganui* and *Maheno* on the 'horseshoe service', along with *Ulimaroa* of Huddart Parker. Since entering service *Maheno* had proved a very popular ship, but extremely expensive to operate.

Early in 1914 *Maheno* was taken out of service for a major refit, during which her original direct drive turbines were removed and replaced with more conventional geared turbines. At the same time the centre one of her three propellers was removed.

When *Maheno* returned to service in September 1914 it was found that her consumption of coal had been greatly reduced, while her service speed was only slightly less than before, despite the loss of one propeller.

Within weeks of the outbreak of war in Europe in August 1914, the 'horseshoe service' was disrupted by the removal of ships for war service. First to go was *Moeraki*, which was taken over by the New Zealand Government one week after war was declared, for service as a troop transport.

On 15 August, *Moeraki*, in company with *Monowai*, departed Auckland carrying the first contingent of New Zealand troops to be sent overseas, to German Samoa, where they landed on 30 August at Apia and secured the island without much opposition. *Moeraki* returned to New Zealand, and was then handed back to the Union Line, resuming her place on the 'horseshoe service', where she remained for most of the remainder of the war.

*Maunganui* was requisitioned by the New Zealand Government in Wellington on 23 August 1914, and converted to carry troops, a task she would perform superbly throughout the war years.

*Manuka* was also requisitioned for trooping duties early in the war, departing on her first voyage to Egypt in October 1914, remaining on this service until 1917.

*Maheno* remained on the 'horseshoe service' until May 1915, then was requisitioned by the New Zealand Government to become that country's first hospital ship. The conversion work was done by the Union Line's own staff at Port Chalmers, with *Maheno* departing Wellington on 10 July for her first voyage overseas, to Egypt and Britain. *Maheno* served in this capacity for the remainder of the war.

The requisitioning of *Maheno* left just *Moeraki* and *Ulimaroa* operating across the Tasman Sea, so the 'horseshoe service' was terminated, and replaced with direct services from Sydney to New Zealand.

In January 1916 the New Zealand Government also requisitioned *Ulimaroa*, despite her being an Australian vessel. She was converted into a troop transport, and painted in the camouflage colours then being used on merchant ships going to war.

Over the next two years *Ulimaroa* made five trooping voyages from New Zealand to Egypt, and was then used to repatriate wounded soldiers from Egypt to New Zealand, her last voyage in this capacity departing Suez on 30 June 1919. For the final years of the war, *Moeraki* was the only vessel operating across the Tasman Sea, but no longer called at Hobart.

The coastal service between Sydney and Hobart was being operated by *Westralia*, *Mokoia* and *Paloona* when the war broke out, following which it was also disrupted. Within weeks of war being declared, *Mokoia* was taken off the Tasmanian service, and converted to transport New Zealand troops, which she did for the rest of the war.

In October 1914 *Paloona* was also taken off the Tasmanian trade, and transferred to the trans-Tasman service as a replacement for larger ships that had been taken for war duty. For the remainder of the war the Union Line service between Sydney and Hobart was suspended, but Huddart Parker kept their *Westralia* on the route throughout the war years.

In December 1918 the Union Line returned to the trade when *Oonah* once again began operating between Sydney and Hobart. At the same time, the Union Line was operating *Taviuni* on a service from Sydney to Burnie and Devonport, while *Wakatipu* was still maintaining the trade from Sydney to Launceston. However, in February 1919 *Westralia* was transferred to the direct service between Melbourne and Wellington, and Huddart Parker temporarily abandoned the Sydney to Hobart trade.

During 1919, as their passenger liners were released from Government service and refitted for commercial trades, the Union Steam Ship Company of New Zealand was gradually able to resume regular services across the Tasman Sea between New Zealand and Australia. However, one pre-war route that was not resumed was the famous 'horseshoe service'; instead the Union Line opted to run several direct services from Sydney or Melbourne to Auckland and Wellington.

Just when it seemed that services were getting back to a semblance of normality, a mass meeting of seamen in Sydney on 20 May 1919 decided to call a strike to support their claim for better working conditions and pay on the coastal services. As Australian ships began arriving at their home port, their crews walked off, and the ships were laid up.

For over two months no headway was made in attempts to settle the strike, which caused enormous hardship to Tasmania, which was totally dependent on ships to transport the necessities of life to the island, and also carry their exports.

With no regular services between Hobart and the mainland, there were occasional voyages between the ports by a variety of small vessels. One such trip, though really outside the confines of this book as it did not carry passengers, is worth recording here.

The vessel involved was the 194 gross ton wooden-hulled excursion boat *Cartela*, built in Hobart in 1912, which normally ventured no further than Bruny Island. However, on 9 July

The Hobart excursion vessel *Cartela* made a trip to Melbourne in 1919 (Maritime Museum of Tasmania)

1919 *Cartela* voyaged from Hobart to Port Huon, where 4,000 cases of apples were loaded, then she set off for Melbourne. Whereas the Union Line and Huddart Parker ships would complete this trip in about 36 hours, it took *Cartela* 21 days.

The voyage was marred all the way by bad weather, forcing the vessel to seek shelter several times. On her first attempt to cross Bass Strait *Cartela* was forced to turn about and seek shelter at Whitemark, on Flinders Island, until the weather abated. Having struggled across Bass Strait, *Cartela* then ran out of coal, and was forced to anchor in Waterloo Bay for ten days until the collier *Moonah* arrived from Melbourne with a load of coal. Having replenished, *Cartela* arrived in Melbourne the next day.

Once the cases of apples had been discharged, *Cartela* loaded a cargo of general merchandise for the return trip. This time the weather was much better, and the voyage took just forty-seven hours to complete, but instead of going directly to Hobart, the vessel was forced to stop at Barnes Bay, on Bruny Island, for quarantine.

This was the only time *Cartela* ventured away from Hobart. Today *Cartela* is still operating excursions on the River Derwent, though now converted to diesel power and greatly altered in appearance, but she is Australia's oldest continually licensed passenger vessel.

In the middle of August 1919 there were signs that the seamen's strike was about to reach a settlement, and at one time there was even an announcement that all ships would be manned again on 18 August. This did not happen, as there were still several issues to be sorted out, but at mass meetings held on 25 August the men did agree to an immediate return to work.

On 27 August *Oonah* left Sydney on a voyage to Hobart, while Huddart Parker decided to send *Riverina* on a special trip to Hobart departing on 30 August, after which the vessel resumed her trade across the Tasman Sea. *Oonah* remained on the trade between Sydney and Hobart for a few more months, but then was replaced by two larger vessels.

The Union Line service from Lyttelton and Wellington to Sydney was being operated by the sister ships, *Moeraki* and *Manuka*. In between each voyage, these ships were also programmed to make a voyage from Sydney to Hobart and back, providing a weekly service. This service was maintained through to the end of 1919, and into the early months of 1920.

By that time *Ulimaroa* had been released from war duties, and following a refit, departed Sydney on 4 March 1920 on her first post-war voyage, to Wellington and Lyttelton. Meanwhile, Huddart Parker also returned briefly to the Hobart trade when *Riverina*, which was then operating between Sydney and Auckland, departed Sydney on 10 March 1920 for Tasmania, but on her return to Sydney resumed her place on the Tasman trade.

On 29 March, *Ulimaroa* departed Sydney on her first voyage to Hobart and back. Subsequently *Ulimaroa* would operate this route once every three weeks, in conjunction with *Moeraki* and *Manuka*.

These three vessels now maintained a combined schedule that provided a weekly departure across the Tasman to Wellington from Sydney, and also a weekly return trip to Hobart, departing Sydney every Tuesday.

For example, *Manuka* took the sailing on 27 April, followed by *Moeraki* on 4 May, *Ulimaroa* on 11 May, *Manuka* again on 18 May and so on. Very occasionally *Riverina* would also make a

*Moeraki* operated between Sydney and Hobart (Author's collection)

voyage to Hobart between her Auckland voyages, one such trip departing Sydney on 14 May.

In August 1920 *Manuka* was temporarily taken off the trans-Tasman service to Sydney, being replaced by *Moana*, which also made the round trip to Hobart from Sydney between trips to New Zealand.

*Manuka* returned to the trade in early September, and was partnered by *Moana* while *Moeraki* was also off the route for maintenance. These two and *Ulimaroa* continued the three-weekly schedule until the end of the November, at which time *Moeraki* returned and *Moana* was transferred to other routes.

On Wednesday, 15 December 1920, members of the Marine Stewards & Pantrymen Union decided to start an immediate strike, which affected Australian owned interstate ships only. *Ulimaroa* had just left on a voyage to New Zealand, but on returning to Sydney the ship had to be laid up when the crew walked off.

However, the ships operated by the Union Steam Ship Company were not affected, so between their trips to Wellington, *Manuka* and *Moeraki* were able to continue to operate a series of weekly round trips between Sydney and Hobart in December 1920 and January 1921. It was not until after the strike was settled on 25 February 1921 that *Ulimaroa*

was able to return to service.

*Manuka*, *Moeraki* and *Ulimaroa* continued to provide a weekly connection between Sydney and Hobart over the next few months, but major changes were happening on the Australian coastal trades.

The introduction of the *Navigation Act* was to eventually prevent non-Australian ships from carrying passengers between Australian ports. This would have a major effect on the Union Line operation to Hobart, which was terminated on 30 June 1921.

*Moeraki* took the last Union Line sailing from Sydney, on 28 June, leaving Hobart on 2 July. When *Ulimaroa* departed Sydney on 5 July, that marked the end of the weekly service to Hobart.

Subsequently *Manuka*, *Moeraki* and *Ulimaroa* only operated a combined service across the Tasman from Sydney, though *Ulimaroa*, being under the Australian flag, could have continued making voyages between Sydney and Hobart.

Instead, Huddart Parker decided to bring back *Westralia* to operate between Sydney and Hobart, but her first departure was not until 18 July 1921.

Instead of providing a weekly departure, *Westralia* made one round trip every ten or eleven days, providing the Tasmanians with just two departures every three weeks, a vastly inferior service to the one they had been enjoying.

# Chapter Seven

# Nairana

In 1913 Huddart Parker had a change of mind about their decision in 1910 to withdraw from the service across Bass Strait. The trade between Melbourne and Launceston was growing steadily, and Huddart Parker decided the time was right to order a new ship which would eclipse *Loongana*, and enable them to return to the Tasmanian service on a very competitive basis.

*Loongana* had been so successful that Huddart Parker went to the same builders, Denny Bros, who were famous for building many of the finest British cross-channel steamers. The design of the new Bass Strait ship was based on the latest of these vessels, and an improvement on *Loongana*.

The new vessel was to be given an extra deck in the superstructure, and also a cruiser stern, which was just beginning to replace the counter stern in shipbuilding, but the same type of machinery would be installed.

Construction of the new vessel commenced at the end of 1913, with delivery scheduled for early in 1915. The vessel was almost complete to the launching stage when the First World War started, at which time all work on non-military ships came to a complete stop at the order of the British Government, who wanted all available workers engaged in the construction of warships.

The unfinished vessel sat on the stocks for the next nine months, but then instructions were received to resume work on it so that it could be launched, which would free the slipway for the construction of more urgently needed warships.

Only a few weeks were required to complete the vessel to launching stage, and she slipped into the water without any ceremony on 21 June 1915, having been named *Nairana*, an aboriginal word meaning 'Golden Eagle' or 'Eagle of the sun'.

Once in the water, though little more than an empty hull, *Nairana* was towed to an anchorage, and left to await future events. For eighteen months the incomplete vessel swung idly at her anchor, but by 1917 the British were in need of more and more ships to meet the demands of the war.

Early in 1917, *Nairana* was requisitioned by the British Government, having been earmarked for conversion into a seaplane carrier. The conversion entailed the erection of a large hangar on the aft section of the ship, complete with a crane to lift the aircraft out of the water.

Meanwhile, forward of the bridge a short, downward, sloping flight deck was installed, to enable the aircraft to take off, and the rest of the superstructure was filled with workshops and maintenance areas. A number of small calibre guns were also fitted fore and aft.

When the conversion was completed, *Nairana* was quite a bizarre looking vessel, an effect that was heightened by the dazzle paint applied,

HMS *Nairana* was a very strange looking vessel (Author's collection)

which was supposed to make the vessel harder to see when it was at sea. On 25 August 1917, the vessel was commissioned into the Royal Navy as HMS *Nairana*.

Having run trials and completed working up exercises the following month, *Nairana* was sent north to Scapa Flow, to join the Grand Fleet. Not a great deal is known about the war service of *Nairana*, apart from one notable incident in August 1918.

British forces had been sent to Archangel in Russia to assist the White Russians in their civil war with the Communists for control of the country. *Nairana* accompanied the British force, anchoring off the Russian port while her seaplanes flew missions attacking the Communist forces holding the town.

The planes bombed the fort that guarded the entrance to the harbour until its guns were silenced, and they also managed to sink the vessel on which a leading Bolshevik was trying to escape.

*Nairana* then came closer in to the port, and used her own guns to engage and knock out six Communist batteries located at the mouth of the river. Throughout the entire incident *Nairana* escaped unscathed.

Soon after the war ended in November 1918, *Nairana* was released by the British Government, and returned to her builder's yard to be completed to the original plans. This was quite a lengthy process, as first all the structures erected during the war had to be removed before work could begin on building the proper superstructure, and then fitting out the interior to its original specifications.

As a final touch, a brass plaque was presented to the vessel by the British Admiralty to commemorate her war career, in particular the part played in the capture of Archangel. The plaque and a photo of the ship as a seaplane carrier were mounted above the grand staircase, where they remained until the end of her commercial career.

The plaque is now in the Wellington Harbour Maritime Museum in New Zealand, while the photograph is in the Launceston Maritime Museum.

It was not until 22 January 1921 that *Nairana* was finally handed over to Huddart Parker, some six years later than the planned delivery date. On 30 January *Nairana*, under the command of Captain Easson, departed Plymouth on her delivery voyage to Australia, arriving in Melbourne on 27 March.

For three weeks *Nairana* sat at Queen's Wharf in the Yarra River while the final touches were made to the interior, and the ship was fully prepared for entry into the service for which it had been designed.

On 18 April 1921 *Nairana* departed Melbourne on her first crossing of Bass Strait, which turned on some heavy weather for the occasion, forcing the vessel to reduce speed, averaging 16.75 knots.

Following an eighteen-hour overnight trip to Launceston, a huge crowd gathered on the wharf the next morning to welcome the ship they had waited so long for.

The return trip to Melbourne was also adversely affected by bad weather, but on

*Nairana* as she appeared when first placed in service (Author's collection)

*Nairana* leaves Melbourne early in her career (WSS Victoria Branch collection)

her second voyage across Bass Strait from Launceston, *Nairana* was able to give a better indication of her speed.

Having passed Low Head, at the mouth of the Tamar River, at 5.50 pm, *Nairana* entered Port Phillip Heads at 3.30 am, having completed the crossing at an average speed of 18 knots, despite running into choppy seas and a north-west wind for five hours.

The vessel operated three round trips a week, departing Melbourne on Monday, Wednesday and Friday evenings, returning from Launceston the following evening, with Sunday spent berthed in Melbourne.

*Nairana* operated on a joint schedule with *Loongana*, which would depart Melbourne on Tuesday and Thursday, with the return trip from Launceston each Wednesday and Friday.

In Melbourne *Nairana* always used Queen's Wharf on the Yarra River, berthing with her bow facing up the river towards the city. On departing, *Nairana* would swing around in a large basin just above Queen's Wharf, then head down the river.

In Launceston, *Nairana* usually proceeded up the Tamar River and berthed at King's Wharf, in the centre of the city.

Sometimes, when river conditions were unfavourable, the vessel could not proceed any further than Beauty Point, near the mouth of the

Tamar River, from where passengers would be transported to Launceston by tender.

The arrival of *Nairana* was greatly appreciated by travellers, but farmers with properties along the edges of the Tamar River were not so happy, complaining about their lands being flooded by the wash from *Nairana* as she swept around the bends of the river.

Comfortable accommodation was provided for 250 passengers in first class and 140 in second class. In peak periods extra passengers were carried, using shakedown berths set up in the lounges at night, and dismantled in the morning.

*Nairana* soon proved she had a good turn of reserve power, being able to reach eighteen knots on some crossings when necessary to make up lost time.

The combined service provided by *Nairana* and *Loongana* was the best the people of Launceston had yet enjoyed.

Three years after the end of the First World War, the Federal Government proclaimed the *Navigation Act*, which would have a major effect on Australian coastal shipping.

This Act had first been promoted as far back as 1904, but progress on developing it had been very slow, and ultimately ceased when war broke out in 1914. In 1919 work on framing the

*Loongana* partnered *Nairana* on the Launceston service (Polly Woodside Museum)

*Navigation Act* resumed, and it became law in 1921.

The *Navigation Act* was the compromise result of trying to serve the interests of both the Australian shipowners and the maritime unions, and basically laid down minimum rates and conditions for seamen working on ships within Australian waters. The Act also prevented ships not owned in Australia from carrying passengers or cargo between Australian ports.

One company to be seriously affected by the *Navigation Act* was the Union Steam Ship Company of New Zealand, some of whose ships were engaged in Australian coastal trades, especially those between Tasmania and the mainland.

Prior to the war, the Union Line had been actively involved in passenger services that connected Melbourne and Hobart and also Sydney and Launceston, being the only company providing these links.

The service between Melbourne and Hobart formed part of the famous 'horseshoe route', but that was abandoned by the Union Line early in the war, and never reinstated.

The trade between Sydney and Launceston had been operated by the Union Line veteran *Wakatipu* since 1899, but on 26 September 1921 *Wakatipu* was laid up in Sydney, and that service closed down as well.

Meanwhile, the service to Burnie and Devonport was still being operated by *Oonah*, by now well and truly into the veteran stage of her career, which departed Melbourne each Tuesday and Friday.

*Oonah* arriving at Devonport (Author's collection)

# Chapter Eight

# Tasmanian Steamers Pty Ltd

During 1921 the Union Steam Ship Company and Huddart Parker began having talks with a view to forming a jointly owned, Australian registered company to operate their Bass Strait ferries. When an agreement was reached, it resulted in the formation of Tasmanian Steamers Pty Ltd, in which each company owned a half share.

The new company was incorporated in Melbourne on 22 December 1921, and commenced operations on 1 January 1922, on which date *Nairana*, *Loongana* and *Oonah* were transferred to their ownership.

The only visible change as far as the ships transferred to the new company were concerned was new funnel colours. These were a combination of those of the two owning firms, a yellow base and black top separated by a wide red band. The Union Line ships retained their dark green hulls, while the hull of *Nairana* continued to be black.

Under the new company, *Loongana* and *Nairana* continued to operate three return trips a week between Melbourne and Launceston, with no departure from either port on Sunday.

However, at Christmas *Loongana* would make a special voyage from Melbourne to Burnie, Devonport and Launceston, while *Nairana* would travel from Melbourne to Launceston, then on to Burnie and Devonport, before returning to Melbourne, with both ships being alongside King's Wharf in Launceston on Christmas Day.

The only problem with the service was the necessity for *Nairana* to have to anchor off Rosevears, fourteen miles down stream from Launceston, when low tide prevented the vessel either arriving or departing King's Wharf at the scheduled time.

On some days when *Nairana* could not proceed as far as Launceston on her arrival from Melbourne, the inconvenience would be exacerbated by the failure of the tender to meet her. The boat used for this was the same one that operated a regular ferry service from Launceston to various places along the river as far as George Town, and the *Nairana* passengers would have to wait until it reached them. Having boarded the passengers from Melbourne, the tender would then make all its usual calls on the way up river to Launceston.

This became such a problem that in the end the Tasmanian Government issued a directive that the tender must always be in attendance when a ferry from Melbourne had to anchor at Rosevears, and then proceed directly to Launceston.

When low tide affected departures, *Nairana* would leave King's Wharf early, and wait at Rosevears for passengers to be brought down river by the tender. However, after Captain McIntyre took command of *Nairana* in 1929, he used the tender twice in his first month of service on the ship, but from then on always made it to and from King's Wharf regardless of the state of the tide.

He was quoted as saying, 'There is nothing wrong with either the Tamar River or the *Nairana*', and criticised previous captains for being too cautious.

Following the formation of Tasmanian Steamers, *Oonah* had continued to operate two round trips a week between Melbourne, Burnie and Devonport, but on odd occasions was called upon to make voyages to Launceston.

In October 1922, *Nairana* was taken out of

*Nairana* in the colours of Tasmanian Steamers (Lindsay Rex collection)

service for overhaul. During the early part of the month *Loongana* operated two trips a week to Launceston, departing Melbourne on Tuesday and Friday, while *Oonah* left on Monday and Thursday for Devonport and Burnie.

However, from 14 October the Launceston Maritime Board began dredging in the Tamar River. To reduce the interference to this caused by larger vessels proceeding up the river, the Bass Strait ships switched their routes, with *Loongana*

departing Melbourne on Monday, Wednesday and Friday for Devonport and Burnie, while *Oonah* would leave on Tuesday and Friday for Launceston.

On the afternoon of Tuesday, 17 October, *Oonah*, under the command of Captain R L Davies, left Melbourne on her first trip to Launceston, carrying 111 passengers, 244 tons of cargo and 500 live sheep.

At 6.23 on the morning of Wednesday, 18

*Loongana* with Tasmanian Steamers colours on her funnels (Lindsay Rex collection)

*Oonah* in the colours of Tasmanian Steamers (Polly Woodside Museum)

October, the vessel passed through Tamar Heads at the mouth of the Tamar River, and began following the twisting channel that led upstream to Launceston. The tide was running in fairly strongly at the time, and *Oonah* did not turn to port quickly enough after passing Bombay Rock, causing it to run aground on Garden Island Reef, off Kelso Spit on the western side of the river almost opposite George Town.

Initial attempts to refloat *Oonah* using the engines full astern proved unsuccessful, so the tug *Wybia* was sent to the scene, but it was also unable to pull *Oonah* free. During the afternoon the excursion boat *Rowitta* was sent down from Launceston to take off all the passengers, and carry them to their destination.

*Oonah* remained stuck fast, so the cargo was off-loaded into lighters, but still the ship remained firmly aground. On the Saturday the coal was also removed from the bunkers, and even the lifeboats removed to further lighten the ship, while arrangements were in hand to bring in salvage gear from the mainland, and the ship's two anchors were laid out astern and attached to cargo winches.

On Sunday, 22 October, there was an exceptionally high tide, and as it reached its peak near noon Captain Davies made another attempt to refloat his ship. With the engines going full astern, and the winches pulling on the anchors, *Oonah* suddenly slipped into deeper water.

*Oonah* then proceeded up the river to Launceston, berthing there at 3 pm. The vessel took on board a large number of passengers and cargo, then left Launceston at 6 am on 23

October and returned to Melbourne.

*Oonah* was drydocked, but was found to have suffered no major damage in the incident. However, the vessel was out of service for several days, resuming her schedule on Friday, 27 October with a voyage to Launceston. When *Nairana* returned to service, *Oonah* reverted to her regular trade to Devonport and Burnie.

During October 1923 the vessel Huddart Parker operated between Sydney and Hobart, *Riverina*, had to go into dry dock, and no suitable replacement was available. As a stopgap measure, *Nairana* was called upon to make two trips on the Sydney–Hobart service.

In her absence, *Loongana* was left to operate two return trips a week to Launceston on her own, departing Melbourne on Tuesday and Friday evening, while *Oonah* continued to make two trips a week to Burnie and Devonport, departing Melbourne on Monday and Thursday at noon.

*Nairana* went to Sydney in late September 1923 for drydocking, being refloated on 11 October. The vessel then made two voyages between Sydney and Hobart, the first departing Sydney on 15 October, arriving in Hobart two days later. Departing Hobart on 18 October, *Nairana* was back in Sydney on 20 October. The second voyage by *Nairana* to Hobart departed Sydney on 24 October, arriving back on 29 October.

For several weeks Huddart Parker had been advertising that *Nairana* would be carrying first and second class passengers on her voyage back to Melbourne, this being described as a

Melbourne Cup trip.

*Nairana* departed Sydney at 4 pm on Monday, 29 October, and made the trip down to Melbourne, where she arrived on the morning of 31 October. The same evening *Nairana* resumed her place on the Bass Strait trade.

In December 1924 and January 1925 almost all the coastal shipping in Australia was brought to a standstill by a seamen's strike. It started off in the first week of December as a strike by stevedores, but over succeeding weeks other maritime unions became involved.

The first Bass Strait vessel to be affected was *Loongana*, which had to be laid up due to lack of sufficient crew on 8 December. *Nairana* and *Oonah* managed to keep going, though the company advertisements indicated that scheduled departures were on a 'circumstances permitting' basis only.

On 12 December *Oonah* was also forced out of service, but *Nairana* still managed to keep operating, though several departures were either delayed or had to be cancelled due to union problems.

Just before Christmas it was thought a settlement had been reached, but several unions did not adhere to the arrangement. Despite this, *Nairana* was still able to operate three trips a week between Melbourne and Launceston over the busy Christmas period, while *Oonah* made a

departure from Melbourne on 24 December to Burnie and Devonport, followed by *Loongana* on 26 December.

From 1 January 1925 *Nairana* was scheduled to make her regular trips to Launceston, while *Loongana* was departing Melbourne on Tuesday and Friday for Burnie and Devonport, and *Oonah* was again laid up.

Within days the strike situation suddenly worsened, centring around a manning dispute. As coastal ships arrived in their home port the crew would walk off, and shipowners were unable to find replacements.

On Monday, 5 January, *Nairana* arrived in Melbourne from Launceston, and her crew walked off. The same thing happened when *Loongana* arrived on the Tuesday morning, so both ships had to be laid up. At the same time the service between Sydney and Hobart also ceased, leaving Tasmania totally isolated.

As this was in the height of the summer tourist season, several thousand visitors found themselves trapped on the island state unable to get home, while hundreds of Tasmanians who had gone to the mainland for a holiday were in a similar predicament.

Because of the provisions of the *Navigation Act* of 1920, under which international passenger liners were banned from carrying passengers between Australian ports, the

*Hobsons Bay* made a special voyage to Tasmania in January 1925 (Author's collection)

situation in Tasmania quickly became desperate. The strike was also affecting the flow of cargo, especially foodstuff, from the mainland, and the State Government made requests to the Prime Minister, Stanley Bruce, and the Federal Government for assistance. The first response to this was an arrangement that would see the liner *Hobsons Bay* make a return trip between Melbourne and Tasmania.

*Hobsons Bay* was a 14,198 gross ton passenger liner owned by the Australian Commonwealth Government Line, one of five sisters built in the early 1920s for the Australian Government to operate between Britain and Australia carrying about 700 migrants and cargo. As it was an Australian owned and registered vessel, it was exempt from the *Navigation Act* ban on international vessels carrying passengers on coastal trades.

In January 1925 *Hobsons Bay* was on a voyage from Britain to Australia, with stops at Fremantle and Melbourne before reaching Sydney. At the same time the Federal Government made arrangements for another vessel of the Commonwealth Government Line, *Largs Bay*, to carry stranded passengers from Sydney to Hobart at the start of its voyage from Sydney back to London, as is described in the next chapter.

By the time *Hobsons Bay* arrived in Melbourne on Friday, 9 January, it had been arranged that the vessel would leave on the Saturday afternoon for Hobart, arriving there on Monday morning, and leaving the same day to return to Melbourne on Wednesday morning.

However, D S Jackson, a Tasmanian Member of Parliament, contacted the Prime Minister with the advice that, should *Hobsons Bay* go to the mouth of the Tamar River instead of Hobart, it would be able to save two days in travelling time.

This was agreed to, much to the chagrin of those in Hobart, and on the evening of 10 January, *Hobsons Bay* left Melbourne for Tasmania, having about 150 passengers bound for Sydney still on board.

For tourists stranded in Hobart, a special overnight train was organised to take 300 of them to Launceston, from where they were transferred at King's Wharf to the excursion steamer *Rowitta* for the trip down the Tamar.

Another 500 potential passengers made the trip from Launceston to George Town, at the mouth of the Tamar, by car or bus, along an unsealed road that was soon clogged with traffic and dust.

When *Hobsons Bay* arrived on the morning of Sunday, 11 January, the captain refused to enter the mouth of the Tamar and anchor off George Town. Instead the ship dropped anchor a mile out to sea.

At 9.30 am about 200 passengers boarded the tug *Wybia* with their luggage at George Town to be taken out to *Hobsons Bay*. Once they were on board the passengers who had boarded the ship in Melbourne to return to Tasmania boarded the tug for the trip to shore.

By then the *Rowitta* had arrived from Launceston, but it had great difficulty in coming alongside the liner due to the choppy sea. The top deck of *Rowitta* kept on hitting the side of the liner, so after about 225 of the passengers had managed to scramble up the accommodation ladder hanging down the side of *Hobsons Bay*, the captain of *Rowitta* decided his vessel was taking too much damage, and he pulled away. There were still over 70 people on board, along with all the luggage.

As *Rowitta* pulled clear of *Hobsons Bay*, *Wybia* came out with a second load of passengers from George Town. The captains of the two vessels conferred, and it was decided that *Wybia* would tie up alongside the liner, with *Rowitta* then going alongside *Wybia*.

This enabled the remaining passengers and all the luggage on *Rowitta* to be taken on board *Hobsons Bay*, along with the passengers and luggage *Wybia* had brought out, plus 70 bags of mail.

At 5 pm *Wybia* pulled away from *Hobsons Bay*, which soon after raised its anchor and headed off for Melbourne, now carrying some 950 passengers.

*Hobsons Bay* arrived in Melbourne the next morning. As soon as the passengers from Tasmania had disembarked, the vessel left to continue its interrupted voyage to Sydney.

This voyage managed to ease the problem facing some tourists in Tasmania, but there were still many other visitors who were stranded on the island, not to mention residents who needed to travel to the mainland. Again the State Government approached the Federal

Government for assistance.

A story in the *Sydney Morning Herald* on Thursday, 15 January recorded an exchange of telegrams between the then Prime Minister, Mr Bruce, and Joseph Lyons, who at that time was the Premier of Tasmania.

Mr Bruce, this week, despatched a telegram to the Premier of Tasmania (Mr Lyons), asking for an exact statement of Tasmania's immediate requirements.

To this telegram Mr Lyons replied as follows: 'Tasmanian Shipping Committee report that 1333 applications for passages have been lodged with shipping offices. Of these approximately 1000 are urgent cases.

Foodstuffs requirements are as follows: Sugar, 550 tons a week; essential foodstuffs and urgent necessities, 350 tons a week.

In addition to the foregoing, Tasmania requires resumption of ordinary passenger steamship services, which at present are completely cut off. Traffic would in ordinary circumstances run to approximately 1000 arrivals a week.

Suggest that *Hobsons Bay* be diverted to Tasmania.'

Mr Lyons wanted *Hobsons Bay* to return to Tasmania to pick up more passengers and carry them back to the mainland across Bass Strait. The report in the *Sydney Morning Herald* continued:

This reply was taken by Mr Bruce before the Cabinet, and after discussion the Prime Minister despatched the following message to Mr Lyons: 'Your telegram today's date received, and the urgent requirements of Tasmania are noted by my Government, which will take all possible steps to meet the present crisis. I shall be glad to receive an assurance that your Government will co-operate in any action that it may be necessary to take.

'With regard to the latter portion of your telegram, I would remind you that members of the Seamen's Union are refusing duty on all interstate vessels, and action by the Government can only embrace the maintenance of urgent and vital services.

'*Hobsons Bay* cannot be diverted, as she proceeded to Sydney.'

The final sentence confirmed that after arriving in Melbourne *Hobsons Bay* had disembarked all the passengers from Tasmania, then gone straight on to Sydney, so was not available for any more trips across Bass Strait.

The *Sydney Morning Herald* story then went on to speculate on the possibility of the Government chartering vessels to re-open the Bass Strait service:

It is expected that the Ministry will ascertain if it can rely upon the Australian Commonwealth Shipping Board to obtain crews for the Tasmanian steamers which will be chartered, and which it is expected will be the *Nairana* and the *Loongana*. Possibly only one of these vessels will be placed in commission, but this will be a matter to be arranged by the Commonwealth Shipping Board.

If the board is unable to obtain the necessary men, the Ministry may take the same course as the Hughes Ministry did in 1917, when it called for free labour to man the vessels rendered idle in the maritime strike. Should any difficulty be encountered in giving effect to the present intentions of the Ministry, the question of summoning Parliament without delay will receive further consideration. The Ministry, however, will of necessity be guided in its future actions by developments from day to day.

On the afternoon of Thursday, 15 January, the Federal Government arranged to charter *Nairana*, and called for volunteers to sign up to crew the ship on Friday morning at the Customs House in Melbourne.

What happened then was reported in the *Sydney Morning Herald* on 17 January as follows:

Complete success followed the Federal Ministry's call for volunteers to man the steamer *Nairana*, and she will leave for Tasmania at noon tomorrow.

Although the hours fixed for selecting volunteers were from 11 o'clock to 2 o'clock, about 50 men had assembled by a quarter to 10 o'clock. From 8 o'clock a large body of policemen were on duty at the Customs House. By 11 o'clock, when the first of the volunteers were dealt with, about 500 strikers had gathered in William Street, but there was no disorder.

Between 11 o'clock and 2 o'clock about 300 men offered themselves for employment, and there was no difficulty in picking a competent crew with coastal experience. Thirty-four stewards and stewardesses formerly employed on the *Nairana*, were signed on in a body.

At 4 o'clock the volunteer crew, guarded by a squad of 45 policemen, marched to the *Nairana*, which is berthed only a few hundred yards from the Customs House. A number of strikers followed, but contented themselves with making jeering and threatening remarks.

Immediately the crew was on board, the secretary of the Stewards and Pantrymen's Association arrived at the ship's side in a taxi cab, and a few minutes afterwards the stewards left the ship. It was learned afterwards that this action followed pressure that had been brought to bear by the Seamen's Union. After a hurried meeting the stewards agreed to man the ship for this trip, but reserve the right to act differently in the future if they receive instructions from their executive.

When the volunteer crew arrived, the Wharf Labourers' Union declared the *Nairana* 'black', and ceased work, but there is coal enough for the voyage. A strong police guard is being maintained all night.

In another story on the same page, the *Sydney Morning Herald* reported:

The Prime Minister (Mr Bruce) expressed pleasure this evening at the excellent response to the appeal made by the Government for a crew to man the *Nairana* for the relief of those stranded and in distress in Tasmania.

Asked whether any other steamers were to be chartered and placed in commission by the Ministry, Mr Bruce replied in the negative. The *Nairana* would, he said, make trips between Melbourne and Launceston as frequently as possible, so that those people who had been stranded on the mainland and in Tasmania would be able to get to their homes. The *Nairana* would not carry any cargo. He believed that the smaller vessels had already relieved the shortage of certain foodstuffs in Tasmania.

The smaller ships this item referred to were mostly sailing vessels, known as the 'mosquito fleet', that maintained cargo services from Melbourne to smaller towns along the north coast of Tasmania. These vessels were mostly family operations, or used non-union crew, so had been able to maintain their services during the strike.

In some cases people desperate to get across Bass Strait paid to travel on these vessels, though in very basic conditions, and the voyage under sail often took two or three days.

On Saturday, 17 January, after twelve days idleness, *Nairana* departed Melbourne for

*Nairana* was chartered by the Federal Government in January 1923 (Lindsay Rex collection)

Launceston once again. Surprisingly, the vessel was not full, probably because many people did not believe the vessel would actually make the trip. The voyage was covered by a reporter from *The Age* who travelled across to Launceston on the *Nairana*:

Few of the passengers who hopefully boarded the *Nairana* at Melbourne today believed that it would leave Melbourne at the scheduled time. Many of them had been stranded in Melbourne for a long time, and had been on vessels that had been held up at the last minute.

'Have the stewards walked off?' 'Has she enough coal to take her across?' Questions like these were asked by every passenger, but the *Nairana* left the wharf at 12 o'clock, and only during the voyage did the passengers learn of the elaborate precautions taken by the Federal Ministry to ensure the departure of the vessel. The *Nairana* carried a double complement of officers in every department. In an emergency the officers could have taken the vessel into the Bay.

At Williamstown was waiting a full crew of naval ratings from the Flinders Depot; each one had been assigned a post, and was carefully instructed in his duties. They could have been transferred to the vessel in half an hour. Nothing unexpected happened. The volunteer seamen swung the vessel efficiently, and at 20 minutes past 12 o'clock it began to steam down the Yarra.

The *Nairana* did not berth at Launceston until 9 o'clock, but the late arrival – the trip usually occupies 17 hours – was no fault of the efficient crew… The delayed arrival was due to the thoughtfulness of the Federal Government, which desired that passengers should have their breakfast on board.

During the day *Nairana* was coaled without any problems, and prepared for the voyage back to Melbourne, scheduled to depart on the Sunday afternoon. For this trip every berth was booked, and temporary berths erected in public rooms. Some people were so desperate to get on board the ship that they camped all Saturday night on the wharf, while others who did not have confirmed bookings sought ways and means to become stowaways. The voyage back to Melbourne went without a hitch, and while a few crew members decided to sign off, they were quickly replaced by more volunteers.

An attempt was made by strikers to prevent the vessel being coaled, but when shoreworkers refused to do the job, the volunteer crew did it.

*Nairana* was scheduled to depart Melbourne again on 21 January, then on 26 January and 30 January. The first two of these voyages were operated, but by then the strike was beginning to crumble. On 27 January a series of mass meetings were held around the country, which voted to return to work.

Immediately the shipping companies began recruiting crews, and *Loongana* was fully manned by 29 January. *Nairana* returned to Melbourne on 29 January, and took the scheduled voyage on 30 January to Launceston. *Loongana* was not ready to depart until 2 February, then *Nairana* left Melbourne again on 4 February.

With conditions back to normal, *Nairana* once again began three weekly departures from Melbourne for Launceston, while *Loongana* left on two days, and *Oonah* again began making two trips a week to Burnie and Devonport. The three ships would maintain these schedules for the next few years.

On the afternoon of 19 August 1925, *Oonah* was returning to Melbourne from Tasmania, and approaching the mouth of the Yarra River. At the same time the Howard Smith Limited coastal liner *Cooma* was coming down the river at the start of a voyage to Queensland.

The rule of the sea says that ships have to pass portside to portside, but as *Oonah* and *Cooma* approached almost head-on, each captain waited for the other to turn to starboard, and effect a safe pass. Too late both captains realised what was happening.

Captain W T Firth on the *Cooma* sounded three warning blasts on his ship's siren, but at almost the same instant Captain Toten on the *Oonah* made the same signal. Both captains then ordered full speed astern, and tried to turn away, but it was too late, and a head-on collision resulted.

This was particularly startling for some passengers on *Cooma*, who were in the dining room enjoying their lunch, while most passengers on *Oonah* were on deck. Fortunately none were injured on either ship.

*Oonah* suffered a large hole in her bow, bent hull plates and twisted railings, while *Cooma* also had a large hole in her bow. Fortunately the

*Oonah* towards the end of her career (Maritime Museum of Tasmania)

damage was above the waterline, but *Cooma* was forced to abandon her voyage and return to her dock, while *Oonah* limped up the river to her regular berth.

*Oonah* was out of service for a month while the damage was repaired. At a subsequent inquiry, both captains were found to have been at fault, but neither lost his ticket over the incident.

Until the early months of 1927, *Nairana* was departing Melbourne for Launceston on Monday, Wednesday and Saturday, while *Loongana* made the trip on Tuesday and Friday. However, when *Nairana* returned to Melbourne from Launceston on Monday, 8 May, the vessel was take out of service for a major overhaul. From then until late October *Loongana* operated to Launceston on her own, providing only two departures a week from Melbourne, on Wednesday and Saturday.

During this period, *Oonah* continued to make two trips a week to Burnie and Devonport, departing Melbourne on Tuesday and Friday at noon.

From time to time the vessels operating across Bass Strait would be affected by bad weather. During her career *Nairana* survived some quite alarming incidents, one of which nearly caused the vessel to be lost.

When *Nairana* departed Launceston on the evening of 24 January 1928, every cabin was fully booked, and extra passengers had to sleep in shakedowns set up in the public rooms. As the steamer passed Low Head and entered Bass Strait, it ran into a severe westerly gale, not an unusual occurrence in these waters.

However, this particular storm was worse than those previously encountered, and *Nairana* was being buffeted so badly that Captain Bates was forced to order a reduction in speed to prevent his vessel being damaged by the huge seas, and try and make the passage more comfortable for the passengers.

During the night a huge rogue wave suddenly struck *Nairana* abeam. The vessel heeled over to an alarming angle, and came very close to capsizing, but fortunately no further waves struck and the ship returned slowly to an even keel. During the heavy roll passengers in cabins were flung from their bunks, while those in the public rooms were tossed around the floor, causing many minor injuries.

One female passenger who had been sick when she boarded the vessel died during the night, and the remaining passengers were extremely relieved when *Nairana* passed through the Rip into Port Phillip Bay the next day, though several hours behind schedule.

Throughout the 1920s, industrial problems arose with monotonous regularity, causing services to be disrupted and at times, as in 1925, totally cancelled for weeks on end. Usually when these industrial problems arose the vessels would remain at their wharves until the matter was settled, but occasionally attempts were made to continue operating, sometimes with disastrous results.

On the whole *Loongana* led a charmed life, causing very few problems for her owners, and retaining her popularity over the years. Apart from the turbine problems encountered in 1917, the one time *Loongana* did encounter major problems at sea was in September 1928, but this was due to no fault of the ship.

*Loongana* had made her regular departure from Melbourne for Launceston on the night of Saturday, 9 September 1928, but on arrival in Launceston on the Sunday morning an industrial dispute prevented the stokeholds being replenished with coal. A thousand tons of coal was sitting on the dock waiting to be taken on board, but no one was allowed to touch it, and the cargo the ship had brought from the mainland remained on board. *Loongana* spent Sunday night alongside in Launceston, and was due to leave on the Monday evening for Melbourne.

During the day company officials and the ship's master decided there was just sufficient coal remaining in the bunkers to get the ship back to Melbourne, provided it operated at a more economical speed. With 200 passengers on board, *Loongana* left Launceston as scheduled, and headed back across Bass Strait, but once away from the shelter of the north coast of Tasmania ran into a heavy sea running beam on to the vessel. Soon after the wind veered to the north, putting further pressure on the engines, and extra coal had to be used to maintain even a slow speed.

About 3 am the officers on the bridge sighted the beam of the lighthouse on Point Lonsdale, at the entrance to Port Phillip Bay, but by then the remaining supply of coal in the bunkers was fast running out. A radio message requesting assistance was sent out as the vessel passed through Port Phillip Heads, and began making her way down the west channel towards Melbourne. *Loongana* was within sight of the city when the final lumps of coal were thrown into the boilers, and soon speed began to fall as the fires in the boilers were extinguished.

With the northerly gale still blowing, *Loongana* was beginning to drift when the tug *Tooranga* arrived, and passed a towline to the stricken vessel. Despite being the most powerful tug stationed in Melbourne, *Tooranga* was able to make little headway in the prevailing gale, which was blowing *Loongana* towards the Williamstown shore.

Shortly after another tug, the *Sprightly*, arrived on the scene and also attached a rope to *Loongana*, and between them the two tugs were able to hold the larger vessel in position, but still did not have enough power to tow it to safety. A third tug, the *James Patterson*, arrived from Port Melbourne, while a fourth tug, the Racer, was sent down to the scene from Victoria Dock.

With *Tooranga*, *Sprightly* and *James Patterson* towing, and Racer standing by if needed, *Loongana* was finally manoeuvred into the entrance of the Yarra River. As the strong northerly wind was still blowing, it was decided to bring *Loongana* alongside the first available berth rather than attempt to tow her all the way to No 4 North Wharf.

Instead of arriving at 9 am as scheduled, *Loongana* was over four hours late, and no doubt the passengers were very relieved when their feet touched dry land again.

The following year *Nairana* survived another very stormy passage. Leaving Melbourne on the evening of Wednesday, 3 April 1929 with 274 passengers on board, the vessel crossed Port Phillip Bay and out through the Rip, then ran into mountainous seas sweeping through Bass Strait from west to east.

Pushed along by wind and wave, *Nairana* approached the northern coastline of Tasmania before dawn the following morning, but driving rain prevented the officers on the bridge from seeing the Low Head light.

In fact, on the previous day the northern regions of Tasmania had been lashed by gale-force winds and torrential rain, which had caused widespread damage, and floods along the Tamar River and its tributaries.

Captain Bates was not prepared to take *Nairana* too close to the shore when he was uncertain of his exact position, but due to the mountainous seas and driving wind he was also unable to anchor and wait for the weather to clear.

Instead the vessel was hove to, bow into the wind and seas, for two hours, but even when daylight finally came the coastline remained invisible.

Eventually Captain Bates decided to take his vessel further out to sea, and for the next twenty-four hours *Nairana* steamed in circles, much to the discomfort of all on board.

After dawn on the morning of Friday, 5 April, *Nairana* again closed on the coast. This time the Low Head light was sighted, and the vessel was able to enter the mouth of the Tamar and proceed up the river to Launceston, berthing at King's Wharf at 10 am.

With the Tamar already in flood, and more water pouring down the South *Esk* River expected to deluge Launceston the following day, *Nairana* stayed in port only a few hours, then left for Melbourne.

Among the passengers who had made the trip back to Melbourne were some who had been on the voyage over to Launceston, and had intended to travel on by road to Hobart. As the south of the island had been totally cut off by flooding, most of these unfortunates were forced to remain on the ship, and suffered another stormy passage back to the mainland.

*Nairana* did not reach Melbourne until early on Saturday, 6 April, but instead of making another trip to Tasmania to make up for the voyage cancelled on 5 April, the vessel remained in Melbourne over the weekend.

On Monday 8 April, *Nairana* departed Melbourne on schedule, but on reaching the mouth of the Tamar next morning, Captain Bates found the river in full flood. Unable to proceed to Launceston, *Nairana* had to berth at Beauty Point, near the mouth of the river.

In fact, for the rest of April and into early May all voyages from Melbourne had to terminate at Beauty Point until it was safe to proceed up the river to Launceston and berth at King's Wharf again.

It was estimated more than twelve inches of rain had fallen in the northern parts of Tasmania over several days, drowning at least 14 people and leaving large areas without gas and electricity.

For many years the vessels operating across Bass Strait had berthed in Melbourne at Queen's Wharf in the Yarra River, but in 1930 the Spencer Street Bridge was built across the river. The new structure was too low for *Nairana* and the other vessels to pass under, so from then on they berthed at North Wharf.

Former *Nairana* crew member Bobby Brookes recalled that, these being the days before aircraft operated across Bass Strait, *Nairana* carried many notable passengers, including the 1934 Australian cricket team, captained by Don Bradman.

After serving as Premier of Tasmania from 1923 to 1929, Joseph Lyons entered Federal Parliament, becoming Prime Minister in 1931, serving in this capacity until his death in 1939. Being from Tasmania, Mr Lyons and his wife, Dame Enid, were frequent passengers on *Nairana* and *Loongana* throughout the 1930s.

*Nairana* had facilities to transport live animals as well, there being four stalls for horses or cattle on the forward well deck. The animals faced inwards towards No 2 hold, away from the weather, and were under cover.

Bobby Brookes recalled a trip he was on from Launceston when they carried a greyhound, called 'Timid Joe', apparently named after an old dog soap. He was unknown at the time, but the crew was told he was very fast, and the owner was hoping to make a killing with him on the Melbourne racing tracks.

As *Nairana* approached the Rip at the entrance to Port Phillip Bay, the owner decided to let the dog out of its kennel for a feed and to stretch its legs. Unfortunately, 'Timid Joe' took off like a rocket along the starboard side of the shelter deck. As the dog reached the stern of the ship, he encountered some early rising passengers walking round the deck in the opposite direction. 'Timid Joe' couldn't stop, so he tried to go round them, but instead went over the rails and into the sea, never to be seen again.

Another animal to disappear on a crossing of Bass Strait was a Tasmanian devil, being transported to Melbourne Zoo. The creature was brought on board in a hardwood crate with a thick metal door, which was placed in one of the horse stalls. In the morning the chief cook

*Nairana* in the Tamar River (Lindsay Rex collection)

went to the stall to feed the Tasmanian devil a piece of steak, but all he found was an empty crate, with a large hole chewed in the side. An extensive search of the ship failed to find any trace of the animal, which was presumed to have gone overboard during the night.

On one trip *Nairana* transported the world's smallest horse, 'Wee Jimmy', who was only two feet high. He came from Patagonia, and was taken over for the Launceston Royal Show, where he was a great success.

Bobby Brookes also recounted another incident that happened during his time on board *Nairana*. Before the ship left Melbourne the last item to be taken on board was the 'ship's box', which contained tobacco products and alcoholic spirits.

While the ship was completing loading, the box would be placed just inside the wharf shed door, opposite No 2 hold. It would then be hoisted on board and placed on top of the mail bags in No 2 hold, and was the first item unloaded in Tasmania.

One day, a few minutes before the box was to be hoisted aboard, two men in a truck carrying a similar looking box on the tray drove up to the wharf shed door, and placed their box alongside the ship's box waiting to be loaded.

The men went to the wharf manager's office, and asked if they were in time to have their box loaded on board *Nairana*. When told they were too late, they went back to the shed door, loaded the ship's box onto the back of their truck, and drove away. The switch was not noticed before the ship departed, and when the other box was opened in Tasmania it was found to contain only telephone books.

*Nairana* was also required to carry bullion from the mainland to Tasmania. Bobby Brookes remembered the differing security arrangements in place at the time. When the bullion was loaded in Melbourne, it was transported to the ship in a heavily armed van, which was brought right to the gangway.

Two men would carry each of the steel boxes containing the bullion up the gangway, then down three flights of stairs. Armed security guards were stationed at the foot and top of the gangway, and on each set of stairs as the bullion was taken to the Bond Room, located on the lower deck.

Once the bullion was in the room, its steel doors

were locked and sealed, then an ordinary wooden door to the room was also closed and locked.

When the ship arrived in Tasmania, an agent from the bank awaiting the bullion would come on board and present his credentials to the ship's purser. He then unlocked the bond room, and wharf labourers were brought down to carry the boxes ashore, with no security guards in sight. Once on the wharf, the boxes of bullion would be loaded onto the back of an open truck, and taken to the bank.

*Nairana* regularly carried cargo across Bass Strait, which could be quite varied. For example, a note in the *Examiner* newspaper in December 1934 listed the cargo loaded on board *Nairana* in Launceston for one voyage to Melbourne.

This comprised 60 bundles of binder twine, 215 cases of fruit, 20 cases of dates, 60 sacks of salt, 16 cases of confectionery, 231 cases of tomatoes, plus sundry other items.

*Nairana* could also carry a small number of cars, which had to be lifted on and off by cranes. Two cargo nets were used, one placed under the front wheels and the other under the rear wheels, and the vehicles were carried on deck.

Bobby Brookes recalled that one of the strangest cargoes to be carried by *Nairana* from Melbourne to Launceston was an early aeroplane, a single-seater Cierva Autogyro, owned by a Mr Gatenby, who flew it around Tasmania.

On a Saturday night in September 1934, when *Nairana* was staying overnight at Launceston, the vessel hosted a 'Pirates Ball', in aid of the St John's Ambulance and the Junior Red Cross. This attracted a large attendance, including among the notables the then Governor of Tasmania, Sir Ernest Clarke, and Lady Clarke.

The vessel was lit up from stem to stern, and flags were draped along each side of the Promenade Deck. An orchestra played music for dancing on the Promenade Deck, and a supper was laid out in the dining saloons, helping to make the night a great success.

During 1934 and 1935 some significant changes occurred in the fleet of Tasmanian Steamers. The veteran *Oonah* was withdrawn from the Bass Strait route she had been operating, from Melbourne to Burnie and Devonport, following her arrival in Melbourne on 12 October 1934.

By the time *Oonah* was withdrawn from service she was almost fifty years old, so it was not surprising that in June 1935 the old vessel was sold to a firm of Japanese shipbreakers. The same company also bought the former Union Line passenger liner *Maheno*, which had been laid up in Sydney early in 1935 after being withdrawn from the trans-Tasman service.

Initially the Japanese planned to have a tug to tow *Oonah* and *Maheno* in tandem to Japan, but then they decided to save some money by having *Oonah* tow *Maheno*. The twin propellers on *Maheno* were removed, and on 3 July 1935 *Oonah* towed *Maheno* through Sydney Heads, and started north on the long trip to Japan.

Five days later the pair ran into heavy weather soon after passing *Moreton* Bay, in Queensland .Throughout the morning the weather worsened and the seas grew rougher. Suddenly the tow rope broke, and *Maheno* was at the mercy of the easterly gale, which drove her towards the Queensland coast.

*Oonah* was having her own difficulties and could do nothing to help, so *Maheno* drifted steadily towards the shore, eventually running aground on a sandy beach on Fraser Island. The eight Japanese seamen who had been on the ship since leaving Sydney spent an anxious night on board as the vessel was pounded by heavy seas, but they were able to get ashore the next morning.

A tug sent to refloat the stranded vessel was unable to approach close enough because of the heavy seas. When the storm subsided, an inspection revealed that *Maheno* had broken its back, and could not be salvaged.

The wreck was abandoned where it lay, and today it is a tourist attraction on Fraser Island, though the rusted and battered remains bear no resemblance to what was a fine liner.

*Oonah* managed to survive the storm at sea, and eventually continued the journey to Japan on her own, being broken up there during 1936.

Following the withdrawal of *Oonah* in October 1934, the service from Melbourne to Burnie and Devonport was operated by *Loongana*, providing two round trips each week on the same schedule that *Oonah* had operated.

*Nairana* maintained the Launceston service from Melbourne throughout the summer of 1934/35 on her own, still operating three return trips a week.

In February 1935 the brand-new *Taroona*

arrived in Melbourne from Scotland, and replaced *Nairana* on the Launceston trade, while *Nairana* was transferred to the service from Melbourne to Burnie and Devonport.

On 6 March 1935, *Loongana* left Melbourne on its last round trip to Tasmania, and was then withdrawn from service. For several months the vessel was held in reserve, but then was offered for sale.

After eighteen months at anchor, *Loongana* was sold to Japanese shipbreakers. On 3 November 1936 *Loongana* left Melbourne for the last time, being towed by the Union Line cargo ship *Kauri*, which had been bought by the same shipbreakers.

*Loongana* departing Devonport (Author's collection)

**Chapter Nine**

# Riverina and Zealandia

As mentioned previously, the Union Steam Ship Company was forced to abandon its service between Sydney and Hobart in June 1921, when the new *Navigation Act* came into effect. This left Huddart Parker as the only company operating on the route, and they had brought back *Lydia* run the service. By this time *Lydia* was over twenty years old, and totally outclassed by newer and larger ships.

Her first departure from Sydney had been on 18 July, but instead of providing a weekly departure, *Lydia* was scheduled to make one round trip every ten or eleven days.

This provided the Tasmanian capital with just two services every three weeks, a vastly inferior service to the one they had been enjoying. This situation continued until the middle of November 1921, at which time *Lydia* was replaced by *Riverina*.

*Lydia* departed Sydney on 11 November, but *Riverina* took the next departure, on 22 November. *Riverina* subsequently became the regular vessel on the trade between Sydney and Hobart.

Being a faster ship, *Riverina* was able to maintain a schedule of weekly departures. However, during the peak holiday period around Christmas 1921, *Lydia* was brought back on the route for two quick trips, carrying passengers only. These departed Sydney on 19 December and 24 December, and were advertised as 'Christmas excursions'. After returning to Sydney again on 31 December, *Lydia* was laid up.

*Riverina* was well suited to the Hobart trade, as she provided pleasant accommodation for passengers in three classes. The comfortable cabins and large and attractively appointed public rooms for the 150 first class passengers were spread over the main, shelter and promenade decks amidships.

The main lounge featured oak-panelled walls inlaid with walnut, while natural light was provided by a superb glass dome. The dining room, located on the shelter deck, spread across the full width of the ship, making it very well lit and airy. There was also extensive open deck space, including an open promenade deck 150 feet/45 m long.

The 120 second class passengers were accommodated in less luxurious facilities towards the stern, with their own lounges and dining room, while rather basic quarters were provided forward of the bridge for a hundred or so steerage class passengers.

Apart from passengers, *Riverina* also could carry large amounts of cargo, including fruit and other perishables, from Hobart. The vessel was powered by a huge triple expansion engine, the low pressure cylinder being a massive 7 feet/2.1 m in diameter.

Although she only had a single propeller, *Riverina* was able to operate very effectively at 16.5 knots, which for many years had made her the fastest ship on the Australian coastal trades. It appeared the vessel was set for a long and successful career serving Tasmania.

For most of the year *Riverina* operated one round trip per week, departing 3 Millers Point in Sydney at 2 pm on Monday, arriving in Hobart on Wednesday morning. The ship would remain there until Thursday afternoon, then head back to Sydney, berthing on Saturday morning.

*Riverina* began operating regularly to Hobart in November 1921 (Author's collection)

These longer stopovers at each port were necessary to enable cargo to be worked, and the ship was also coaled in Sydney. During the winter months *Riverina* worked an easier schedule, providing two return trips to Hobart every three weeks. One trip would depart on Monday from Sydney, returning on Sunday, but the next trip would not leave until Friday, returning to Sydney the following Thursday.

After being taken off the Hobart service, *Westralia* was laid up in Sydney, but then returned to service with a departure from Sydney on 18 August 1922 for Hobart. The vessel made several more trips while *Riverina* was used on other services, but as the summer approached *Riverina* resumed its place on the route.

*Westralia* spent the next few years laid up or operating coastal services as required, but in 1927 the vessel was sold to W R Carpenter & Co. With her engine removed, the vessel was towed to Rabaul, and served as a storeship for copra from local plantations. During a Japanese air raid on Rabaul on 22 January 1942, *Westralia* was hit by a bomb and sunk.

The introduction of the *Navigation Act* in 1921, which had effectively ended the participation of the Union Steam Ship Company of New Zealand in the Australian coastal trades, also affected the liners operated by such companies as P & O and the Orient Line.

They had previously made occasional calls at Hobart, and carried passengers on coastal voyages, but this now ceased, even though the ships continued to make visits to Hobart to load cargo. The only foreign-going vessels not affected by the Act were the five 'Bay' liners owned by the Australian Commonwealth Government Line, which were all registered in Australia, and operated regular services between Britain and Australian ports.

The result was a sudden shortage of availability on the route from Hobart to Sydney, while there was now no service at all between Hobart and Melbourne. Occasionally people would be forced to adopt desperate measures to secure a passage to the mainland.

One such instance concerned a lady in Hobart who needed to get to Melbourne urgently, but could not secure a passage on any of the Bass Strait vessels. In desperation she signed on to a British ship in Hobart as an assistant steward so she could get to Melbourne.

Such instances of signing on as temporary crew became increasingly common, but on the whole the residents of Hobart, and indeed the rest of Tasmania, felt very harshly treated by the *Navigation Act*.

Every two years *Riverina* would be taken out of service for a drydocking and overhaul. Usually there would be no spare passenger ship to maintain the Hobart service during this period, but in October 1923 a ship was available.

The Bass Strait ferry *Nairana* was due to come to Sydney at the end of September 1923 for overhaul and drydocking, leaving *Loongana* to maintain the service between Melbourne and Launceston on her own. After the drydocking was completed *Nairana* ran trials on Thursday,

*Nairana* arriving in Hobart in October 1923 (Maritime Museum of Tasmania)

11 October, making two trips out to sea during the day. *Riverina* returned to Sydney the same day, and after disembarking her passengers and unloading cargo went into the vacated dry dock.

*Nairana* was then prepared for her first trip to Hobart, being berthed at 3 Millers Point. *Nairana* departed the berth at noon on Monday, 15 October, on her first trip to Hobart, carrying first and second class passengers, but no cargo. She arrived in Hobart on 17 October, remaining there two days, then returned to Sydney on 21 October.

At noon on Wednesday, 24 October, *Nairana* left Sydney on her second trip to Hobart, arriving back in Sydney on the morning of Monday, 29 October.

For several weeks Huddart Parker had been advertising the trip from Sydney back to Melbourne by *Nairana* as available to passengers. *Nairana* departed Sydney at 4 pm on 29 October, and made the trip down to Melbourne carrying a large number of passengers, many going south for the running of the Melbourne Cup. She arrived in Melbourne on the morning of 31 October, and the same evening resumed her place on the Bass Strait trade.

By that time the work on *Riverina* had been completed, and she departed Sydney for Hobart on Wednesday, 31 October, then maintained a weekly service, departing Sydney each Wednesday throughout the summer.

As 1924 came to an end, a series of strikes involving maritime unions which began in a small way escalated into a major situation that threatened to bring the coastal trades to a complete standstill. *Riverina* was scheduled to depart Sydney for Hobart on Monday, 8 December 1924, but on returning was to be transferred to the service between Sydney and Fremantle for a month. This would enable the larger *Zealandia* to be taken off the Fremantle trade and make four round trips to Hobart, departing Sydney on 17, 23 and 31 December and 7 January, with *Riverina* returning to take the 14 January departure.

The strike began with stevedores at the major ports refusing to work cargo, and gradually brought other sections of the maritime industry into the dispute. *Riverina* completed her scheduled voyage to Hobart, and left for Fremantle, while *Zealandia* took on the rest of the December departures as planned.

However, in early January the strike intensified into a manning dispute, and ships began being laid up due to insufficient crew being available. *Zealandia* was ready to depart on 7 January with a full complement of 250 first class and 50 second class passengers on board, but was two crewmen short, and the rest of the crew refused to depart short handed. *Zealandia* was forced to remain at her berth, and the sailing was cancelled. A similar situation applied to *Riverina*, which was in Fremantle.

The Commonwealth Government Line vessel *Largs Bay* was also in Sydney, due to leave on Saturday, 10 January for Britain, but stopping along the way at Hobart, Melbourne and Fremantle.

A large number of the passengers from *Zealandia* were rebooked on *Largs Bay* to Hobart, and duly boarded the ship, along with several hundred others destined for Melbourne and Fremantle as well as London.

Just as *Largs Bay* was due to leave her berth at Darling Harbour, 20 crewmen slipped over the side and left the ship. Although the vessel pulled away and headed down the harbour, it had to drop anchor as the remaining crew refused to take her any further.

Attempts to obtain replacements failed, and after four days sitting in the harbour, the frustrated passengers found themselves back at the Darling Harbour wharves on the Wednesday The departure of *Largs Bay* was cancelled indefinitely when replacement crew could not be obtained, and the entire crew was then dismissed.

The strike dragged on until a mass meeting of seamen on 27 January voted to return to work. However, the end of the strike did not bring about an immediate resumption of services, as ships that had lain idle for several weeks needed to be prepared for service again.

*Zealandia* had been sitting in Sydney for three weeks, and did not depart until 4 February for Hobart. Meanwhile *Riverina* had to come back east from Fremantle, and on returning to Sydney resumed her place on the Hobart trade

on 11 February, while *Zealandia* went back to the Fremantle service. Over the next two years, *Riverina* made regular weekly trips between Sydney and Hobart.

Saturday, 16 April 1927, was a gala day in Hobart, as in the morning the battle-cruiser HMS *Renown* arrived, berthing at Ocean Pier. On board were the Duke and Duchess of York, later King George VI and Queen Elizabeth, who were on their way to Sydney from Britain, and due to open the new Parliament House in Canberra later that month. All the vessels in port were decked out in flags and bunting, as was the fleet of excursion boats packed with sightseers that crowded around the warship.

That same Saturday morning *Riverina* departed King's Pier, Hobart at noon on a voyage north to Sydney, having on board 142 passengers.

In the holds were 19,352 cases of fruit, mostly apples, and 496 tons of general cargo. This included a large consignment of chocolate bars from the Cadbury factory near Hobart, and over a million wooden clothes pegs.

Next day the weather gradually worsened as the ship crossed the eastern end of Bass Strait and closed in on the Victorian coastline.

*Riverina* berthed at Queens Pier in Hobart in the 1920s, with a Blue Funnel vessel at Kings Pier. (*The Mercury*)

*Riverina* aground, with Gabo Island in the background. (Maritime Museum of Tasmania)

Driving rain reduced visibility to almost zero, while south-easterly winds blowing at gale force whipped up heavy seas, making life on board most uncomfortable for both passengers and crew.

As darkness approached on 17 April, *Riverina* neared the border of Victoria and New South Wales, and the officers on the bridge searched in vain for the beacon of the Gabo Island lighthouse so they could accurately ascertain their position. However, in the heavy rain and deep darkness the light could not be seen, so Captain Parry was unaware his ship was several miles west of its planned course.

Shortly after 7 pm, *Riverina* suddenly shuddered, and came to a quick halt, having run aground on the unseen shoreline. There was no panic on board, as the ship was sitting upright and in no danger of capsizing or sinking.

Attempts at refloating using the engine in full reverse failed to move the stricken vessel at all. Eventually all efforts to refloat the vessel that night were abandoned, and passengers and crew settled down for an anxious night on board, while waves continually pounded the vessel, and rain fell steadily.

At daylight next morning the position they were in finally became clear. *Riverina* was hard aground a short distance off a long stretch of beach just south and west of Gabo Island.

Daylight also brought the first rescuers to the scene, but there was very little they could do. High seas continued to pound the ship, and

made it impossible for any boats to be lowered, or sent out from shore, so those on board the vessel were forced to remain where they were for a second night.

During the day the cargo steamers *Port Nicholson* and *Iron Baron* hove to off the shore, being joined later in the day by the Huddart Parker cargo vessel *Goulburn*, but none of them could do anything to assist the stranded ship or its passengers.

*Riverina* aground, as seen from the beach (Author's collection)

By the following morning the seas had moderated sufficiently for one of the ship's lifeboats to be lowered on the landward side. A line was passed to the shore and attached to the bow of the lifeboat, while another line was attached to the stern and connected to the ship.

Over several hours the passengers were ferried ashore in the lifeboat, along with some of the crew. Once ashore they made their way by foot some eight miles along the beach to the small township of Mallacoota, where they were looked after by the residents.

The passengers were later taken by road to Eden, where they boarded another coastal liner, *Bombala*, which took them to Sydney.

Salvage work commenced immediately and at first hopes were high that the ship could be floated off the beach without too much damage. In the meantime all the perishable cargo had to be thrown overboard, and other items were removed to the shore in an attempt to lighten the ship.

For a month salvage workers strove to refloat *Riverina*, but to no avail. On 21 May, Huddart Parker abandoned the ship to the underwriters, who in turn sold the vessel at auction for £2,225 to Riverina Salvage Ltd, a small syndicate specially formed to refloat the ship.

Riverina Salvage commenced work on the vessel on 6 July. By that time *Riverina* was sitting well away from the water except at high tide. The chief engineer on the project, G E Arundel, noted that, 'Upon emptying ballast tanks and inspecting hull plating, I found that the bottom plating was dented in a few places, but there were no fractures. There was slight leakage only at the margin plates of ballast tanks in bilges.'

On 13 July the steamer *Kurrara* arrived on the scene, having brought in an array of heavy equipment, but due to bad weather it was not until 16 July that a line could be put ashore from *Kurrara*. Next day a wooden punt was used to transfer the salvage gear to *Riverina*.

The salvors then set about lightening the ship still further. Everything that could be removed or thrown overboard was, including most of the coal from the bunkers. At the same time, *Kurrara* laid two sets of three anchors to seaward of *Riverina*.

The actual salvage operation was under the control of a Dane, Captain Andersen. He noted when arriving on the scene that at high tide waves came around the stem and stern of *Riverina*, and met nearly amidships on the landward side of the ship. This was causing sand to build up amidships, which ultimately could cause the vessel to break in two.

To combat this, Andersen had a sandbag wall built inshore, parallel with the ship, which had the effect of increasing the depth of water on that side of the ship. High pressure water jets were also used to disperse sand building up against the hull of the vessel.

The propeller also posed a problem, as it had become buried in sand up to the boss. It took eight days hard work removing the build-up of sand before the propeller could be turned. Then, with steam in four of the six boilers, the propeller was used to remove sand from under the after section of the ship.

Over a period of days the ship was slowly moved, by hauling on the anchors, a distance of 135 feet towards the sea, but it was still aground.

An extra effort was made to refloat the ship on the night of 17 August, and, after much work and expense, the salvage workers finally managed to get the vessel afloat again just after midnight.

*Riverina* was then anchored a short distance out to sea to await the delivery of coal which was being brought down from Eden. The chief engineer noted that on 29 August *Riverina* was rolling and pitching in a strong south-west wind and sea, but there was not enough coal on board to enable the ship to steam to Eden.

The ketch *Nell* arrived on 7 September with coal, but bad weather prevented it being loaded onto *Riverina* for some time. That night a gale swept through the area, and the *Nell* had to return to Eden for safety. *Riverina* remained anchored off the beach for the next two weeks, but the *Nell* did not return.

In the end the wooden punt that had been used to ferry salvage gear ashore *Kurrara* was broken up, to be used in the furnaces, along with any other wooden items available.

On the morning of 25 September, *Riverina* was being manoeuvred out to sea when, at 10.30 am, the anchor chain broke, and the ship was pushed onto a sandbank a short distance off the beach. Another steamer, the *Glenreagh*, was engaged to lay fresh anchors and cables, and a few days later

With her back broken, *Riverina* lies abandoned on the beach (Maritime Museum of Tasmania)

another attempt was made to refloat *Riverina*, but yet again this was unsuccessful.

Soon after more gales began sweeping through the area again, and the salvage crew had to cease work on *Riverina*. Much to their horror, the vessel was swept right back onto the beach, suffering a badly broken rudder.

Over the next few days huge waves continued to pound the helpless vessel; eventually her back was broken, and the ship was declared a total loss.

The Riverina Salvage consortium sold the wreck to a Melbourne businessman in 1928, and he salvaged what worthwhile fittings and furnishings were left on board, then had the ship broken up where it lay.

The lower sections of the hull were left on the beach, and remained visible for many years. During the Second World War these remains were used for target practice by aircraft of the Royal Australian Air Force. Today there are no visible signs left of the wreck.

An unusual sidelight to the loss of the *Riverina* is that it occurred within sight of the spot where, on 27 January 1890, another vessel named *Riverina* was also wrecked, that one having been owned by the Blue Anchor Line.

The sudden loss of *Riverina* caused major problems to Huddart Parker, as the vessel could not be quickly replaced from their own fleet. For several weeks there was no service at all between Sydney and Hobart, but then the *Zealandia* was transferred from its regular trade between Sydney and Fremantle to fill the gap.

The second vessel of the name, *Zealandia* at 6,683 gross tons was larger than *Riverina*, providing accommodation for about 200 first class, 120 second class and 120 third class passengers, as well as a large cargo capacity. Built in Scotland in 1910, *Zealandia* was originally intended to be placed on the trans-Tasman trade, as her name implied.

However, on arriving in Australia from Britain, *Zealandia* was chartered out to the Union Steamship Company of New Zealand, and placed on their Canadian-Australasian Line service across the Pacific from Sydney and Auckland to Honolulu and Vancouver.

It was not until April 1913 that the vessel was returned to her owners, and then placed on the coastal trade between Sydney and Fremantle, on which she replaced *Riverina*.

*Zealandia* remained in this trade until being requisitioned in May 1918 for service as a troop transport. Returned to Huddart Parker in July 1919, *Zealandia* returned to the coastal service on 13 December 1919, and operated between Sydney and Fremantle for the next seven years, apart from four trips between Sydney and Hobart in the summer of 1924/25.

Following the loss of *Riverina*, *Zealandia* began operating regularly between Sydney and Hobart, her first departure being on Saturday, 14 May 1927 from 3 Darling Harbour at 11 am.

Being a larger vessel, *Zealandia* required more time in port for cargo handling, so was placed on a schedule of fortnightly departures from Sydney until the end of October. From Wednesday, 9 November, *Zealandia* began operating weekly departures from Sydney for the peak summer travel period, reverting to the fortnightly schedule again in April.

*Zealandia* continued to operate between Sydney and Hobart until the end of June 1928, then returned to the service between Sydney and Fremantle.

As Huddart Parker had no other passenger vessel available, the Hobart service was taken over by the cargo vessel *Yarra*, which departed Sydney for the first time on 29 June. *Yarra* remained on the Hobart trade for the next six months, carrying cargo only.

*Zealandia* returned to the Hobart service in January 1929, but the following month had to go back to the Fremantle trade following the sinking of the coastal liner *Kanowna* in Bass Strait on 17 February.

With Huddart Parker again having no other ship available, the Hobart passenger service

*Zealandia* replaced *Riverina* on the Hobart service (Author's collection)

was terminated once more, this time until September 1929, when the new Huddart Parker liner *Westralia* entered the Fremantle service.

*Zealandia* was then able to return to the trade between Sydney and Hobart, on which she would serve for most of the next ten years, apart from one six month period when she was again away from the trade.

On 24 March 1932, *Ulimaroa* left Sydney on her final voyage to New Zealand, returning on 4 April, then being withdrawn and laid up. As no replacement was immediately available, *Zealandia* was taken off the Hobart service and began operating between Sydney and New Zealand ports. This was the first time she actually ran on the service for which she had been built.

Her first voyage departed Sydney on 8 April for Wellington, and on 22 April to Auckland. For the next six months the passenger service between Sydney and Hobart was abandoned, with only a cargo service being maintained by

*Ulimaroa* was placed on the Hobart trade in late 1932 (Author's collection)

the *Yarra*. It left Sydney on 1 April on its first voyage to Hobart, and subsequently made one round trip every two weeks through the winter.

One reason for Huddart Parker temporarily abandoning the Hobart passenger trade was that, unlike previous years, the company was now facing some major competition on the route.

The *Navigation Act* of 1920 had specifically excluded liners operating international services from carrying passengers between Australian ports. This had meant that passengers from overseas wishing to travel to Tasmania had to disembark in either Melbourne or Sydney, then travel on an Australian coastal liner to their destination, or make the reverse trip to join a liner going overseas.

This provision applied even when the particular liner was scheduled to call at a Tasmanian port, usually on the voyage back to Britain, to load a cargo of fruit and dairy products.

During 1932 several provisions of the *Navigation Act* had been relaxed, and permission was granted for some overseas liners to carry passengers between Sydney and Hobart, though initially this only applied during the tourist season.

The first company to take advantage of this was P & O, which began scheduling their liners to include a monthly call at Hobart on their voyages between England and Australia and return.

Among the ships to do this were *Cathay*,

which departed Sydney on 9 February for Hobart, followed by *Maloja* on 8 March and *Mooltan* on 5 April. The minimum one-way fare was £5 10s 0d first class and £4 15s 0d second class, compared to the minimum third class return fare of £8 10s 0d charged by Huddart Parker for *Zealandia*.

With the coming of spring and summer it was essential that a regular passenger vessel be placed on the route until *Zealandia* was able to resume it. As a result *Ulimaroa*, which had been laid up in Sydney through the winter, was reactivated to operate the Hobart trade.

Her first departure from Sydney was on 29 October 1932, and she operated two further trips the following month, departing Sydney on 12 November and 26 November. Through December *Ulimaroa* maintained a weekly service, departing Sydney every Wednesday, and on 4 January 1933, her final arrival in Sydney being on 9 January.

On 11 January *Zealandia*, having been replaced on the trans-Tasman route by the brand new *Wanganella*, resumed her place on the Hobart trade, again operating weekly departures. *Ulimaroa* remained laid up until being sold to Japanese shipbreakers in 1934.

*Zealandia* now maintained a regular service between Sydney and Hobart, the vessel usually leaving Sydney every Wednesday, and Hobart on Saturday.

From time to time Huddart Parker decided to try sending the vessel on occasional short cruises from Hobart during the days it would otherwise be idle in port. An itinerary provided to passengers on such a trip made by *Zealandia* stated the vessel would depart Hobart at 10pm on Friday, 10 November 1933, bound for Port Davey and then Port Arthur, returning to Hobart on the night of 12 November.

The itinerary stated that on 11 November *Zealandia* would drop anchor at Port Davey early that morning, and a note advised "passengers desiring to leave the ship may do so at their own risk and expense, circumstances permitting."

The vessel would leave Port Davey at 4pm to travel through the D'Entrecasteaux Channel to Huon Island, where it would anchor overnight, and "music will be broadcast for dancing from 8pm."

On 12 November *Zealandia* would depart the anchorage early in the morning, continuing on up the D'Entrecasteaux Channel and on to Port Arthur, where again passengers could land at their own risk and expense. Departing Port Arthur at 7pm, *Zealandia* returned to Hobart a couple of hours later.

The vessel then departed Hobart on Monday for Sydney, arriving on Wednesday morning, and leaving the same day on another voyage to Hobart.

On Monday, 15 January 1934, *Zealandia* left Sydney for Hobart, arriving there on 17 January, but the same evening departed on a cruise to Coles Bay and Port Arthur. Passengers making the round trip could either stay on board the ship for the entire trip from Sydney, including the cruise, or leave the ship in Hobart for a few days, then join the return trip to Sydney.

*Zealandia* made another overnight cruise from Hobart to Coles Bay, departing on 26 January 1935, returning the next day.

Huddart Parker Ltd also sent their newest and largest liner, *Wanganella*, to Hobart on occasional cruises. The first of these departed Sydney on 26 December, going first to Hobart and then Melbourne, while a second left Sydney on 20 February 1934 on the same itinerary. The fares were advertised as from £9 first class and £7 10s 0d second class. Newspaper advertisements stated passengers could 'Cruise in comfort on this luxurious liner', whose features included 'Deck games, Dancing, Talking Pictures, Swimming Pool.'

In July 1934 *Zealandia* was taken out of service briefly for overhaul, and on 23 July *Wanganella* left Sydney on a special relief voyage to Hobart, arriving and departing on 25 July, returning to Sydney on 27 July.

*Wanganella* made several visits to Hobart (Author's collection)

*Wanganella* made two further cruises to Tasmania in the summer of 1935/36, the first departing Sydney on 21 December 1935, going first to Melbourne and then Hobart, returning to Sydney on 28 December. The second cruise left Sydney on 18 February 1936, visiting Hobart first and then Melbourne, returning to Sydney on 24 February.

Other companies showed an occasional interest in serving Tasmania. The Australasian United Steam Navigation Company scheduled *Orungal* to make a special voyage to Hobart, departing Sydney on 8 January 1934, in the course of one of its regular trips between Sydney and Melbourne. The one-way fare was £4 10s 0d, but the standard of accommodation offered was not on a par with the Huddart Parker vessels.

During the summer and autumn tourist season of 1934 the Melbourne Steamship Company returned to the Tasmanian trade. Previously the company had been operating a small cargo/passenger steamer, the *Sydney*, on the service from Sydney to northern Tasmania, but it had ceased trading in 1916.

After the First World War the Melbourne Steamship Company fleet was reduced to a single small passenger vessel, the 3,886 gross ton *Dimboola*, built in 1912, which maintained a secondary service between Sydney and Fremantle.

In November 1929 *Dimboola* was placed on the east coast trade between Melbourne and Cairns while a regular trader, the *Orungal*, was out of service for repairs.

Unfortunately *Dimboola* was so slow it could not maintain the full schedule, and its voyages were terminated at Townsville instead of Cairns. When *Orungal* returned in June 1930, *Dimboola* was laid up, and remained idle apart from a few voyages to Fremantle in the summer of 1931/32.

*Dimboola* was reactivated in December 1933, and scheduled to make eleven round voyages from Sydney to ports in northern Tasmania. *Dimboola* provided rather simple accommodation for 72 passengers in first class and 74 in second class, and also had a considerable cargo capacity.

The two-week voyages were from Sydney to Melbourne, then across Bass Strait to Stanley, Burnie, Devonport and Launceston, then back to Melbourne and Sydney.

The first of these voyages left Sydney on 30 December 1933, going first to Melbourne, then

*Dimboola* at Burnie (Author's collection)

reaching Stanley on 2 January 1934, and Burnie the following day at 3 pm. The local *Examiner* newspaper reported that the ship was carrying a 'complement of passengers' on the round trip from the mainland.

Leaving Burnie on 4 January, *Dimboola* made the short trip to Devonport, then arrived in Launceston on Friday, 5 January, where local produce and general cargo was loaded for the mainland.

Passengers could be carried in either direction between the mainland and Tasmania, and the round trip was also heavily advertised as a cruise, the fare charged being £14 for first class and £8 second class.

*Dimboola* continued to operate these voyages until early June 1934, then returned to the Fremantle trade, on which it remained until being replaced in 1935 by the much larger *Duntroon*.

*Dimboola* was subsequently sold to buyers from Hong Kong, and survived the Second World War, not being broken up until 1953.

From 1935 the overseas lines were allowed to carry passengers to and from all Tasmanian ports throughout the year, though the larger liners were only able to berth in Hobart and Burnie.

The P & O liner *Strathnaver* berthed in Hobart in 1938 (Maritime Museum of Tasmania)

Numerous P & O liners, including the 22,547 gross ton sisters *Strathnaver* and *Strathaird*, along with the slightly larger *Strathmore*, *Stratheden* and *Strathallan,* called at Tasmanian ports in the late 1930s.

Other callers included the five Orient Line 20,000 gross ton sisters *Orama, Oronsay, Otranto, Orford* and *Orontes*, and the newer *Orion* and *Orcades* also became familiar visitors to Hobart and Burnie over the next few years. However, all these liners could only make available on the coastal trade those berths that were not booked for the whole overseas voyage.

*Zealandia* was the regular vessel operating between Sydney and Hobart during the late 1930s, remaining on this service without a break for seven years.

Then, on 21 June 1940, *Zealandia* was requisitioned by the Australian Government for service as a troop transport. Her last departure from Hobart had been on 15 June.

With no ships available as a replacement, the trade between Hobart and Sydney was suspended, and would not be resumed on a regular basis for twenty-five years.

*Zealandia* was refitted to transport 900 troops by the Cockatoo Docks and Engineering Company in Sydney, and over the next eighteen months made numerous trips to Darwin and also to Singapore. On 19 February 1942, *Zealandia* was lying at anchor in Darwin Harbour when Japanese aircraft attacked the city.

*Zealandia* was singled out as a target by two Japanese bombers, which set the vessel ablaze. Luckily only three of the 145 persons on board the ship lost their lives in the attack, and a short while later *Zealandia* sank, leaving only her mast tops showing above the water.

Ironically, the wreck was raised by a Japanese firm during 1959, and broken up.

*Zealandia* on fire and sinking in Darwin harbour on 19 February 1942 (Author's collection)

# Chapter Ten

# Taroona

When *Loongana* and *Oonah*, the Union Steam Ship Company of New Zealand Ltd contributions to the fleet of Tasmanian Steamers Pty Ltd, were due for replacement in the 1930s, the Union company decided to build just one larger ship for the trade.

The general design of the new ship, with a raked bow, cruiser stern, two funnels and two masts, was based on *Rangatira*, which had been built in 1931 for the Union Line overnight ferry service between Wellington and Lyttelton in New Zealand. Though this service was shorter than that from Melbourne to Launceston, and mostly followed the coastline of the South Island, it did include a crossing of Cook Strait, which could be as turbulent a stretch of water as Bass Strait. It was considered that the same type of ship would be suitable to both services, especially as *Rangatira* had proved a great success.

*Rangatira* had been built in England by Vickers-Armstrong Ltd at their Barrow-in-Furness shipyard, but when the contract for the new ship for the Bass Strait service was awarded, it went to Alexander Stephen & Son of Glasgow.

The keel of the new vessel was laid down in September 1933, and when launched in June 1934 was named *Taroona*, derived from the

The Union Line ferry *Rangatira* (Author's collection)

Aboriginal word for a seashell, and also the name of a suburb of Hobart.

Completed in January 1935, *Taroona* measured 4,297 gross tons, almost twice the size of *Loongana*, and was 354 feet/107.9 m long, with a beam of 50 feet/15.2 m.

*Taroona* was fitted with three oil-fired Yarrow water tube boilers with superheaters, which drove six single reduction steam turbines, geared to twin propeller shafts. The vessel achieved a maximum of 18 knots on speed trials, though her service speed would be 16 knots.

Built at a cost of £350,000, a huge amount in those days, the new vessel provided comfortable cabin accommodation spread over five decks for 302 first class and 105 second class passengers. In peak periods a further 36 first class and 40 second class passengers could be carried in temporary berths.

The first class accommodation, located in the forward and midships areas, was decorated in the finest woods, including deluxe cabins panelled in birch and sycamore. The public rooms were particular notable, and even the embarkation lobby was panelled in walnut.

Most of the promenade deck was taken up by the first class lounge and smoking room, which were connected by wide passageways on either side of the ship. Both these rooms and the dining room featured upholstered walnut furniture, and were panelled in fine wood.

The smoking room was particularly attractive, the walls being lined with oak, and having concealed lighting, a high clerestory roof, and a large marble fireplace. There was also an adjoining bar. Stairs led down from the smoking

*Taroona* as she appeared when first built (Author's collection)

room to the dining room, panelled in elm, on the main deck.

Second class cabins and facilities, which included a lounge, bar and dining room, were fitted out in a less lavish style, and located in the after end of the vessel.

A section of number one hold was refrigerated for the transporting of fruit from Tasmania to the mainland. Space under cover was also provided for about 30 cars, which had to be lifted on and off the deck by the ship's cargo gear.

Under the command of Captain Evan Evans, *Taroona* left Greenock on 26 January 1935, for her delivery voyage to Australia, via the Mediterranean and Suez Canal, arriving in Melbourne on 28 February.

Over the next ten days final touches were completed to the interior of *Taroona*, whose entry into service brought about a major change in the Bass Strait trade. The new ship would be placed on the prime route between Melbourne and Launceston, which brought about changes affecting the two older vessels.

On 6 March *Loongana* left Melbourne on her final voyage to Burnie and Devonport, having been on this route since *Oonah* was withdrawn the previous October, arriving back in Melbourne on 8 March. *Loongana* was then laid up in Melbourne, being held in reserve in case any problems should befall the other two vessels.

As *Taroona* was to replace *Nairana* on the Launceston trade, on 9 March *Nairana* made her final scheduled departure from Launceston, arriving back in Melbourne the following morning. *Nairana* was then transferred to the service from Melbourne to Burnie and Devonport.

On 12 March 1935 *Taroona* departed her berth at North Wharf in the Yarra River at 4.45 pm on her maiden crossing of Bass Strait, docking at King's Wharf, Launceston at 9.15 am next day. The ship was greeted by thousands of people lining the river bank and thronging the wharves, and an official welcoming function was held on board during the day.

*Taroona* operated a regular schedule of three return trips per week during most of the year, departing Melbourne on Monday, Wednesday and Saturday afternoons, returning from Launceston on Tuesday, Thursday and Sunday afternoons. The vessel remained in Melbourne on Friday nights.

In the winter months the timetable was reduced to two trips a week. The ship usually managed to run to schedule, though this was sometimes disrupted by severe weather.

*Nairana* departed Melbourne for Burnie and Devonport on Tuesday and Friday. The vessel would arrive in Burnie on the Wednesday and Saturday morning, then move on to Devonport later that day, and stay overnight.

On the Thursday and Sunday evenings, *Nairana* would leave Devonport, arriving back in Melbourne on the Friday and Monday mornings, with Monday night spent alongside in Melbourne.

Although *Taroona* carried the colours of Tasmanian Steamers on her funnels, the hull was painted Union Line green. After a short time in service it was found necessary to raise the height of the funnels, which also improved her overall appearance.

*Taroona* soon became very popular with the travelling public. Captain Evans remained in command of the vessel until his retirement in 1936, when he was succeeded by Captain Robert Huntley.

It had been planned that *Nairana* would return to the Launceston trade from time to time, sometimes to meet the demand for extra berths, and also when *Taroona* was undergoing annual overhaul. Also, at Christmas special trips would be operated, with both ships scheduled to spend Christmas Day alongside King's Wharf at Launceston.

However, in December 1935 most of the Australian coastal ships were affected by a national seamen's strike. When the crew on *Nairana* walked off, the vessel had to be taken out of service and laid up in Melbourne, but sufficient volunteer crew was found to keep *Taroona* going. *Taroona* spent Christmas Day 1935 alone in Launceston.

Going into 1936 it appeared that the Bass Strait service being operated by *Taroona* and *Nairana* would be more than adequate to meet passenger demand. The two ships seemed set for many successful years together, but within the space of six weeks both nearly came to a sudden end in unexpected disasters.

Probably the worst incident to affect *Nairana* during her entire career occurred on what appeared to be a perfectly calm day. On the morning of 12 April 1936, which was also Easter Sunday, *Nairana* was approaching the entrance to Port Phillip Bay in remarkably placid seas. A few early rising passengers were already on deck to see the ship pass through the Rip into the bay when, without warning, a huge wave suddenly rose out of the calm sea.

Moving towards the vessel from the starboard quarter, it first caused the bow of *Nairana* to dip alarmingly, then the steamer rolled heavily to port, almost on her beam ends, with water reaching as high as the boat deck, which was normally forty feet above the water line.

All but a few of the eighty-eight passengers on board received injuries, some serious, and there were four fatalities. Three passengers who had been standing on the promenade deck, Mr and Mrs Parsons and their 20-year old daughter, were swept overboard when the huge wave struck, and never seen again. Another passenger on a lower deck was flung against the side of the superstructure so violently he was killed instantly, though his wife, who was holding their infant, survived despite being trapped in waist-high water.

In the engine room, several stokers narrowly escaped death when they were pinned down by wheelbarrows, shovels and coal. In the dining room, every item laid on the tables for breakfast was swept away, while public rooms and cabins were left in disarray.

When the wave struck *Nairana* the helmsman was flung from the wheel into a corner of the wheelhouse. For what seemed an eternity *Nairana* lay on her port side, then slowly came upright and swung heavily to starboard, again almost lying on her side, until Captain McIntyre himself was able to seize the wheel and bring his ship back on an even keel.

Once the situation was under control, *Nairana* was able to enter Port Phillip Bay and proceed to her berth in the Yarra River. Amazingly, the vessel suffered very little structural damage in the incident, though some parts were damaged by water.

In her early years the operation of *Taroona* was affected by several unfortunate incidents, the first of which could have ended her career very early. This occurred on 10 May 1936, when the ship was docked in Melbourne, and a fire broke out in the first class accommodation.

*Taroona* had been operating regularly across Bass Strait for a year, but on 18 April left Melbourne to go to Sydney for overhaul. While she was away *Nairana* operated the entire Bass Strait service on her own, departing Melbourne for Launceston on Monday and Friday, with one trip a week to Burnie and Devonport leaving Melbourne on Wednesday.

*Taroona* returned to Melbourne from Sydney on Saturday, 9 May, berthing at North Wharf, and was due to resume its place on the Launceston trade on Monday, 11 May. However, shortly after 9 am on Sunday, 10 May, an explosion occurred on board the ship, causing a major fire. The incident was reported by the *Sydney Morning Herald* the following morning, which stated:

Damage estimated at between £8,000 and £10,000 was caused by a fire on the Bass Strait passenger steamer, *Taroona*, this morning while the ship was moored at North Wharf. The ship … arrived on Saturday from Sydney where it had been overhauled completely. When an explosion occurred, two stewards were blown from the interior of the ship to the wharf, but were not injured.

It is believed that the fire was caused by the fusing of electrical apparatus. At one stage it was feared that the whole ship would be destroyed, but skilful firefighting by the fire brigades and seamen enabled the fire to be contained to two decks amidships.

The second steward (Mr J Somerwell), who was the first to discover the fire, said: 'I was sitting in the dining saloon on C deck writing out my list when I heard the crackling of fire. Rushing up the staircase to B deck I found the staircase from B deck to A deck blazing fiercely. The fire had a strong hold on the polished wood on both sides of the staircase. I thought that I could extinguish the blaze, and I did not give the alarm until I found that the fire was getting out of control. Another steward, H Campbell, rushed up and we grabbed fire extinguishers from the walls, each using two extinguishers.'

As Somerwell and Campbell were directing streams of extinguishing liquid on the blazing woodwork there was a loud report and a terrific blast of smoke and hot gas lifted the two men from their feet, and swept them through the open embarkation door at the side of the ship, and dashed them on to the wharf more than 20 feet from where they had been standing. Somerwell escaped with a severely bruised wrist, and Campbell suffered a shaking. Fire brigade officials said that the explosion was caused by the compression of smoke, hot air, and inflammable gases in a small area.

As the flames raced along the alleyway on A deck the alarm bells were rung, and members of the crew and a gang of painters ran from all parts of the vessel to the scene of the fire amidships. Mr H Lawler, who was in charge of 30 painters who were painting aft in preparation for the departure of the ship tomorrow, shouted to the watchman on the wharf, who summoned the fire brigade.

Valuable veneer wood was crackling and clouds of suffocating smoke were swirling around the furniture in the lounge-room and the smoke-room when Lawler and W Wilson, a painter, burst open the door of the smoke-room. A strong current of smoke and gases blew them from their feet when they broke a window to reach the seat of the fire. They were forced to retreat.

The crew, who were formerly members of the Royal Australian Navy, went to their allotted stations and directed hoses and chemical extinguishers on to the flames. All the lights had been extinguished, but in the darkness of the engine-room the chief engineer (Mr R Graham) and the second engineer (Mr J Mullock) connected the pumps and started them to supply water to the ship's hoses.

Within three minutes of the alarm being given all the fireproof doors were closed and sprinklers drenched the interiors. Despite the splendid work of the crew, the fire spread rapidly, and clouds of smoke were sweeping over the Yarra as machines from three city fire stations reached the ship. When the firemen added eight large hoses to the six ship hoses, about 2,000 gallons of water a minute were being poured onto the blaze. The fire was under control at 10.57 am, 30 minutes after the alarm had been received.

The heat was intense and the pitch in the deck seams began to boil. Several seamen, who were standing on the upper deck beneath the forward starboard lifeboat, were startled when the wooden deck beneath their feet began to bulge upward. Fearing an explosion, they ran to the other side of the deck.

Amidships the vessel was an inferno. Windows and portholes cracked and smashed in the intense heat, and in the charred and blackened alleyways water swirled a foot deep. Lifeboats were scorched and blistered, and the cabins occupied by the engineers were buckled and burnt. A chest containing life-jackets on the boat deck was destroyed. Canvas weather cloths were burnt and other fittings on the boat deck were damaged or destroyed.

Fortunately most of the serious damage was restricted to the lounge and smoking room at the forward end of the promenade deck, and the fire was extinguished before it could spread any further. As the newspaper reported, there were fears the ship could be totally destroyed, and it was only due to the superb efforts of the ship's crew and the fire brigades that a total disaster was averted.

*Wollongbar* berthed at Burnie (F Reid photo; R W Brookes collection)

The vessel was out of service for several months while repairs to the fire and smoke damaged sections were completed.

*Nairana* had been scheduled to return to its twice-weekly service to Burnie and Devonport from 12 May, but had be put back onto the Launceston trade. The vessel continued to operate two trips a week to Launceston, and one round trip to Burnie and Devonport.

Tasmanian Steamers was then able to charter *Wollongbar*, which was owned by the North Coast Steam Navigation Company, and usually operated between Sydney and Byron Bay in northern New South Wales.

*Wollongbar* was built in 1922 to replace the first ship of the name, which was wrecked at Byron Bay on 14 May 1921. The second *Wollongbar* was 2,239 gross tons, and could carry two hundred passengers in two classes.

By the end of the 1930s the trade to Byron Bay was in decline, following the completion of a railway line to the area from Sydney, and *Wollongbar* was often laid up in the winter months. The charter of the ship to Tasmanian Steamers was very welcome for the North Coast company. *Wollongbar* made its first departure from Melbourne on Friday 30 May 1936.

The arrival of *Wollongbar* enabled *Nairana* to operate three return trips a week to Launceston, departing Melbourne on Monday, Wednesday and Saturday. *Wollongbar* operated two return trips a week to Burnie and Devonport, leaving Melbourne on Tuesday and Friday. *Wollongbar* spent almost three months operating across Bass Strait, her final departure from Melbourne being on 21 August, by which time repairs to *Taroona* had been completed.

*Wollongbar* returned to her regular trade, though the vessel continued to spend lengthy periods each year laid up. When the war came, *Wollongbar* was kept on the coastal service, and on the evening of 28 April 1943 was torpedoed

*Taroona* after the fire damage was repaired (Lindsay Rex collection)

by a Japanese submarine off Crescent Head, sinking in less than a minute, with the loss of 32 lives from the 37 persons on board at the time.

While *Taroona* was being repaired, a few alterations were made to the arrangement of the windows in the main lounge at the forward end of the promenade deck. The vessel resumed service from Melbourne on the evening of Wednesday, 26 August 1936. Her next departure from Melbourne was on the Saturday evening.

However, the winter service to Launceston in 1936 was not as frequent as in the previous year, *Taroona* not departing Melbourne again until Wednesday, 2 September, then on the following Sunday, while the next voyage did not leave until Thursday, 11 September.

*Nairana*, however, resumed its usual twice-weekly departures for Burnie and Devonport on Tuesday and Friday.

On the evening of Sunday, 14 September 1936, *Nairana* departed Devonport on schedule, but faced a stormy passage across Bass Strait. Captain McIntyre had been feeling unwell when the vessel sailed, and went to his cabin once the vessel was safely into Bass Strait.

Captain McIntyre returned to the bridge as *Nairana* approached Port Phillip Heads early the next morning, running into a strong northerly gale. As the vessel was entering Port Phillip Bay,

Captain McIntyre collapsed on the bridge. He was carried to his cabin, while the chief officer took over and ordered full speed as the ship crossed Port Phillip Bay, which was quite rough.

It is claimed *Nairana* reached a top speed of 20 knots during this crossing of the bay. As soon as *Nairana* berthed, Captain McIntyre was rushed ashore and taken to hospital, where he recovered and eventually resumed command of *Nairana*.

In October 1936 *Taroona* began a more frequent service to Launceston, departing Melbourne every Monday, Wednesday and Friday, returning from Launceston the following day, spending Sunday night in Melbourne.

This lasted through the summer and autumn months, but when winter came again the schedule was reduced, with irregular sailings from Melbourne and Launceston.

At Christmas in 1936 *Nairana* made a special voyage from Melbourne to Burnie and Devonport, then went on to Launceston, being there with *Taroona* on Christmas Day.

On the evening of Monday, 5 July 1937, *Taroona* left Launceston on a regular voyage to Melbourne, but on entering Port Phillip Bay the following morning was enveloped in a thick fog. Despite this, the vessel continued to steam up the bay towards Melbourne, following the western channel as it usually did.

*Taroona* and *Nairana* in Launceston, probably at Christmas 1936 (R W Brookes collection)

However, in the fog *Taroona* began to stray from the marked channel, veered off course towards the shore, and ran aground on a sandbank off Point Cook. The vessel was brought to a shuddering halt, but there was no immediate danger to passengers and crew.

The engines were put into full reverse power, and after a brief period aground, *Taroona* was refloated. *Taroona* then proceeded at slow speed, and soon after entered the mouth of the Yarra River, berthing at North Wharf. Passengers were disembarked, and some cargo was offloaded, but during the afternoon the vessel went into Duke & Orr's dry dock, a short distance upstream from North Wharf.

It was not until the dock had been pumped dry at 5 pm that an inspection revealed damage to the underwater sections of the hull. This chiefly centred on the starboard bilge keel, which suffered buckled plates for a length of about 40 feet/12.2 m from just below the bridge.

A full survey of the damage could not be completed until the next day, and this revealed more damage, including a dent in the forefoot. Of more serious concern was the discovery that the starboard bilge tanks and several frames had also been damaged in the grounding.

*Taroona* had been scheduled to depart Melbourne the same day, Wednesday 7 July, but that sailing was cancelled. Initially it was estimated that repairs to *Taroona* would take about a week, so arrangements were made to bring Nairana back on to the Launceston run again.

Nairana had left Melbourne for Devonport and Burnie on Tuesday afternoon, 6 July, and was due back in Melbourne on Thursday, 8 July at 10.30 am. It was arranged that Nairana would make a quick turnaround, and depart Melbourne at 4 pm the same day on a voyage to Burnie and Launceston, carrying all the passengers who had been booked on *Taroona*.

Also on board would be passengers booked on Nairana's scheduled Friday service to Devonport and Burnie who could leave a day earlier. The return trip left Launceston early on the afternoon of Saturday, 10 July, and included another call at Burnie before the overnight crossing of Bass Strait, arriving in Melbourne at 10.30 am on Sunday, 11 July.

The next day, Monday 12 July, Nairana left Melbourne at 2.45 pm again bound for Burnie and then Launceston, arriving there on the Tuesday morning. However, the return trip was directly back to Melbourne, arriving at 10.30 on the Wednesday morning.

*Nairana* departing Devonport in the late 1930s (F Reid photo - R W Brookes collection)

It had been planned that Nairana would then resume her regular service to Devonport and Burnie with a departure from Melbourne that afternoon. However, news from the dry dock indicated that repairs to *Taroona* would take longer than anticipated.

So Nairana left Melbourne at the scheduled time, but again went to Burnie and Launceston, returning to Melbourne on the morning of Friday, 16 July. After another quick turnaround, Nairana left the same day at 4 pm on a direct voyage to Launceston, returning to Melbourne on the Monday morning.

By then the repairs to *Taroona* were almost finished, and she was scheduled to resume service on Wednesday, 21 July. It is possible that it was during this drydocking that a change was made to the paint scheme on *Taroona*, with the top section of the hull being repainted white, which greatly improved her appearance.

*Taroona* came out of the drydock on 20 July, going to 7 North Wharf, while the same afternoon

Nairana left 10 North Wharf on a regular voyage to Devonport and Burnie. *Taroona* left as scheduled at 4 pm on 21 July, and the two ships then resumed their regular schedules.

Later in July *Taroona* suffered engine trouble, this time in the Tamar River while departing Launceston, and had to be towed back to King's Wharf for repairs. In February 1938, shortly after departing Melbourne, there was another engine breakdown, and once again the vessel had to be towed back to her berth, resuming service the next day.

Fortunately this would be the last major problem to affect *Taroona* for some time. The vessel was able to settle down to regular service between Melbourne and Launceston.

At the same time, Nairana was able to maintain the service from Melbourne to Burnie and Devonport without any further disruptions for the rest of 1938, and into 1939. However in September that year the situation changed again.

*Taroona* with a changed paint scheme in the late 1930s (Author's collection)

# Chapter Eleven

# World War 2 and the Post-War Years

When war in Europe broke out in September 1939 it had no immediate effect on the schedules operated by the vessels trading across Bass Strait. By the end of 1939 both *Taroona* and *Nairana* began carrying large numbers of military personnel, which meant they could only transport a restricted number of commercial passengers.

As a safety precaution, the ships were painted grey all over, including the windows and portholes, and a crow's nest was installed high up on the foremast. The vessels still operated their voyages overnight, but no navigation lights were shown, and on the inside of doors that opened onto outside decks there was only a purple light.

After several ships hit mines in Bass Strait during November 1940, *Taroona* and *Nairana* were also equipped with paravanes. These were streamed over the side when the ship was at sea, to cut the cables of anchored mines and ward off floating mines.

Bobby Brookes was serving on board *Nairana*, and recalled that the ship was fitted with her

*Nairana* in wartime grey departing Devonport (R W Brookes collection)

own armament. Aft on the promenade deck, the emergency steering wheel was removed, and a 4-inch Mk VIII anti-submarine gun mounted.

This weapon dated from 1910, and had originally been fitted to the first HMAS *Parramatta*. It was mounted on a pedestal, and did not have a protective shield. A gunner was posted to the ship, and he was assisted by members of the regular crew.

When drills were held, the gun would first be loaded with a practice projectile and fired. The second shot would use live ammunition, aimed to straddle a smoke float released from the stern of the ship.

An Oerlikon anti-aircraft gun was also fitted, atop the deckhouse aft of the mainmast, while a number of .303 rifles were also carried, to puncture and sink floating mines. *Taroona* was a fitted with a similar variety of armaments.

The entry of Japan into the Second World War in December 1941 brought the conflict much closer to Australia, and would eventually have a major effect on the Bass Strait trade.

Although registered in Melbourne, *Taroona* was nominally part of the fleet of the Union Steam Ship Company of New Zealand, and was requisitioned on 5 January 1942 by the New Zealand Government. *Taroona* was undergoing an engine overhaul in Melbourne when the message from New Zealand was received.

As a result of herculean efforts by those involved, the engines were quickly put back together, and *Taroona* left Melbourne on 7 January for Auckland, arriving there three days later. However, no changes were made to the accommodation, which remained in its civilian configuration.

On 12 January, a contingent of New Zealand troops, comprising 36 officers and 644 other ranks, embarked on *Taroona* in Auckland. Escorted by the Union Steam Ship Company trans-Tasman liner *Monowai*, which had been converted into an armed merchant cruiser, and was also carrying troops, *Taroona* left Auckland on 13 January, reaching Fijian waters three days later.

As the two ships neared Suva on 16 January, they were attacked by gunfire from a surfaced Japanese submarine, but neither was damaged, and they docked in Suva the same day.

Arriving back in Auckland on 19 January, *Taroona* boarded a number of New Zealand military personnel, who were carried back to Melbourne. Returned to her owners on 30 Jan-uary, *Taroona* resumed her place on the Launceston trade in February, while *Nairana* went back on the service to Burnie and Devonport, though not for long.

On 12 March 1942, *Taroona* was requisitioned again, this time by the Australian Government, and converted into a troop transport, with a capacity of 678 officers and other ranks. The ship was given a quick refit, during which the top section of the aft funnel was removed to provide a better arc of fire for anti-aircraft guns mounted on the top deck.

On entering military service, *Taroona* was based at Townsville, from where her first voyage

*Taroona* was painted grey when war broke out in 1939 (Robert J Tompkins collection)

Changed appearance of *Taroona* when serving as a troop transport (Author's collection)

was to Port Moresby, arriving there on 25 March. When leaving the port next day, *Taroona* went aground on Nateara Reef, being held fast from the bow to below the bridge on the port side.

Initial attempts to refloat *Taroona* failed, and most of the fuel and cargo on board had to be removed to lighten the ship. During this time Japanese bombers were making frequent raids on Port Moresby, but amazingly they did not notice the ship stranded at the harbour entrance, which could easily have become a target. *Taroona* was finally pulled clear three days later, returned to port to refuel, then headed back to Townsville, where repairs were effected.

Over the next four years *Taroona* operated a shuttle service from Townsville to New Guinea, making 94 round trips in all, carrying 93,482 men and steaming 204,500 miles. She made 74 visits to Milne Bay, 46 to Port Moresby and 19 to Lae, with occasional calls at eleven other island ports.

During the war *Taroona* was manned by her regular officers and crew. The strain of this service eventually took its toll on Captain Huntley, who collapsed and died on the bridge when the ship was off Townsville. Command of *Taroona* was then shared by Captain D M Keith and Captain C W Ostenfeld.

With *Taroona* gone, the whole burden of maintaining the service across Bass Strait fell upon *Nairana*, which returned to the Launceston

trade for the next few years, while also making occasional trips to Burnie and Devonport.

*Nairana* was not considered suitable for military service, as she was still a coal-burner, and emitted clouds of black smoke from her two funnels that could be seen for miles. Despite this, *Nairana* had a very hectic time during the war years.

The number of passengers being carried was greatly increased, far in excess of available berths, and many people had to find a chair to sleep in, or lie on the floor of one of the public rooms. For safety purposes, four wooden liferafts were placed on board, one pair being located either side of the foremast, the others on either side of the mainmast, above the deck railings. So great was the demand for passages that a priority system had to be introduced.

At first half the available berths on every departure were reserved for military personnel, but later in the war civilian passengers were only carried in an allocation on every third trip, or in other words, once a week.

*Nairana* operated without letup and with minimal maintenance throughout the war years. In 1943, *Nairana* was entering the Tamar River when she ran aground in Whirlpool Reach, caused by the rudder jamming. Refloated some two hours later at high tide, the vessel continued up the river to Launceston, and returned to Melbourne as scheduled, but then spent the next

*Taroona* looked quite different after the war with only one funnel (Author's collection)

thirteen days in the Williamstown graving dock undergoing repairs.

Early in 1944, *Nairana* made her fourth and last visit to Sydney, again going to Cockatoo Island for overhaul. During the period the vessel was away in Sydney there was no passenger service operated at all between the mainland and Tasmania.

Arriving at Cockatoo Island on 22 February, *Nairana* was berthed at the Plate Wharf on the northern side of the island. *Nairana* just missed meeting up with her Bass Strait partner in Sydney, as *Taroona* had been undergoing turbine repairs at Cockatoo Island from 29 November 1943 to 18 February 1944, then resumed her role as a troop transport.

The work on *Nairana* involved re-blading of the turbines, removal of the guns installed earlier in the war, and some minor hull alterations. *Nairana* left Cockatoo on 5 April 1944, and resumed her place on the Bass Strait trade when she returned to Melbourne.

Even when the war ended there was no letup for *Nairana*, as *Taroona* was retained on Government service in the first months of peace, repatriating Australian troops.

On 4 February 1946 *Taroona* arrived in Sydney carrying 644 troops returning home from New Guinea. The ship was then paid off by the Navy, and remained in Sydney to be refitted for a return to commercial service.

The Bass Strait service continued to be operated by *Nairana*, her last departure from King's Wharf at Launceston being on 20 September 1946. Her

subsequent voyages terminated at Beauty Point, near the mouth of the Tamar River.

The work took just over six months to complete, and on 26 September *Taroona* left Sydney for Melbourne. Although much the same internally, externally she looked quite different, with only a single tall funnel.

On the evening of Thursday, 3 October 1946, *Taroona* departed Melbourne on her first crossing of Bass Strait in over four and a half years. In command was Captain *Nelson* Bonetti, who would remain with the ship for the rest of her Bass Strait career. *Taroona* was greeted by a huge crowd on arrival in Launceston the next morning, and a civic reception was held at the Town Hall to welcome the ship back. *Taroona* then resumed her pre-war schedule of three return trips a week between Melbourne and Launceston, and *Nairana* went back to operating two trips a week from Melbourne to Burnie and Devonport.

For the summer season of 1946/47 an attempt was made to revive a service between Sydney and Hobart, which had ceased when *Zealandia* was requisitioned for war duty in June 1940. The vessel placed on the route was *Ormiston*, owned by the Australasian United Steam Navigation Company (AUSN).

*Ormiston* was one of a pair of cargo/passenger vessels built in Scotland in 1922/23 for the Khedivial Mail Steamship Co, based in Egypt but owned by the P & O Group. Originally named *Famaka* and *Fezara*, the two ships were transferred within the P & O organisation in

*Ormiston* was placed in service between Sydney and Hobart in late 1946 (Author's collection)

1927 to the AUSN, being renamed *Ormiston* and *Orungal*.

The pair was fitted out with accommodation for 240 passengers in one class, and placed on the Australian east coast route between Melbourne and Cairns. At various times both ships were used on other trades, and they made occasional visits to Hobart on voyages between Sydney and Melbourne during the 1930s.

Between January and April 1937 *Ormiston* made six cruises from Sydney to various Tasmanian ports. These must have been quite successful, as they were repeated in 1938 and 1939. *Orungal* was wrecked near the entrance to Port Phillip Bay on 21 November 1940. *Ormiston* was used on a variety of coastal and island services during the early years of the war.

On 12 May 1943, *Ormiston* was torpedoed off the New South Wales north coast, but managed to reach Coffs Harbour safely, and later moved to Sydney for repairs. It was not until February 1944 that *Ormiston* returned to service, being used to transport troops around the Australian coast under the auspices of the Shipping Control Board.

When the war ended, there was a shortage of passenger ships on the Australian coast, and *Ormiston* was placed on a route between Melbourne, Sydney and Brisbane, carrying 107 passengers in rather austere accommodation on B and C decks only. Still under the Shipping Control Board, for the summer of 1946/47 *Ormiston* was placed on the Sydney to Hobart route, initially scheduled to make five round trips on a fortnightly schedule. As *Ormiston* was quite a slow vessel, with a service speed of only 15 knots, it spent two days at sea in each direction.

*Ormiston* departed Lime Street Wharf in Sydney on its first trip for the season on Friday,

15 November 1946, berthing at No 1 Princes Wharf in Hobart on the morning of Monday, 18 November. At the same time another vessel made a voyage from Sydney to Hobart with passengers, but in this case only a dozen. However, the event was sufficiently noteworthy for the following item to appear in the *Mercury* on 19 November, under the heading 'Shipping Milestone':

The arrival at Hobart in the past four days of two ships with passengers direct from Sydney – the first since 1941 – must be regarded as an important milestone on the road back to normal in shipping. It was perhaps fitting that the first oversea vessel to bring interstate passengers should be the *Port Hobart* on her maiden voyage, and it is hoped she is but the first of many oversea ships which will make calls at Hobart soon. More important to Hobart, however, was the arrival yesterday of the interstate liner *Ormiston*, which inaugurated a fortnightly service, until the middle of January, between Sydney and Hobart. Although air travel to some extent minimised the inconvenience caused Hobartians with the removal from the passenger service of the *Zealandia* in 1941 there is little doubt that a sea link with Australia's largest city is vital to Tasmania. It is hoped additional trips by the *Ormiston* can be arranged until a passenger vessel is placed on the Sydney–Hobart service permanently.

The return trip by *Ormiston* left Hobart on 22 November, arriving back in Sydney three days later. The vessel then spent six days in Sydney before departing on its second voyage. This schedule was eventually extended to ten round trips over four months, the final voyage departing Sydney on 28 March 1947, being in Hobart from 31 March to 3 April, arriving back in Sydney on 6 April. *Ormiston* was then withdrawn from service for reconditioning to peacetime standards.

Apart from the occasional voyage between Sydney and Hobart by an overseas cargo vessel with very limited accommodation, it would be almost twenty years before another passenger ship was placed on a regular passenger service between Sydney and Hobart.

*Ormiston* remained trading on the Australian coast until January 1955, when she was sold to a Greek concern, Typaldos Line, who would later also buy *Taroona*. *Ormiston* was renamed

*Atlantic*, but her new career was extremely short, as she arrived at La Spezia in Italy on 30 November 1957 to be broken up.

Meanwhile, Tasmanian Steamers had decided that from the end of December 1947 *Taroona* would no longer proceed up the Tamar River to berth at King's Wharf in Launceston. Instead the vessel would terminate its trips at Beauty Point, close to the mouth of the river, berthing at Inspection Head, the wharf where large liners

*Nairana* at Burnie in 1946 (F Reid photo; R W Brookes collection)

berthed. This move was most unpopular with Launceston residents, as it took the best part of an hour to drive from the city to Beauty Point, and there was no rail connection.

When *Taroona* had resumed her place on the Launceston trade in October 1946, *Nairana* was in desperate need of a major refit, but Tasmanian Steamers were of the opinion that the expense could not be justified. In the immediate post-war years regular air services were being established across Bass Strait, and the number of passengers using the two ships had begun to decline. So *Nairana* was given a basic overhaul, then returned to service.

Tasmanian Steamers eventually reached the position where the use of two ships on the Tasmanian trade could no longer be justified. *Nairana* departed Devonport on her final crossing of Bass Strait on 13 February 1948, arriving in Melbourne the following morning, and being withdrawn from service.

At first *Nairana* was laid up at No 1 South Wharf, but then it was towed to an anchorage

in Hobson's Bay. Despite being offered for sale at a very low price, no offers were forthcoming for the old vessel, which sat idle for the next two years, with only a watchman on board.

When *Nairana* was taken out of service, *Taroona* was left to operate the Bass Strait services on her own, and was placed on a new schedule.

Though still operating three round trips a week, the Monday night departure from Melbourne went to Beauty Point, while the Wednesday night trip was to Burnie and the Friday night sailing to Devonport.

On each voyage the ship returned to Melbourne the next night, with Sunday spent tied up in Melbourne.

Early in 1951 *Nairana* was sold to a Williamstown firm, Wm Mussell Pty Ltd, who planned to gradually scrap the vessel. However, before any work could start, on the night of 18 February 1951 a huge storm struck Melbourne.

*Nairana* was torn from her moorings, swept over two sandbanks, and driven aground a short distance from Prince's Pier. Attempts at refloating failed, so all saleable gear and fittings were removed and sold at auction.

In 1953 work began on cutting up *Nairana* where it lay, and by the middle of 1954 the only visible part of the ship was the double bottom. By the end of the year that had gone too.

On 11 May 1951, *Taroona* arrived in Sydney for an extensive overhaul, being out of service for about ten weeks, during which time there was no replacement vessel on Bass Strait.

In July 1951, Huddart Parker briefly took *Wanganella* off the trans-Tasman trade from Sydney for two special trips to Tasmania.

*Nairana* aground off Port Melbourne (R W Brookes collection)

*Wanganella* visited Hobart and Burnie in July 1951
(Author's collection)

*Moonta* replaced *Taroona* for six months in 1955
(Author's collection)

Leaving Sydney on 6 July, *Wanganella* arrived in Hobart two days later carrying 85 passengers, 40 of whom disembarked, while 70 joined the ship.

Wanganella left Hobart on 10 July for Burnie, berthing there next day, then made an overnight voyage to Melbourne. Leaving again on 12 July, *Wanganella* voyaged overnight to Burnie, then went on to Hobart, arriving on 15 July, and embarking 128 passengers for the trip back to Sydney, which left Hobart on 17 July.

In the early post-war years a number of fledgling air services were established between the mainland and Tasmania. One such venture involved a company called Trans Oceanic Airways, which in 1952 was advertising flights direct from Sydney to Hobart in 3½ hours in a 'luxurious Solent Flying Boat, landing on the Derwent River at Hobart'.

During the early 1950s *Taroona* continued to maintain the Bass Strait passenger service on its own, with three round trips a week.

In June 1955 *Taroona* was taken out of service again for a much longer overhaul, but this time a replacement was provided. This was the diminutive Adelaide Steamship Company coastal vessel Moonta, which was much smaller than *Taroona* at 2,693 gross tons, and provided cabin accommodation for only 140 passengers, but at least it was better than nothing.

Built in Denmark in 1931, *Moonta* was designed for the service from Adelaide to various ports in Spencer Gulf, including Port Lincoln, Port Germein, Port Pirie, Port Augusta and Port Hughes. *Moonta* remained on this trade until February 1955, when she was withdrawn and offered for sale. With no buyer immediately forthcoming, the Adelaide Steamship Company was more than pleased to be able to charter the ship to Tasmanian Steamers.

On 6 June 1955, *Moonta* departed Melbourne on her first voyage across Bass Strait, working to the same schedule as *Taroona*, with three round trips a week. The work on *Taroona* lasted much longer than had been anticipated, and it was not until early December that she returned to the Bass Strait trade, much to the relief of passengers.

*Moonta* completed her final crossing of Bass Strait in Melbourne on 8 December, and then Taroona resumed her regular schedule. By that time *Moonta* had been sold to a Greek company, Hellenic Mediterranean Lines, who took over the ship in Melbourne on 21 December.

Renamed *Lydia*, she left Melbourne three days later for Piraeus, and spent the next ten years operating in the Mediterranean. In June 1967 the vessel was berthed in a basin gouged out of the beach at Le Barcares, on the French Mediterranean coast. The basin was then filled with sand, leaving the vessel high and dry on the beach, where she remains to this day as a nightclub and entertainment centre.

In 1956 there were reports that the Tasmanian Government had begun negotiations with Huddart Parker Ltd to have placed on a service between Sydney and Hobart during the coming summer tourist season.

Built in 1929, the 8,108 gross ton *Westralia* had operated for most of its career on the major interstate passenger service from east coast ports to Fremantle, but as the 1950s progressed this trade was slowly dying as more people chose to travel by plane.

With *Taroona* unable to meet the demand for passages to Tasmania in the summer months, a ship such as *Westralia*, which could carry about 350 passengers, would have provided a very welcome increase in available berths. However, the talks came to nothing, and *Taroona* remained the sole passenger shipping connection between the mainland and the island state.

The number of passengers wanting to take their cars with them to Tasmania increased

*Taroona* berthed at Burnie (F Reid photo; Devonport Maritime Museum)

steadily in the late 1950s. *Taroona* had space to carry between thirty and forty cars, depending on their size, but they had to be lifted on and off the ship one at a time by crane, which was a slow and tedious business.

It was becoming increasingly clear that a new vessel capable of carrying a large number of vehicles as well as passengers was needed for the trade. However, Tasmanian Steamers was unable to obtain subsidies from either the Tasmanian or Federal Goverments to enable them to build a new ship.

So in 1957 the company announced that *Taroona* would be withdrawn from service in 1959, and no replacement would be provided. As a result, the Federal Government requested Australian National Line take over the trade, and build a new vessel for which a subsidy would be provided.

While the new ship was building, *Taroona*, now referred to as 'The Grand Old Lady', continued to ply back and forth across Bass Strait, until the time came for her to be withdrawn in September 1959.

Wal Lane recalled his first visit to Tasmania in March 1958, which was his first holiday since leaving school and starting work. He booked himself on *Taroona* in an outside single berth cabin in first class, the return fare costing him the princely sum of £11, which included dinner and breakfast in both directions.

His ticket, issued by the Sydney office of the Tasmanian Government Tourist Bureau, showed the voyage to Tasmania would berth in Devonport, but no port was shown for his return trip, and he was advised to check on this while in Tasmania. Wal travelled from Sydney to Melbourne by train, and joined the ship at its

berth in the Yarra River on 10 March.

This was his first voyage on anything larger than a Sydney ferry, and the first time he had crossed open water. After passing through the Rip, Wal recalled that the sea was quite rough, with white caps on the waves, but he thought that was just the normal thing. He managed to have dinner, and then went to his cabin for the night.

Next morning he jumped out of bed to look out the porthole to see if the Tasmanian coastline was visible, and it was only then he felt unsteady on his feet, and decided to climb back into bed.

A few minutes later the steward knocked on the cabin door, and entered to enquire if Wal would be going down to breakfast. Feeling quite off-colour by then, Wal said he would not be having breakfast, to which the steward replied he would not be the only one. It turned out that most of the passengers were laid low by seasickness, and no doubt longing for the voyage to end.

In mid-morning *Taroona* arrived in Devonport, berthing on the western side of the harbour as usual. Wal was quite relieved to disembark, and walked the short distance to the railway station, where he was due to catch a train later in the day to Burnie. He had to collect his ticket from the station office, and the station master invited Wal to join him in a cup of tea, but him was still not feeling the best, and declined.

With time to spare, Wal wandered around the shops of Devonport, but it was early afternoon before he felt game enough to eat something, buying a sandwich and going down to the reserve by the river to eat it. Sitting on a bench, he overheard a couple sitting nearby say how bad the trip on *Taroona* had been. Wal got into conversation with them, and they said they had been coming to Tasmania for a holiday every year for the past ten years, but the trip the previous night on *Taroona* had been the roughest they had ever endured.

Wal spent ten days touring around Tasmania, mostly by train, and a few days before he was due to return to the mainland contacted the Tasmanian Government Tourist Bureau to find out where he should join *Taroona*.

At that time the vessel was running a rather irregular pattern of voyages from Burnie, Devonport and Beauty Point, but Wal was very surprised when he was informed that the vessel would be leaving from Bell Bay, which was located on the eastern shore of the Tamar River opposite Beauty Point.

On Saturday, 22 March, Wal and other passengers assembled outside the Launceston railway station at 1 pm. They were put on board three buses and driven almost the full length of the Tamar river to Bell Bay, where *Taroona* was alongside the berth usually used by cargo ships loading alumina products.

Fortunately the voyage back to Melbourne was much smoother, and Wal was able to enjoy his breakfast before disembarking at Princes Pier. As he was walking away from the ship, Wal stopped to take a picture of it. Since then Wal Lane has travelled on many ships, and that

*Taroona* at Princes Pier on 23 March 1958 (Wal Lane photo)

voyage on the *Taroona* remains the only time he has been seasick.

The ship took her leave of Tasmania over a period of several days, with crowds of well-wishers farewelling her on the final departures from each port.

She left Burnie for the last time on 22 September, then three days later came her farewell to Launceston. Following a function on board the vessel at Beauty Point, *Taroona* slowly drew away from the wharf, with bunting flying.

On her arrival at Melbourne next morning, Captain Bonetti was ill, and had to be taken to hospital, so for her final voyages across Bass Strait the vessel was commanded by Captain C H George.

*Taroona* departed Melbourne for her final trip to Tasmania on 28 September, arriving in Devonport the next morning. It was a cold, rainy day, but that evening thousands turned out to farewell the old steamer as she left Tasmania for the last time, arriving back in Melbourne on Wednesday, 30 September.

By that time *Taroona* had already been sold, to a Greek company, Typaldos Line. A Greek crew had been flown out to Melbourne, and took over the ship almost immediately.

Her name was changed to *Hellas*, and on 12 October 1959 the steamer left Melbourne for the last time, bound for the warmer waters of the Mediterranean. At that time *Hellas* was the largest vessel in the Typaldos fleet, and she became their flagship.

Following her arrival in Greece, the old ship was given an extensive refit. The superstructure was extended aft to provide a new lounge and an

*Taroona* departing Beauty Point on 3 January 1959 (Lindsay Rex photo)

outdoor swimming pool on the promenade deck.

The accommodation was altered to carry 150 first class, 125 second class and 150 tourist class passengers, and all cabins were fitted with air conditioning.

Each class was allocated a separate lounge and dining room, but all shared the swimming pool. The hull was painted white with a narrow black band, and the varnished wood bridge was retained.

The funnel was painted in Typaldos colours, yellow with the company emblem on each side. Despite her age, the vessel looked very smart in the new livery.

In April 1960 *Hellas* entered service between Italy, Greece and Turkey. *Hellas* served on this route for two years during the tourist season, being laid up in winter. She was then transferred to another route, making weekly departures from Venice to Split, Patras, Piraeus and Heraklion, in Crete. This was also a seasonal trade, from April to November, with the vessel being laid up in the other months.

Commencing in April 1965, *Hellas* began operating on a new fortnightly cruise service from Venice to Alexandria, in Egypt, with calls at various Greek island ports along the way. This lasted only a single season, as in 1966 *Hellas* was transferred to another service, from Venice to Haifa, in Israel.

On 3 November 1966, *Hellas* arrived in Venice to complete her final voyage for the season, then went to Greece to be laid up for the winter at Perama, near Piraeus. It was not realised at that time that *Hellas* had finished her active career, and would spend the next twenty-three years laid up.

On the night of 12 December 1966, another vessel owned by Typaldos Line, the inter-island ferry *Heraklion*, sank during a severe storm, with heavy loss of life. The blame for this tragedy was laid totally on the owners, who later went to jail, and the entire Typaldos operation ceased.

Several vessels owned by Typaldos Line were sold to other operators, but *Hellas* attracted no buyers, and remained idle in Perama Bay, growing shabbier with each passing year.

In May 1989, *Hellas* was sold to Turkish shipbreakers. Towed out of Perama Bay, she arrived at Aliaga on 23 May, and was pulled ashore on the beach there. By the end of the year nothing remained of the vessel that had once been the pride of the Bass Strait trade.

*Hellas* laid up in Perama Bay in 1978 (Stephen Berry photo)

# Chapter Twelve

# Princess of Tasmania

The ferry service across Bass Strait between Melbourne and ports in northern Tasmania had been operated since 1922 by Tasmanian Steamers Pty Ltd, jointly owned by Huddart Parker Limited and the Union Steam Ship Company of New Zealand.

During the 1950s this service was maintained by just one ship, *Taroona*, which had adequate accommodation for 400 passengers, but could carry only 30 cars, which had to be lifted on and off by cranes. This was totally inadequate to meet the growing demand for the transportation of private vehicles between the mainland and Tasmania, and a totally new type of ship was required.

Tasmanian Steamers were well aware of this, and made plans to operate a drive-on drive-off vessel on the route, but were unable to obtain subsidies from either the Tasmanian or Federal Governments to enable them to build a new ship. Instead, in 1957 the company announced that *Taroona* would be withdrawn from the Bass Strait service in 1959, and no replacement provided.

It was essential to maintain a regular passenger shipping connection between the mainland and the island state, so the Federal Government decided that the Australian Coastal Shipping Commission should take over the service, for which they would provided with a subsidy.

The Australian Coastal Shipping Commission had been established on 1 October 1956 after the passing of the *Australian Coastal Shipping Commission Act.*

The new organisation took over the fleet of some forty ships previously operated by the Australian Shipping Board, which itself had been formed on 1 January 1946 by the Australian Government. The transfer took place on 1 January 1957, and the new organisation operated as Australian National Line.

An order was placed in October 1956 with the New South Wales State Dockyard at Newcastle for the construction of a new vessel, which would be the first drive-on drive-off car ferry in the southern hemisphere.

The keel of the vessel was laid on 15 November 1957, and it was launched on 15 December 1958, being named *Princess of Tasmania*.

Fitting out continued through the first half of 1959, and on 20 July the vessel left Newcastle for the first time, spending three days at sea on trials. *Princess of Tasmania* then paid a fleeting visit to Sydney on 24 July, proceeding as far up Sydney Harbour as Fort Denison before returning to sea, and heading back to Newcastle. Further fitting out work continued over the next two months, followed by final sea trials.

*Princess of Tasmania* on the slip just before being launched (Devonport Maritime Museum)

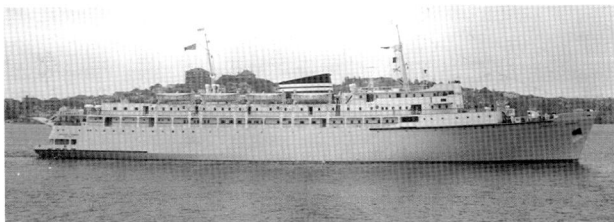

*Princess of Tasmania* arriving in Sydney Harbour on 17 September 1959 (Fred Roderick photo; Author's collection)

*Princess of Tasmania* was handed over to Australian National Line in Newcastle on 14 September 1959. As completed the vessel measured 3,964 gross tons, having a length of 372 ft/113.4 m and beam of 58 ft/17.6 m.

The two propellers were powered by a pair of 8,600 bhp, 9 cylinder, 2-stroke cycle single acting Nohab Polar type diesels, built by Nydqvist & Holm A/B, of Trollhattan in Norway, which could push the ship along at a service speed of 16 knots.

*Princess of Tasmania* left Newcastle on 17 September, under the command of Captain W B Williams, and proceeded south to Sydney, berthing at No 2 Circular Quay for two days. During this time the vessel was inspected by over 6,000 visitors.

It then continued its voyage to Melbourne, but on entering Bass Strait for the first time encountered strong winds and high seas. While other ships were forced to seek shelter, *Princess of Tasmania* proved her worth and seakeeping ability, ploughing on through the heavy seas.

The ANL cargo ship *Noongah*, sheltering in the lee of Wilson's Promontory, sent a message to the new ship that read, 'Congratulations on your inaugural voyage. Would you please open your car deck and let me in. I am running late.'

Entering Port Phillip Heads at 5.30 am on 21 September, *Princess of Tasmania* hugged the eastern shoreline as she proceeded up Port Phillip Bay to Melbourne, her port of registry, berthing for the first time at 9.30 am at Webb Dock, which had been specially built to handle the ship.

Instead of following the irregular schedule operated by *Taroona*, of trips to each of Beauty Point, Burnie and Devonport, *Princess of Tasmania* would be operating three round trips a week to Devonport only, due to its central location.

To facilitate this, a new terminal had been built at East Devonport, similar to the one constructed at Webb Dock in Melbourne. Both terminals incorporated a large parking area for cars waiting to drive on board the ship, a loading ramp, and a terminal building.

As *Princess of Tasmania* was only going to operate a fourteen-hour overnight voyage in each direction, the facilities provided for the maximum of 334 passengers were quite simple.

Breakfast would be the only meal served on board, so instead of a dining room there was a cafeteria, in which 80 seats were provided at three U-shaped islands. Unfortunately, when the ship was full the queue for breakfast would wind up the access stairs and along adjacent companionways, making moving around the ship quite difficult.

The only other amenity was a small smoking room and bar located aft on the boat deck. Passengers also had access to an open observation deck forward of the bridge, with another area of open deck aft on the top deck. It was thought that as the voyage across Bass Strait would always be overnight, there would be little need for larger facilities.

Accommodation for 178 passengers was provided in cabins, 26 single berth, 27 twin berth and 18 four berth, as well as two suites, which were the only cabins to have private facilities. There were also 156 aircraft-style reclining seats located in three lounges, two of which were at the forward end of the boat deck, while the third was next to the cafeteria on the upper deck.

The vehicle deck, which was 325 ft/99 m long, almost the full length of the hull, could accommodate up to 142 cars, depending on their size, with access through a stern door only, enabling loading or discharge to be completed within an hour. At peak periods extra cars could also be carried in a two-tier lower hold, linked to the vehicle deck by an electric lift.

To counter the rough seas often experienced in Bass Strait, *Princess of Tasmania* was the first Australian coastal vessel to be fitted with fin stabilisers. There were also twin rudders and a Voith-Schneider bow thruster to assist the vessel to turn when docking, which was always done stern first. A crew of 67 was carried. The vessel also introduced the new ANL creamy yellow hull colour.

*Princess of Tasmania* arriving in Devonport (Nancy Jacobs photo)

On the evening of Wednesday, 23 September 1959, *Princess of Tasmania* left Melbourne on her first voyage across Bass Strait to Tasmania. This was a special test trip, with only 180 invited guests aboard, including Dame Pattie Menzies, wife of the then Prime Minister, numerous politicians and media representatives. There were also 100 new cars on the vehicle deck being delivered to dealers in Tasmania.

Escorted on the voyage by HMAS *Quiberon*, *Princess of Tasmania* went first to Emu Bay, near Burnie, to give local residents a brief look at the new ship, which then proceeded to Devonport, berthing at 10 am. The arrival was witnessed by over 8,000 people lining both banks of the Mersey River.

*Princess of Tasmania* remained in Devonport, and on the afternoon of 26 September the then Premier of Tasmania, Eric Reece, officially opened the new terminal at East Devonport, which was named the Sir Robert Cosgrove Bass Strait Ferry Terminal. When this ceremony

*Princess of Tasmania* (Author's collection)

Travel to and from TASMANIA by SEAROAD

on the M.V. "Princess of Tasmania"

OWNED AND OPERATED BY THE AUSTRALIAN NATIONAL LINE
PRINCIPAL AGENTS: TASMANIAN STEAMERS PTY. LTD

Cover of an early brochure promoting *Princess of Tasmania* (Author's collection)

was over, *Princess of Tasmania* was opened for public inspection, and 12,000 people took the opportunity to have a look at the new ship, which then returned to Melbourne.

The ship *Princess of Tasmania* was replacing, *Taroona*, completed her final crossing of Bass Strait on Wednesday, 30 September. On Friday 2 October, *Princess of Tasmania* departed Melbourne on her first commercial voyage to Devonport.

The vessel was programmed to make three return trips a week, departing Melbourne on the evening of Monday, Wednesday and Friday, and Devonport on Tuesday, Thursday and Sunday, with Saturday spent alongside in Devonport.

Departure time for all trips was originally set for 8 pm, but it was soon changed to 7.30 pm, though the arrival time remained unchanged at 10 am.

Advertised as the 'Searoad' service, it soon became very popular with the travelling public, and during the first three weeks of operation the vessel carried 3,903 passengers and 1,313 vehicles.

During her first five months *Princess of Tasmania* carried 37,152 passengers and 13,666 vehicles; in her first year of operation the vessel transported 64,836 passengers, 16,978 cars and 7,808 commercial vehicles.

In 1961 Captain Williams retired, being replaced by Captain Harry Hadley, who remained with the ship for the remainder of its service in Australian waters.

The operation of the ship quickly settled into a steady pattern, with no notable interruptions. The introduction of the new ship soon resulted in a considerable increase in the number of people wishing to travel to Tasmania and take their cars with them.

However, the vessel also provided motor dealers in Tasmania with a convenient way of having their new cars delivered from the mainland, which took up considerable space on the vehicle deck, and prevented many potential tourists from travelling.

Within a year of *Princess of Tasmania* entering service it was obvious that the vessel could not adequately meet the demand for drive-on drive-off freight vehicles, as priority on the car decks was given to passenger's cars.

As a result, Australian National Line decided to order a second vessel for the Bass Strait trade, though in this case it would just carry general cargo and freight vehicles, and accommodation would only be provided for drivers accompanying their trucks.

The new vessel was built by the Newcastle State Dockyard, and when completed in 1961 was named *Bass Trader*. Although shorter than *Princess of Tasmania* at 322 ft/104.2 m, her gross tonnage of 4,129 was larger.

*Princess of Tasmania* arriving in Devonport (Devonport Maritime Museum)

*Princess of Tasmania* berthed at the new Bass Strait Ferry Terminal at East Devonport (Devonport
Maritime Museum)

*Bass Trader* was placed in service from
Melbourne to northern Tasmania, making
one trip a week to each of Bell Bay, Burnie and
Devonport. The vessel could carry sixty semi-
trailers and also twenty standard size containers
on the upper deck, though these had to be lifted
on and off by shore crane.

*Bass Trader* was fitted with twin controllable
pitch propellers powered by a pair of 18 cylinder,
2-stroke cycle single acting Deltic diesel engines,
built by D Napier & Son of Liverpool, England.

These engines were unique at the time, as
*Bass Trader* was the first vessel in the world to be
fitted with machinery designed on the principle
of engine repair by replacement. Each of the
diesel engines weighed only five tons, and if
one was suffering problems it could be removed

*Bass Trader* carried cargo and vehicles only across
Bass Strait (Lindsay Rex collection)

and replaced within a matter of a few hours by
a spare engine kept ashore. This meant the ship
would not have to be taken out of service for
mechanical repairs.

Most of the time *Princess of Tasmania* operated
across Bass Strait without any problems, but
occasionally the ship would be affected by the bad
weather the area is notorious for, especially during
the winter months. On some trips the vessel would
find itself battling through high seas and strong
winds, which caused great discomfort to the
passengers, and occasionally injury or damage to
people, animals, cars and freight.

Robert Buckton recalled making several trips
on *Princess of Tasmania* during the 1960s. He
usually travelled in a reclining chair rather than
a cabin, and remembered how sometimes the
vessel would start pitching and rolling as soon
as it passed through Port Phillip Heads. Often
by early the following morning the ship would
be steaming along through calm waters as they
approached Devonport.

Robert worked for a Melbourne firm that
built and restored organs, and he recalled one
particularly bad trip in the late 1960s. He and
some work colleagues had been to Tasmania to
dismantle a church organ, pack the parts into a
large box trailer and bring it back to Melbourne
for restoration.

When the restoration work was completed,

the organ was again disassembled into numerous parts, packed back into the box trailer, and driven down to Webb Dock to be taken on board *Princess of Tasmania* for the trip back to Tasmania.

Once the towing vehicle and the box trailer had been driven onto the garage deck of *Princess of Tasmania*, the trailer was disconnected and both vehicles lashed down for the voyage. Also taken on board that night for the trip were several horse trailers, each containing two or three racehorses on their way to a meeting in Tasmania.

Robert and his workmates found the seats they had been allocated and settled down for the overnight trip. As they passed through Port Phillip Heads they encountered extremely rough seas, and soon the ferry was being tossed around like a cork. It was very uncomfortable for the passengers, but down on the vehicle deck the movement had a disastrous effect.

The lashings broke on some of the horse trailers, causing them to topple over, killing or badly injuring the horses inside. The box trailer carrying the parts of the restored organ also toppled over, and was not put upright until the vessel finally docked in Devonport after a harrowing voyage.

When Robert and his workmates looked

### TIME-TABLE

The following time-table will be adhered to:

**TO DEVONPORT**

| Depart Melbourne | Monday | 7.30 p.m. |
| Arrive Devonport | Tuesday | 10 a.m. |
| Depart Melbourne | Wednesday | 7.30 p.m. |
| Arrive Devonport | Thursday | 10 a.m. |
| Depart Melbourne | Friday | 7.30 p.m. |
| Arrive Devonport | Saturday | 10 a.m. |

**TO MELBOURNE**

| Depart Devonport | Tuesday | 7.30 p.m. |
| Arrive Melbourne | Wednesday | 10 a.m. |
| Depart Devonport | Thursday | 7.30 p.m. |
| Arrive Melbourne | Friday | 10 a.m. |
| Depart Devonport | Saturday | 7.30 p.m. |
| Arrive Melbourne | Sunday | 10 a.m. |

THE ABOVE SCHEDULES WILL VARY OVER CHRISTMAS AND THE NEW YEAR, WHEN IT IS USUAL TO INCLUDE EXTRA VOYAGES.

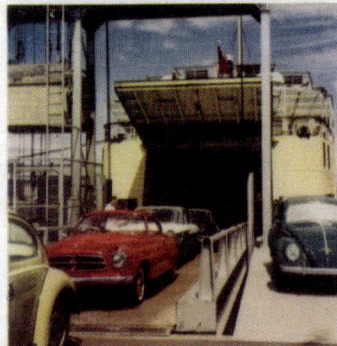

**EASY ACCESS FOR MOTORISTS**

It's so simple to put your car on board. Drive straight on to the vehicle deck, park your car under supervision and walk up to the passenger lounge. In addition to the stabilizers, patent lashings engage in "buttons" on the deck to prevent movement of vehicles while at sea and a massive steel stern door seals off the vehicle deck, forming a watertight compartment.

**CABIN ACCOMMODATION**

One-, two-, and four-berth cabins are available for those who so prefer. The cabins are well appointed and equipped with hot and cold water.

**HOW TO BOOK**

Tasmanian Steamers Pty. Ltd., who are represented by Union Steam Ship Co. or Huddart Parker Ltd. at main ports, are the principal agents, or you can apply to any recognized travel agency. It is wise to book ahead to ensure your car space, and accommodation, etc., and agents will be pleased to help you with your booking.

It is important to advise the date you wish to leave and return, the number of people in your party, the type of accommodation you require on board and if taking your car, the make and year.

**SELF-ADJUSTING RECLINING CHAIRS**

For all travellers, except those who require cabins, comfortable self-adjusting reclining chairs are provided. Rugs and pillows are also available from the steward.

**EXPERT ASSISTANCE**

To assist motorists, the R.A.C.V. and R.A.C.T. have representatives in the Terminals both on the arrival and departure of the "Princess of Tasmania".

**TOURIST ADVICE**

A representative of the Tasmanian Government Tourist Bureau and the Tasmanian Railways is in attendance at the Devonport Terminal.

Page from an early *Princess of Tasmania* brochure (Author's collection)

inside the box trailer, they realised that many of the restored parts had been severely damaged, and there was no alternative but to take the organ back to Melbourne and do the job all over again.

Through the 1960s the demand for passages across Bass Strait by passengers taking their cars with them steadily rose, and in 1969 a second passenger vessel, *Australian Trader*, joined *Princess of Tasmania* on the trade.

However, before that occurred, another new vessel had been built to operate to Tasmania from Sydney.

*Princess of Tasmania* and *Bass Trader* in Webb Dock, Melbourne (Lindsay Rex collection)

# Chapter Thirteen

# Empress of Australia

When Australian National Line took over the Bass Strait passenger trade in 1959, and *Princess of Tasmania* was placed on the route between Melbourne and Devonport, the service proved highly successful, so it was soon decided that a regular passenger service between Sydney and Tasmania should be re-established.

Plans were drawn up for the construction of what would be a most notable ship, far in advance of her time, which would cost almost £3,500,000. It would be the first large drive-on drive-off passenger and car ferry to be built in the world, and the largest passenger vessel ever built in Australia.

When tenders were called for the construction of the vessel, it was quite a surprise that the winning bid came from Cockatoo Docks & Engineering Company Pty Ltd, located on Cockatoo Island in Sydney Harbour. The actual order for the vessel was placed on 21 February 1962, under a fixed price contract.

Cockatoo had a long tradition of building naval ships, but had not been involved in constructing large commercial vessels since 1946, when the

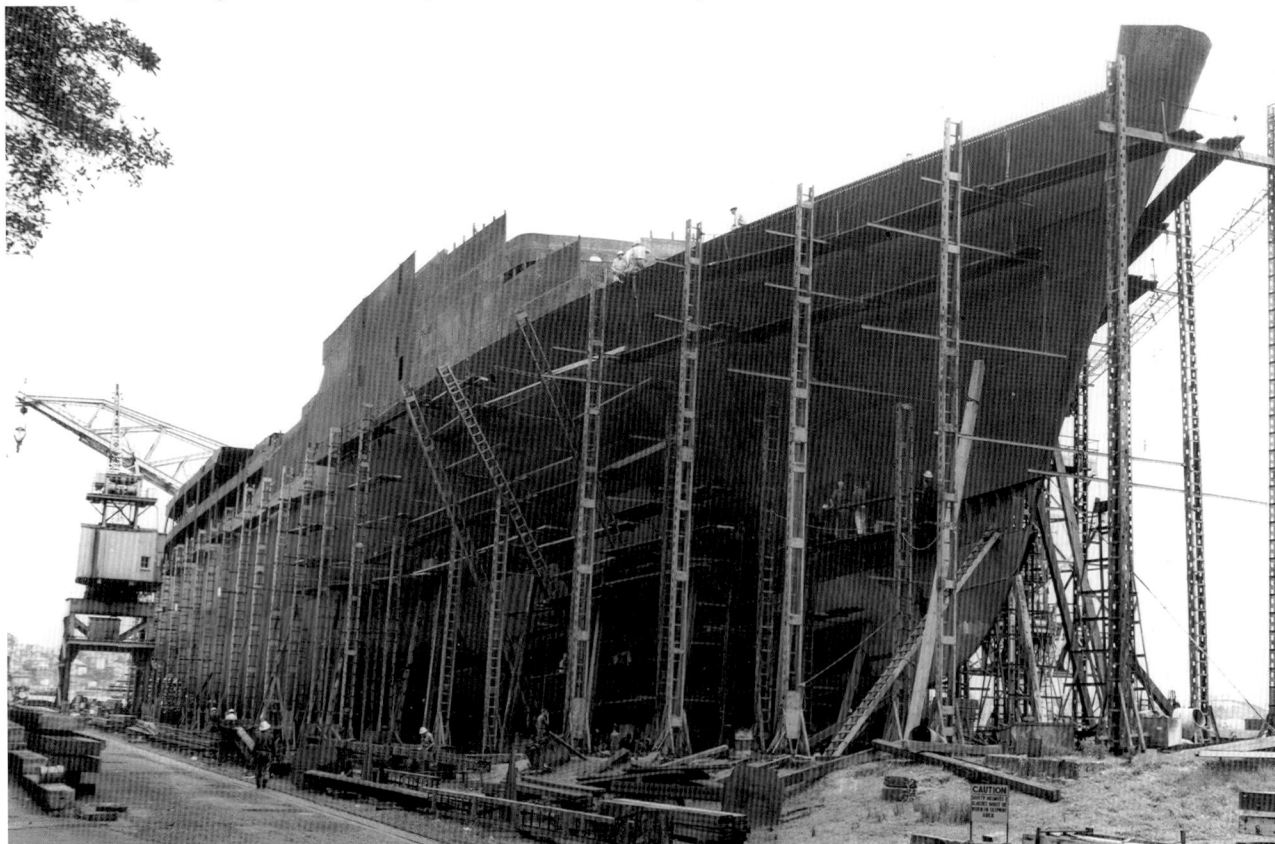

*Empress of Australia* under construction at Cockatoo Island (*The Mercury*)

cargo ship River Hunter was completed. By the 1960s there was very little naval construction work available, so Cockatoo began tendering for commercial work, with the Tasmanian ferry being their first successful bid.

The keel of the new ship was laid on 11 September 1962, on No 1 slipway, located on the northern side of the island. This slipway had been established in 1912 to enable the cruiser HMAS *Brisbane* to be built, and it was widened in the early 1920s when two cargo ships, *Fordsdale* and *Ferndale*, were built for the Australian Government. However, to enable the new vessel to be built, the slipway had to be widened again to accommodate it.

Completion of the ship was originally scheduled for late 1964. Although designated yard No 220, the vessel was referred to by dock workers as the 'Duchess of Woolloomooloo'.

The vessel was launched on 18 January 1964, being christened *Empress of Australia* by the Hon Catherine Sidney, daughter of the then Governor-General, Lord de L'Isle.

Fitting out was expected to take ten months, and the maiden voyage was scheduled for 5 December 1964. In preparation for the introduction of the ship, new terminals had to be built in Sydney, Hobart, Bell Bay and Burnie. Initially it was proposed to locate the Sydney terminal in Woolloomooloo Bay, on the site of the Domain swimming pool, but this was abandoned in favour of Clark's Point, Woolwich. This was also abandoned, and a final decision made to build the terminal on the western side of Mort Bay, in the suburb of Balmain.

A timetable was formulated that provided for three return trips from Sydney every two weeks. There would be one return trip from Sydney to Hobart every second Saturday, followed by two return trips to Bell Bay and Burnie, departing Sydney on the Thursday of one week and the next Tuesday. The minimum fare for a one-way trip was set at £17, for a share of a four berth cabin, with accompanied cars being charged £27.

In September 1964 it was announced that the first thirteen trips were all booked out in both directions. Unfortunately all did not go to plan, and delays in completing the ship forced the cancellation of the scheduled maiden voyage, and the following eight trips until the middle of January 1965.

On 2 December 1964, *Empress of Australia* left her builder's yard for the first time to undergo preliminary tests, though at that time the stern door had still not been installed. A contract had been awarded to B A Boyle & Associates to design and

*Empress of Australia* being launched and at the fitting out berth (Author's collection)

Aerial shot of *Empress of Australia* running trials off Sydney in December 1964 (Lindsay Rex collection)

supply the hydraulically operated stern door, which was manufactured by Newcastle Engineering Pty Ltd.

The door was delivered and fitted in place, but failed to operate properly during trials and had to be removed. Alterations included modifying the door structure, the insertion of new hydraulic rams and new gear quadrants, while the door track on the ship was also modified. Once these changes had been made the door was again fitted, and this time worked acceptably.

Later in December full sea trials were conducted off the New South Wales coast, during which a maximum speed of 21.5 knots was achieved, well in excess of the contracted service speed.

It was not until 8 January that *Empress of Australia* was handed over to Australian National Line, the same day the new terminal at Mort Bay was officially opened.

As previously mentioned, Cockatoo had constructed *Empress of Australia* under a fixed price contract. As John Jeremy noted in his fine book on Cockatoo Island, while the vessel was an excellent product, 'the transition from the construction of warships (which since the war had been built at cost) to commercial construction (at a fixed price) was not a happy

*Empress of Australia* at Mort Bay on 8 January 1965 (Author's collection)

The "Empress" is a twin screw motor ves...
12,037 tons, 443 feet in length, with a b...
70 feet. She carries 250 passengers in 4, 2,
ually designed, are tastefully furnished and
berth and deluxe cabins all of which were
with individual temperature controls. The "En...
is, of course, air conditioned throughout. She
at 17 knots, has a maximum speed of 20

and covers the journey between Sydney and Tas...
in 36 to 44 hours, depending on the port of
Like the "Princess", the "Empress of Austral...
equipped with the latest navigational and safet...
and is fully stabilized.

A voyage on the "Empress of Australia" is a ne...
be-forgotten experience — the holiday you
always dreamed about. Your travel agent will
you make that dream come true.

THE MILK BAR, MEETING PLACE FOR THE YOUNGER FOLK

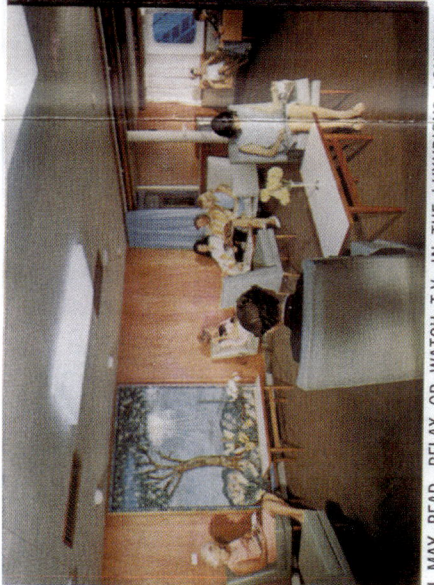

THE SMOKE ROOM IS THE SOCIAL HUB OF THE SHIP

YOU MAY READ, RELAX OR WATCH T.V. IN THE LUXURIOUS LOUNGES

SUPERB MEALS IN THE SUMPTUOUSLY APPOINTED DINING ROOM

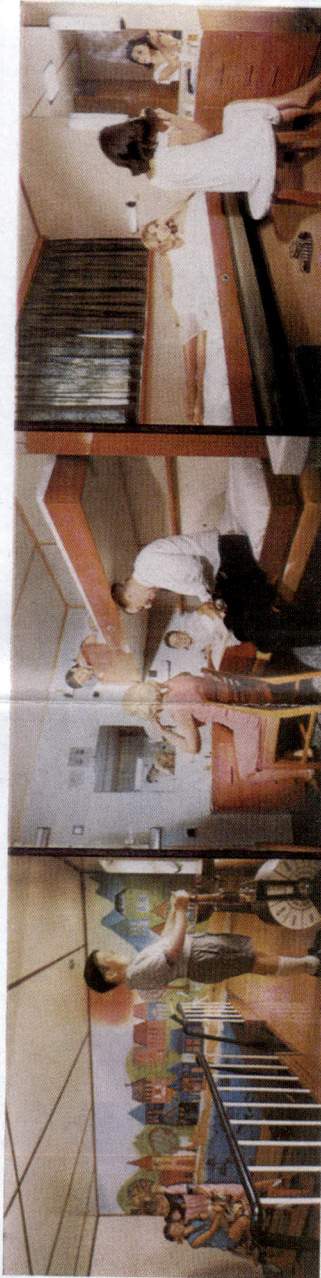

Page from the first brochure produced to promote *Empress of Australia* (Author's collection)

*Empress of Australia* approaching Hobart on 18 January 1965 (The Mercury)

*Empress of Australia* berthing at 4 Princes Wharf on 18 January 1965 (Lindsay Rex collection)

one for the shipyard, and Cockatoo lost a substantial amount of money on the contract."

As completed, *Empress of Australia* measured 12,037 gross tons. The hull was 445 ft/135.6 m long with a maximum beam of 70 ft/21.5 m. A pair of 10-cylinder turbo-charged two-stroke MAN diesels powered twin propellers, providing

a service speed of 18.5 knots. The vessel was also fitted with twin rudders and a side thrust propeller near the bow, to assist in turning in confined spaces.

At the time *Empress of Australia* was completed, the 625 mile route between Sydney and Hobart was the longest being operated by a

*Empress of Australia* entering Sydney Harbour (Jim Freeman photo)

drive-on drive-off ferry in the world.

Although marketed as a ferry service, the route was in open water, and required two nights at sea in each direction, so all of the 250 passengers were provided with cabins.

Top of the range were four deluxe suites with twin beds and private facilities, and five slightly smaller two-bed suites with private facilities. There were also 83 standard 2-berth cabins, four single-berth cabins and seventeen with four berths, in all of which the lower berths could be converted into day lounges.

Public amenities included two large lounges, a dining room, writing room, smoking room and children's playroom. All the cabins and public rooms were fully air-conditioned. For extra comfort a pair of fin stabilisers was fitted.

The vessel was only fitted with a stern door that provided access to the garage space for up to 90 cars, or 51 cars and 16 trucks, as well as 160 containers.

Prior to entering service, *Empress of Australia* departed Sydney on 12 January for a two-day shakedown cruise along the New South Wales coast, carrying 170 invited guests.

At 9 pm on Saturday, 16 January 1965, *Empress of Australia*, under the command of Captain M V Langdale, departed Mort Bay on her maiden voyage. Averaging 18 knots, the ship reached Hobart on Monday, 18 January in the record

*Princess of Tasmania* (Author's collection)

# M.V. EMPRESS OF AUSTRALIA

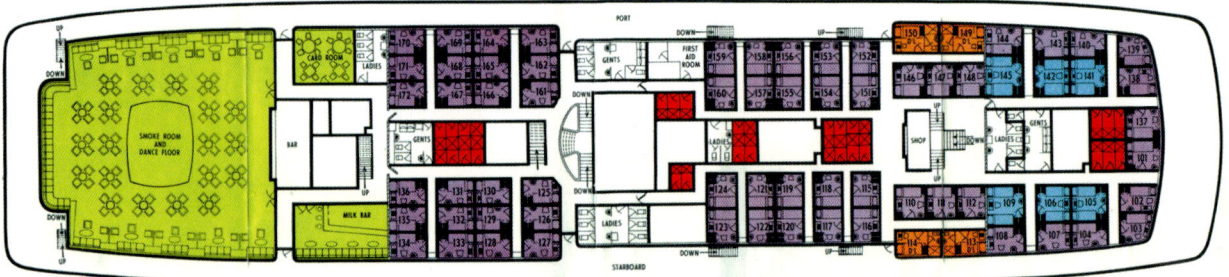

**BOAT DECK**

**BRIDGE DECK**

# M.V. PRINCESS OF TASMANIA

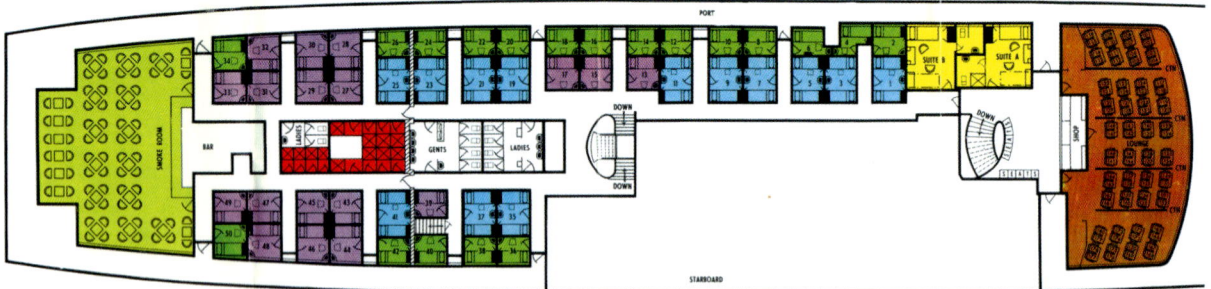

**BOAT DECK**

**UPPER DECK**

Deck plans of *Express of Australia* and *Princess of Tasmania* (Author's collection)

SHELTER DECK

SPORTS DECK

## M.V. EMPRESS OF AUSTRALIA

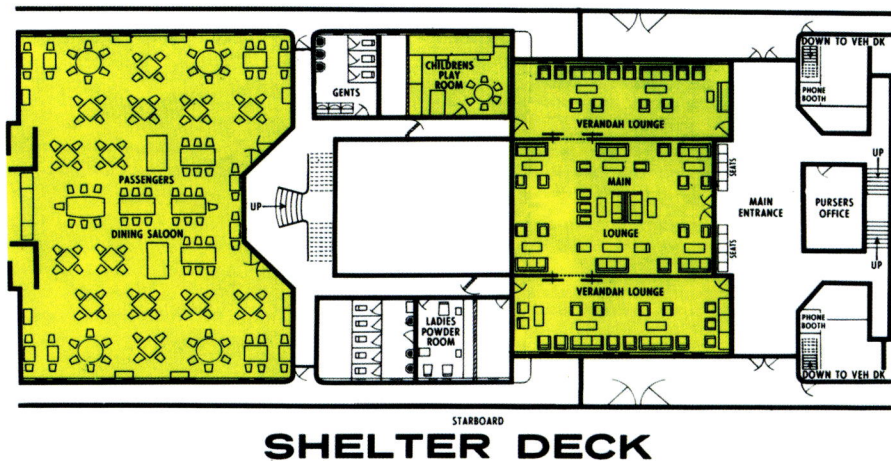

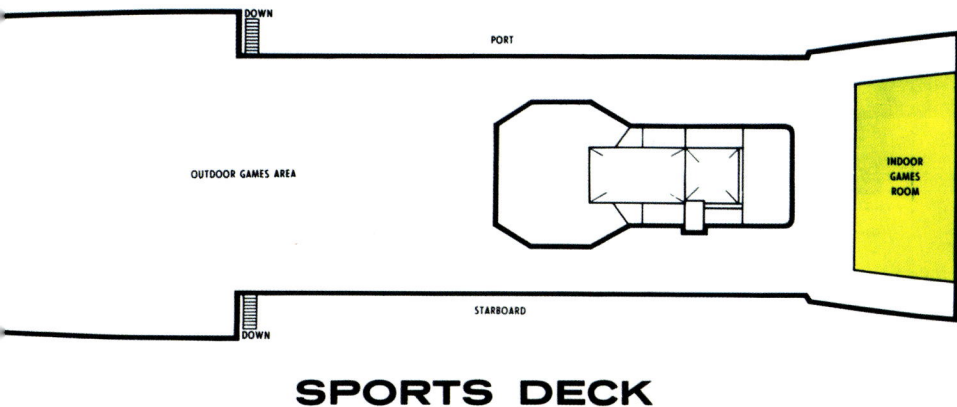

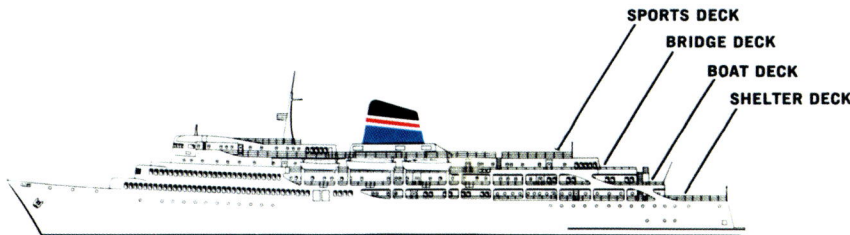

SPORTS DECK
BRIDGE DECK
BOAT DECK
SHELTER DECK

### LEGEND

| | | |
|---|---|---|
| 1 PASSENGER CABIN | 2 PASSENGER CABIN | 4 PASSENGER CABIN |
| 1 PASSENGER DE LUXE CABIN | SUITES | DINING ROOMS LOUNGES, ETC. |
| 2 PASSENGER DE LUXE CABIN | SHOWERS | RECLINING SEAT LOUNGES |

BED
DRESSING TABLE
WARDROBE
WASH BASIN
WARDROBE
CHAIR
SHOWER
W.C.
RECLINING SEAT
STOOL

## M.V. PRINCESS OF TASMANIA

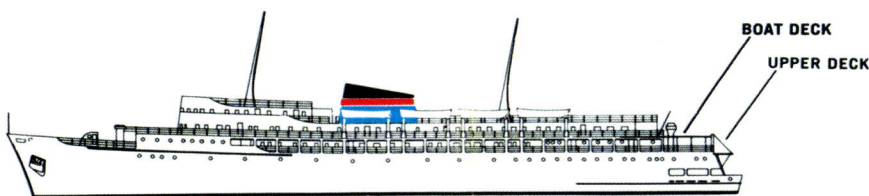

BOAT DECK
UPPER DECK

time of 37½ hours, which was 11½ hours faster than the previous record set by *Zealandia* in the 1930s.

*Empress of Australia* arrived in Hobart, which was also her port of registry, to a gala reception at 10 am on 18 January, on which day the new terminal built there, No 4 Prince's Wharf, was officially opened.

After a twelve hour stay, the vessel departed for Sydney, arriving back early on the morning of Wednesday, 20 January. Following an overnight stay in Sydney, *Empress of Australia* departed on the morning of Thursday, 21 January, and entered the Tamar River on the afternoon of 22 January. She received another gala welcome as she berthed at Bell Bay, being escorted by a flotilla of small boats, while several aircraft from the Tasmanian Aero Club flew overhead.

The ship departed Bell Bay at 6 am the next day for Burnie, arriving four hours later to another enthusiastic welcome. Departing at 8.30 pm the same day, *Empress of Australia* arrived back in Sydney on the morning of Monday, 25 January.

The same evening the vessel left on her third trip, arriving in Bell Bay on the morning of Wednesday, 27 January, continuing on to Burnie the next morning, and departing that night to arrive back in Sydney on the morning of Saturday, 30 January. This completed her first fortnightly schedule, which she would maintain throughout her career operating from Sydney.

The service between the mainland and Tasmania provided by both *Princess of Tasmania* and *Empress of Australia* was advertised as the 'Searoad' service.

In 1970 I joined Union Travel, the Sydney travel office of the Union Steamship Company of New Zealand, who were the booking agents for the 'Searoad' service.

My first job with Union Travel was in the 'Searoad' section, taking bookings over the counter and sometimes on the telephone for the services to Tasmania from both Sydney and Melbourne. As I soon found out, the name 'Searoad' sometimes was not properly understood by the general public.

One day a lady of indeterminate age came up to the counter, and asked me to provide her with information on driving her car to Tasmania on the searoad. When I began to explain that it was actually a shipping service, she gave me a strange look, and in so many words told me I was talking nonsense, and that she would not travel by ship, but was determined to drive to Tasmania.

Despite my best efforts, I was unable to convince her that there was no road across Bass Strait, and after again questioning my intelligence, she stormed off.

The reservation plans for *Empress of Australia* were looked after by a team of young ladies located in a large room on the first floor of our building, located on George Street opposite the junction with Bridge Street. These reservation plans were large sheets of paper, one for every voyage, with reservations being taken up to a year in advance.

When a request was made, I would have to telephone the reservation section, the young lady I was speaking to would find the plan for the appropriate date, and advise me of availability. If the type of accommodation being requested was available, the names of the passengers would be written in against the cabin number, and also the relevant car details. The same procedure would have to be followed for a return trip from Tasmania, so it was quite a lengthy business. Once everything had been confirmed, the customer would either pay a deposit to secure the booking, or be given a week to pay it, otherwise the reservation would be cancelled.

By far the most requested trips each year were just before and after Christmas. We would take advance bookings for these up to fifteen months ahead of the departure date, and usually when the actual reservation plan was opened, it would be filled up almost immediately. There was also a waiting list provided for each sailing, and sometimes these Christmas sailings would have 250 confirmed passengers and another 250 on the waiting list.

When requests were made for bookings on the *Princess of Tasmania*, we had to send a message off to our Melbourne office, where the reservation plans were held in a similar fashion to those in Sydney.

This procedure could take some time, especially if the required sailings were not available, but this was typical of the way such work was done before the computer revolution.

By far the most enjoyable part of my job involved being in attendance at Mort Bay when *Empress of Australia* either arrived or departed. Usually two or three of us would go from the office, first walking down to the Union Line wharf in Darling Harbour. There we would board one of the company workboats for the trip across the harbour to Mort Bay.

Once there, if it were a departure we would be responsible for checking in all the passengers, and ensuring all the cars and freight got on the ship. In those days only the driver would remain with in car, any passengers having to pass through the terminal and board via the gangway. Once the car had been driven on board the driver would climb a flight of stairs from the garage deck to the accommodation areas.

Sometimes the departures went without a hitch, but frequently there would be a last-minute problem, usually union related. The crew on *Empress of Australia* belonged to a variety of unions, and they seemed to delight in taking it in turns to bring up some matter of dispute just before the ship was due to depart.

One day it would be the stewards, next time the seamen, then the officers, and sometimes even the shore workers would get in on the act. They probably thought it was doing them some good, but in the end it was just this type of constant union trouble that brought about the end of the Australian National Line service from

Sydney, and cost most of the men their jobs, but that was all in the future.

The arrival of *Empress of Australia* in Sydney was always a spectacular sight. The vessel would pass under the Sydney Harbour Bridge and round Goat Island, then do a 180 degree turn in its own length, using the bow thruster and twin rudders before gliding gracefully stern first into the berth, until it was just touching the vehicle ramp.

Unfortunately this did not always happen as planned, and I once witnessed an arrival where the ship came in a bit too fast, and hit the vehicle ramp with a resounding crash. The shore ramp was pushed out of line, and repairs lasting several hours had to be effected before it could be placed in position, enabling passengers to drive their cars off.

Public acceptance of *Empress of Australia* was immediate, and she enjoyed capacity passenger loadings on most trips in her first year of operation, though numbers tended to decline somewhat in the winter months. The round trip to Tasmania from Sydney was also offered as a cruise, which proved quite popular.

The first major problem to affect the ship occurred on Saturday, 13 January 1966, when she was docked at Bell Bay. A fire broke out in the engine room switchboard, which was brought rapidly under control by crew members using hand held extinguishers. However, the damage caused by the fire put the ship out of service for a week, and it had to return empty to Sydney for repairs.

The fire could not have happened at a worse time, as the vessel was due to go to Burnie the same day and embark a full load of passengers and cars for the trip to Sydney. The next round trip from Sydney also had to be cancelled, disrupting the travel plans of a further 500 passengers, but repairs were completed in time for the scheduled departure from Sydney on 20 January to Hobart.

It was in April of 1966 that *Empress of Australia* carried what was claimed to be the largest single piece of cargo loaded by the drive-on method in Australia up to that time. This was an 84 foot long dredge 'ladder', weighing 40 tons, which was transported to Burnie to be installed in a dredge being built for the Burnie Marine Board.

On one occasion *Empress of Australia* carried at least one less-than-honest passenger. While the ship was at sea on the night of 8/9 October 1968, someone managed to enter the purser's

**M.V. EMPRESS OF AUSTRALIA**
**M.V. PRINCESS OF TASMANIA**

**SEAROAD**

SERVICE TO AND FROM TASMANIA

OWNED AND OPERATED BY THE AUSTRALIAN NATIONAL LINE
Principal Passenger Agents: UNION STEAM SHIP CO. OF N.Z. LTD.

office, open the safe and steal about $10,000, then slip away unseen. The theft was intensively investigated, but no culprit was ever identified.

As the 1960s came to a close it seemed that Australian National Line had found the right formula to operate successful passenger services from the mainland to Tasmania. The service from Sydney was being very well patronised, while the trade across Bass Strait from Melbourne had grown to such an extent that a second ship was required to meet demand.

# Chapter Fourteen

# Australian Trader

The Australian National Line Bass Strait passenger ferry service being operated between Melbourne and Devonport by *Princess of Tasmania* was enjoying great success in the mid-1960s, and it was decided that a second ship would be required to cater to the growing passenger trade to and from Tasmania. However, while the new ship would be twice the size of *Princess of Tasmania*, it would carry fewer passengers, but have a greatly enlarged cargo capacity.

When tenders were called for the construction of the new vessel, the order went to the New South Wales State Dockyard in Newcastle, which had built the *Princess of Tasmania* ten years previously, and construction commenced in 1968. Built at a cost of over $8 million, the new vessel was given the same hull design and dimensions as *Empress of Australia*, though with a much smaller superstructure.

Launched on 17 February 1969, the vessel was

*Australian Trader* about to be launched on 17 February 1969 (Lindsay Rex collection)

christened *Australian Trader* by Lady Williams, wife of the chairman of Australian National Line, Sir John Williams. There was a minor hitch during the ceremony, as after the traditional bottle of champagne had been smashed against the hull of the vessel, nothing happened.

A shipyard official standing next to Lady Williams was seen to lean out of the official box and bark some instructions to workers below, who discovered a launch pin had not been removed. Once this was done, the vessel slid gracefully down the slipway into the waters of Newcastle Harbour.

Completion of the ship was delayed by a series of industrial disputes and the late arrival of necessary parts from overseas. It was not until late May 1969 that sea trials could be conducted off the New South Wales coast.

At 5 am on Sunday, 1 June, *Australian Trader* left her berth in Newcastle for her first major trip, to Sydney and back. Unfortunately the vessel ran aground in Newcastle Harbour, and it took tugs one and a half hours to refloat her. A quick inspection indicated no major damage had been inflicted, so *Australian Trader* left Newcastle and headed south to Sydney, berthing at the Mort Bay terminal usually used by *Empress of Australia*. Here a number of officials of the Australian Shipping Board boarded the ship, which then departed for the trip back to Newcastle.

As *Australian Trader* was departing through Sydney Heads there was a major mechanical malfunction in one engine, which had to be shut down. The vessel proceeded north on just one engine, and instead of undergoing a series of engine trials as had been planned, went straight back to Newcastle, berthing at 8 pm, four hours earlier than planned.

As a precaution, *Australian Trader* was drydocked to check that the hull had not been damaged in the earlier grounding. At the same time repairs were carried out on the defective engine. *Australian Trader* resumed her final sea trials on Friday, 6 June, and once these were successfully completed, *Australian Trader* was handed over to her owners, and proceeded first to Sydney for a promotional visit before going to Melbourne to enter service.

Instead of joining *Princess of Tasmania* on the route to Devonport only, it had been decided that *Australian Trader* would operate to three ports, Bell Bay, Burnie and Devonport, in rotation. A schedule was formulated which had the ship operating three return trips a week from Melbourne. There would be a Sunday evening departure for Burnie, Tuesday to Bell Bay and Thursday to Devonport. The return voyage would be made the following evening from each port, with the vessel remaining in Melbourne on Saturday night at Webb Dock, where it shared the terminal with *Princess of Tasmania*.

*Australian Trader* measured 7,005 gross tons, and was 135.6 m/445 ft long with a beam of 21.5

*Australian Trader* (Jim Freeman photo)

m/70 ft. A pair of Denny Brown stabiliser fins was fitted, and a Voith-Schneider bow thruster to assist with manoeuvring.

Power was provided by a pair of 16 cylinder 4-stroke cycle single acting Pielstik type diesel engines, which had been built in France by Chantiers de l'Atlantique at St Nazaire, and gave the vessel a service speed of 17.5 knots.

The accommodation provided for the 190 passengers *Australian Trader* could carry was a combination of that provided on the two other ANL vessels. There were single and two-berth cabins, some with private facilities, provided for 140 passengers. Some of the two-berth cabins had interconnecting doors so they could be used by families. The remaining 50 passengers were allocated aircraft style reclining chairs in a lounge.

Public amenities included an 80-seat observation lounge and a smoke room with bar on the boat deck, while the upper deck contained two 38-seat lounges, a tavern and shop, and a large cafeteria, as breakfast was the only meal served on the ship.

All the passenger cabins and public rooms were fully air-conditioned, but there was a rather limited amount of open deck space. The crew numbered 69.

When it came to garage space, the lessons of *Empress of Australia* had not been learnt, as access to the vehicle deck was through a stern door only. Covered garage space for about 110 cars was provided. A further 15 cars could be parked on portable platforms, six in the hold and 11 on the orlop deck during peak travel periods. There was also space for 30 motorcycles in the upper tween deck forward.

In addition, there was an area for trailers and low-loaders on the open deck at the stern. Specially designed containers could also be carried, being loaded by forklift trucks.

On the evening of Tuesday, 24 June 1969, under the command of Captain G A Hunt, *Australian Trader* departed Melbourne on her maiden crossing of Bass Strait. This was a special voyage to Devonport, where the ship arrived the following morning in howling winds and pouring rain.

The gloomy weather matched the atmosphere of the arrival, as only a few days earlier the then Federal Minister for Shipping and Transport, Mr Ian Sinclair, had made a statement in Parliament in which he had expressed doubts about the ecoNomic viability of the new ship.

He also hinted that the Government was considering the removal of the subsidy that enabled Australian National Line to maintain their Tasmanian passenger services.

*Australian Trader* returned to Melbourne, and on Sunday, 29 June departed on her first scheduled voyage, arriving in Burnie the following morning.

The vessel was due to make her inaugural trip to Bell Bay from Melbourne on the evening of 1

*Australian Trader* berthed in Devonport (Devonport Maritime Museum)

July, but a strike by stewards delayed the departure by twenty-four hours. When *Australian Trader* did finally arrive in Bell Bay on the morning of 3 July she received a gala welcome, but it had been an inauspicious start for the ship.

As if these problems were not serious enough for Australian National Line, *Empress of Australia* had been strikebound for days in Sydney at the same time, while negotiations with unions dragged on.

Passengers booked on cancelled voyages had to be put up in hotels at the expense of ANL. Eventually some of them were flown to their destinations in Tasmania, again at the expense of ANL.

With two passenger vessels operating across Bass Strait, there were departures six nights a week from Melbourne to northern Tasmania,

## "Empress of Australia"

### TIME-TABLE

(Subject to alteration without notice)

The time-table is based on a fortnightly schedule allowing for three sailings from Sydney and three from Tasmanian ports as follows:

**SYDNEY**
Depart 9.00 p.m. Saturday
(Note: Passengers with cars should arrive at the ship from 7 p.m. and **no later** than 8 p.m. Other passengers may board from 7 p.m.)

**HOBART**
Arrive 10.00 a.m. Monday
Depart 10.00 p.m. Monday
(Note: Embarking passengers with cars should arrive at the ship between 8 p.m. and 9 p.m. Other passengers may board from 8 p,m.)

**SYDNEY**
Arrive 11.00 a.m. Wednesday
Depart 9.30 a.m. Thursday
(Note: Embarking passengers with cars should arrive at the ship between 8 a.m. and 8.30 a.m. Other passengers may board from 8 a.m.)

**LAUNCESTON (BELL BAY)**
Arrive 4.30 p.m. Friday
Depart 10.00 a.m. Saturday
(Note: All embarking passengers should arrive at the ship not before 9 a.m. Saturday.)

**BURNIE**
Arrive 1.00 p.m. Saturday
Depart 10.00 p.m. Saturday
(Note: Embarking passengers with cars should arrive at the ship from 7 p.m. and **no later** than 8 p.m. Other passengers may board from 7 p.m.)

**SYDNEY**
Arrive 7.00 a.m. Monday
Depart 9.00 p.m. Tuesday
(Note: Embarking passengers with cars should arrive at the ship from 7 p.m. and **no later** than 8 p.m. Other passengers may board from 7 p.m.)

**LAUNCESTON (BELL BAY)**
Arrive 7.00 a.m. Thursday
Depart Noon Thursday
(Note: Embarking passengers with cars should arrive at the ship between 10 a.m. and 11.30 a.m. Other passengers may board from 10 a.m.)

**BURNIE**
Arrive 4.00 p.m. Thursday
Depart 11.00 p.m. Thursday
(Note: Embarking passengers with cars should arrive at the ship from 7.30 p.m. and **no later** than 9 p.m. Other passengers may board from 7.30 p.m.)

**SYDNEY**
Arrive 9.00 a.m. Saturday
(The time-table is then repeated as above.)

NOTE: In all cases where a night departure is involved passengers should dine before embarking as no late meal will be served on board. In cases of morning departures embarking passengers are advised that lunch will be the first meal on board.

## "Princess of Tasmania"

### TIME-TABLE

(Subject to alteration without notice)

Three departures weekly from Melbourne and three from Devonport, as follows:

**MELBOURNE**
Depart 7.30 p.m. Monday

**DEVONPORT**
Arrive 10.00 a.m. Tuesday
Depart 7.30 p.m. Tuesday

**MELBOURNE**
Arrive 10.00 a.m. Wednesday
Depart 7.30 p.m. Wednesday

**DEVONPORT**
Arrive 10.00 a.m. Thursday
Depart 7.30 p.m. Thursday

**MELBOURNE**
Arrive 10.00 a.m. Friday
Depart 7.30 p.m. Friday

**DEVONPORT**
Arrive 10.00 a.m. Saturday
Depart 7.30 p.m. Sunday

**MELBOURNE**
Arrive 10.00 a.m. Monday

## "Australian Trader"

### TIME-TABLE

(Subject to alteration without notice)

Three departures weekly from Melbourne and three from Northern Tasmanian ports as follows:

**MELBOURNE**
Depart 7.30 p.m. Sunday

**BURNIE**
Arrive 10.00 a.m. Monday
Depart 7.30 p.m. Monday

**MELBOURNE**
Arrive 10.00 a.m. Tuesday
Depart 7.30 p.m. Tuesday

**BELL BAY**
Arrive 10.00 a.m. Wednesday
Depart 7.30 p.m. Wednesday

**MELBOURNE**
Arrive 10.00 a.m. Thursday
Depart 7.30 p.m. Thursday

**DEVONPORT**
Arrive 10.00 a.m. Friday
Depart 7.30 p.m. Friday

**MELBOURNE**
Arrive 10.00 a.m. Saturday

NOTE: Passengers with cars should present themselves at the "Princess of Tasmania" or "Australian Trader" at the time stated on the ticket. Other passengers may board any time after 6 p.m. but not later than 7 p.m.

*Australian Trader* (Author's collection)

four of which were to Devonport, while one went to Bell Bay and another to Burnie.

This revived the type of passenger service that had been operated during the 1930s by *Taroona* and *Nairana*, and even earlier by Nairana and *Loongana* in the 1920s.

*Australian Trader* was a fine vessel, but never managed to gain the popularity of *Princess of Tasmania* with the travelling public. Despite this, the service seemed to be thriving in the early 1970s, and *Princess of Tasmania* carried her one millionth passenger across Bass Strait in September 1971.

Unfortunately, it was also during the early 1970s that a continual succession of industrial disputes began to upset the sailing schedule of all three passenger vessels operating the services to Tasmania.

On numerous occasions a vessel would have boarded passengers and be ready to depart when a strike would be called by one department of crew members, which would prevent the ship from leaving.

Often these problems could be sorted out relatively quickly, and the ship would be only a few hours late, but on other occasions the passengers would have to return to shore, and the entire trip be cancelled.

The ships also had to contend with the stormy weather encountered with monotonous regularity in Bass Strait, and other problems too. On 3 June 1971, *Australian Trader* was disabled in Port Phillip Bay when a cable wrapped around one propeller shaft as she was departing. The voyage was cancelled, and she made a quick trip to Sydney to be drydocked for repairs.

Just a few weeks later, on 6 July, while coming in to Webb Dock in Melbourne, *Australian Trader* collided with the berthed ANL cargo ship *Darwin Trader*, but only minor damage was caused to both vessels.

Despite the bright prospects envisioned when *Australian Trader* entered the Bass Strait trade in 1969, the service did not develop in the manner expected, and within three years the Australian National Line services to Tasmania were in considerable trouble.

The threatened removal of the Federal Government subsidy did not occur, but the three -ship operation was not proving to be ecoNomic, and changes had to be made. When they were announced, early in 1972, there were quite drastic, involving a total reorganisation of the entire operation that affected all three ships.

# Chapter Fifteen

# All Change

Early in January 1972 Australian National Line announced a drastic change in their ferry operations. *Empress of Australia* was to be transferred to the service from Melbourne to Devonport, while *Australian Trader* would replace her on the Sydney trade, and *Princess of Tasmania* would be withdrawn altogether, and sold.

The first of the ships to be affected was *Australian Trader*, which berthed in Melbourne for the last time on the morning of 7 April 1972. The vessel then returned to her builder's yard in Newcastle to undergo several alterations prior to entering her new service.

Because the route from Sydney to Tasmania required two nights at sea, the airline style reclining seats were removed, reducing her capacity to just the 140 passengers that could be accommodated in cabins.

As these cabins had been designed for a short overnight trip only, they were quite small, and not really suited to the longer voyage.

The public rooms were all refurbished, while the cafeteria had to be upgraded into a proper dining room. In order to provide the open deck space that would be required for the passengers on the days the ship was at sea, an extra deck was built on to the after end of the superstructure.

However this addition limited the height of trucks that could be carried on the vehicle deck below. The work was completed in a couple of weeks.

*Australian Trader* berthed in Hobart after alterations (Lindsay Rex collection)

On Saturday, 26 April 1972 *Australian Trader* departed on her first voyage from Sydney, to Hobart. The two-week schedule the ship would follow was the same as that followed by *Empress of Australia*, with one return trip to Hobart departing Sydney every second Saturday, followed by two round trips to Bell Bay and Burnie.

*Empress of Australia* arrived in Sydney from Tasmania for the last time on 24 April 1972, then also went to Newcastle for major alterations at the State Dockyard.

The original cabin accommodation was retained, but the dining room was converted into a cafeteria. Both the existing lounges and an extra space built on the after end of the superstructure were fitted with 190 aircraft style reclining seats, increasing passenger capacity to 440, about 100 less than the combined capacity of the two vessels she would be replacing. After being rebuilt the vessel was remeasured, and surprisingly the new gross tonnage was shown as 8,196.

On 26 June 1972, *Princess of Tasmania* departed Melbourne on her final voyage to Devonport. The following evening the ship left Tasmania for the last time, farewelled by several thousand people. Her arrival back in Melbourne on the morning of 28 June marked the completion of her 3,886th voyage on the trade.

During her thirteen years crossing Bass Strait, *Princess of Tasmania* did not miss one scheduled voyage because of mechanical problems, and she carried over one million passengers while travelling nearly as many miles. The vessel was then laid up in Melbourne, awaiting a buyer.

In September 1972 *Princess of Tasmania* was sold to Bahamarine Ltd, based in Nassau. Without a change of name, though now registered in London, *Princess of Tasmania* left Melbourne for the last time on 7 October. Crossing the Pacific Ocean and passing through the Panama Canal, she headed for the east coast of Canada.

Her new owners had arranged to charter the vessel to Canadian National Railways, and with virtually no alterations she began operating between North Sydney, Nova Scotia and Argentia in Newfoundland. This was an eighteen-hour overnight service, not unlike that for which she had been built. The route was only operated for eight months of the year, with the ship being laid up during the winter.

*Princess of Tasmania* was renamed *Marine Cruiser* in 1975 (Author's collection)

Surprisingly, her name was not changed until 1975, when she became *Marine Cruiser*. By that time a few structural alterations had been made to the stern section, which increased her tonnage to 4,141 gross. She looked very smart in the CNR colours, with a deep blue hull and funnel.

Instead of being laid up for the winter of 1976/77, *Marine Cruiser* was placed on the Bay of Fundy service between Yarmouth, Nova Scotia and Portland in Maine, a ten-hour crossing. For the next eight years, though, *Marine Cruiser* operated only on the Nova Scotia to Newfoundland seasonal trade, being laid up in winter.

In 1984 *Marine Cruiser* was sold to Dolphin International Shipping Co, of Malta, and crossed the North Atlantic to the Mediterranean. Renamed *Majorca Rose*, the vessel entered service on 25 May 1984 between Port Vendres in France and Alcudia on the island of Majorca.

She served on this route through the 1984 summer season, but was then moved to Greece and laid up. At the end of 1984 the vessel was sold to another Maltese concern, *Equator* Shipping Co Ltd, and renamed *Equator*, but remained laid up in Greece.

In 1985 came a sale to third Maltese company, Progress Marine Ltd, who initially renamed the vessel *Nomi*, though this was soon changed to *Adriatic Star*, at which time she was also transferred to Greek registry.

The vessel returned to service again, operating

*Adriatic Star* (Author's collection)

on ferry routes between Greece and Italy during the summer months only, being laid up in winter. On 14 September 1987, *Adriatic Star* was laid up in Perama Bay, close to Piraeus.

Ironically, lying close by was another Greek flag ferry, *Hellas*, which was the former *Taroona* that *Princess of Tasmania* was built to replace.

Early in 1988 the vessel changed owners again, being bought by Menik Maritime (Pte) Ltd, of Sri Lanka, but she remained idle at Perama and was not renamed. By the end of 1988 the vessel was under the Italian flag, having been acquired by her sixth owner, Traghetti delle Isole SpA.

Renamed *Lampedusa*, she returned to service in 1989, again operating between Greece and Italy on the summer seasonal trade. She continued in this service in the summer of 1990.

*Lampedusa* (Author's collection)

In 1991 the vessel changed owners, flag and name yet again. Purchased by a Saudi Arabian firm, Fayez Trading & Shipping, reputedly for US$4 million, and renamed *Shahd Fayez*, she entered service in the Red Sea, mostly carrying pilgrims from Egypt to Jeddah, the port for Mecca.

However, in 1992 her name was changed by the new owners to *Al Mahrousa*, under which she spent the next eight years. In 2000 the vessel acquired its tenth name, *Tebah 2000*, again without change of owner, remaining under the Saudi Arabian flag, and at the time of writing is still operating under that name.

Meanwhile back in Australia, *Empress of Australia*, under the command of Captain Harry Hadley, who had transferred from *Princess of Tasmania*, made her first departure from Melbourne on 30 June, to Devonport.

The Bass Strait crossing was a far cry from her original route, taking just fourteen hours overnight. The vessel made three return trips per week, departing Melbourne on Monday,

Wednesday and Friday, and Devonport on Tuesday, Thursday and Sunday, with a layover in Devonport on Saturday.

The entrance to the River Mersey at Devonport is quite narrow and in strong winds can be quite tricky to navigate. Several times early in her Bass Strait career *Empress of Australia* encountered problems while entering or leaving port, though without incurring any major damage.

*Empress of Australia* ploughed steadily back and forth in all weathers across Bass Strait, which can be one of the stormiest bodies of water in the world. Despite this the vessel was seldom late arriving, though occasional mishaps did occur.

During one stormy night in June 1976, a huge wave struck the ship. Captain Hadley was hurled across the bridge, being knocked unconscious and suffering a dislocated shoulder. On the vehicle deck a dolly-wheel collapsed under a semi-trailer, whose load then fell onto a camper trailer, which was demolished. But in general the service progressed without a hitch, and proved quite popular and successful.

Unfortunately, *Australian Trader* was not having nearly as good a reception on the trade from Sydney, as it quickly became obvious the vessel was totally unsuited to her new service due to the inadequate passenger facilities.

One letter written to a Sydney newspaper by an irate passenger who had previously travelled on *Empress of Australia* said in part:

> The atmosphere on board is awful, with low ceilings and no natural light in the dining room. The lounge is sited amidships with corridors on either side and no natural light.
>
> With a family to cater for, I found no nursery for the children, and no laundry, drying or ironing facilities. Morning and afternoon tea or coffee is only obtainable from a vending machine.
>
> The garage facilities are primitive, with wire mesh and tarpaulin as the only protection…to offer her as a substitute for the *Empress* is an insult to the intelligence of the travelling public.

The letter writer was not alone in his condemnation of the ship, and passenger loadings fell dramatically. In addition, a constant series of strikes by various maritime unions

*Empress of Australia* as rebuilt for the Bass Strait trade, shown here berthed at Devonport (Bruce Miller photo)

further affected the operation of the ship, and deterred passenger traffic even more.

There were also occasional problems caused by weather, including one voyage in August 1972. *Australian Trader* was bound for Bell Bay when the weather became so bad the ship was forced to seek shelter in the lee of Deal Island.

The worst weather encountered by *Australian Trader* was on a voyage to Hobart that departed Sydney on 8 June 1974. As the ship headed south it ran into gale force winds that were whipping up huge seas, and the ship was forced to reduce speed.

Despite this precaution, a section of steel railing near the bow was bent double, and there was flooding in several passenger cabins and the crew quarters. Cargo stored on the open section of deck at the stern was also affected by water damage. Such was the ferocity of the storm that

*Empress of Australia* departing Melbourne (Chris Mackey photo)

it delayed the arrival of the ship into Hobart by 27 hours, and it was a very relieved group of passengers who disembarked.

*Australian Trader* remained on the trade from Sydney to Tasmania for four years, but in June 1976 Australian National Line suddenly announced that the service would be terminated the following month. It was stated that a ship then under construction in Newcastle would take over the route, but carry no passengers, only cargo. The new ship would be reviving the name *Bass Trader*, the previous vessel of that name having been sold in 1975.

Owing to delays in the completion of *Bass Trader*, *Australian Trader* was retained in service past the 3 July date originally given for termination, and it was not until 27 July 1976 that the vessel left Sydney on her final voyage, to Bell Bay and Burnie.

The decision to remove *Australian Trader* from service caused uproar in Tasmania, and also with the maritime unions, as many of their members would lose their livelihoods.

When *Australian Trader* reached Bell Bay on 29 July the crew went on strike, and refused to allow the ship to be moved, effectively blocking the main discharge ramp at the port.

Despite the fact that disruptions to the service caused by the unions had been a major factor in the decision to terminate the service, the crew

*Australian Trader* at Bell Bay (Kingsley Barr photo - Dale Crisp collection)

sought local support from the public, but this was not forthcoming.

For almost two months *Australian Trader* remained idle in Bell Bay while the crew refused to budge. Finally, on 24 September, they gave up, and the ship left, having been alongside for 57 days. *Australian Trader* returned directly to Sydney, arriving on 26 September. The vessel was laid up at Woolloomooloo, and offered for sale.

In October 1976 representatives of the Royal Australian Navy inspected the ship, and decided to purchase it for use as a training vessel. The sale was completed on 16 January 1977, and work began soon after on converting the ship for its new role. Some initial conversion work was done at Garden Island in Sydney, during which the entire vessel was painted navy grey. On 25 August 1977 the ship was officially commissioned into the Royal Australian Navy as HMAS *Jervis Bay*, pennant number 203.

From 26 September three days of engines trials were conducted, then on 14 October the vessel arrived at the Balmain yard of Storey & Keers (Ship Repairs) Pty Ltd to undergo fourteen weeks of further conversion work. This included the addition of a new navigating bridge over the existing bridge and other structural alterations. Internally, all the cabins were retained, while sections of the car deck were transformed into classrooms and lecture halls. The stern door was retained, to enable vehicles and heavy equipment to be transported when required.

On 17 January 1978 *Jervis Bay* left the Storey & Keers shipyard and returned to Garden Island. The overall cost to the Navy of purchasing the ship and the conversion work was $8 million.

Now ready to enter service in her new role, *Jervis Bay* took over from HMAS *Duchess* as the Royal Australian Navy training ship. The vessel departed Sydney on 10 February 1978 on her first training cruise. She was based at Garden Island, and spent lengthy periods alongside the wharf there, earning the nickname 'building 203'.

Apart from serving as a training ship, *Jervis Bay* was sometimes used in other roles. The longest voyage undertaken by *Jervis Bay* commenced on 24 December 1992, when the vessel departed Townsville, carrying 110 soldiers and a full load of supplies, bound for Somalia to help with the famine relief programme being conducted by the United Nations.

*Jervis Bay* was decommissioned on 7 April 1994 in Sydney and officially put on the sales

HMAS *Jervis Bay* (Peter Plowman photo)

market in October 1994, with interest being shown from firms in Greece, Indonesia, Scandinavia, Great Britain, India and Singapore as well as Australia. On 23 December a sale was finalised with a Liberian registered firm, Voyager Marine Ltd. Renamed *Agios Andreas*, and showing Kingstown in St Vincent as its port of registry, the vessel left Sydney on the morning of Saturday, 14 January 1995. It made the long voyage to Greece on only one engine, as the starboard engine had been dismantled, and was still in pieces.

On arrival in Greece, the vessel underwent an extensive rebuilding, during which the superstructure was extended aft, providing extra berths and public rooms. Once the rebuilding was completed, the vessel measured 11,109 gross tons, and could accommodate up to 1,120 passengers, though only 316 were provided with beds in cabins. *Agios Andreas* entered service on the trade between Greek and Turkish ports operated by Med Link Lines. The vessel

*Agios Andreas* (Author's collection)

survived until the end of 2003, then was sold to shipbreakers in Greece.

The withdrawal of *Australian Trader* left *Empress of Australia* as the sole passenger vessel connecting Tasmania to the mainland, a reversion to the situation that had existed through the 1950s.

During her first five years of operation across Bass Strait, *Empress of Australia* enjoyed particularly good passenger loadings. In the year ending 30 June 1977, the vessel carried 111,622 passengers, an occupancy level of 83 per cent.

Despite these good figures the service could only be sustained with the assistance of a $2 million Federal Government annual subsidy.

The service across Bass Strait was only infrequently disrupted by union actions, and the occasional accident. On 11 January 1978, while loading was in progress in Melbourne,

fire broke out in the electrical switchboard on board *Empress of Australia*. Although the blaze was quickly extinguished, the resulting damage caused the ship to enter the Melbourne floating dock for repairs. She returned to service on 16 January, but the incident caused major problems for hundreds of passengers who had been booked on the cancelled voyages.

On the morning of Saturday, 15 July 1978, *Empress of Australia* was approaching Devonport on a regular voyage from Melbourne, with 280 passengers and 98 cars on board, as well as 100 crew, being due to berth at 9.30 am. A strong north-easterly wind was blowing and a heavy swell running on an ebbing tide as *Empress of Australia* entered the channel at the mouth of the Mersey River, but as the vessel slowed down it was pushed towards the western shoreline by the combined wind and swell. An anchor was dropped to try and keep the vessel in the channel, but before this could take effect, *Empress of Australia* went aground at 9.10 am some 400 metres inside the river entrance.

The Devonport tug *Gawler* was quickly on the scene, and attached a rope to the stricken ferry, but was unable to pull it free. As the tide ebbed, *Empress of Australia* developed a list to port, and remained firmly aground, though the passengers were in no immediate danger.

Calls for extra assistance brought the Burnie tug *York Syme* to the scene, and shortly after two more tugs, *York Town* and *Wybia*, arrived from Launceston. As the next high tide approached

Two views of *Empress of Australia* aground off Devonport on 15 July 1978 (Devonport Maritime Museum)

With the help of four tugs, *Empress of Australia* is refloated (Devonport Maritime Museum)

its peak at 3pm, all four tugs were brought into action, despite the atrocious weather, with pouring rain being driven by a strong north-north-west wind, and heavy seas running.

With three tugs attached to the bow and one at the stern, they were able to pull *Empress of Australia* free, and the vessel was soon back in the main channel. After a short pause to check for damage, *Empress of Australia* was able to proceed down the river and finally berthed at 3.15 pm.

An inspection of the hull located no leaks, and *Empress of Australia* was able to depart Devonport on schedule at 7.30 pm for the voyage back to Melbourne. Fortunately this was scheduled to be the last Bass Strait crossing by the ship before it went into dry dock at Westernport for annual survey and maintenance.

*Empress of Australia* returned to service on schedule, and for the next few years operated without any problems. During October 1980, *Empress of Australia* carried a banner on the superstructure just behind the bridge, celebrating the 21st anniversary of the introduction of the ANL Searoad service across Bass Strait.

With *Empress of Australia* approaching twenty years of service, thoughts had begun turning to the provision of a replacement vessel. During 1982 four companies expressed an interest in providing a replacement service to that of *Empress of Australia*, these being Brambles, TNT Bulkships Ltd, Tasmanian Shipping Services and Celsiunator (SA) Pty Ltd, of Port Adelaide.

Each of their proposals was for either one or two passenger and cargo vessels, and some stated they would not require a Government subsidy. All of these proposals, along with that of ANL, were rejected by the Federal, Victorian and Tasmanian Governments.

On 10 May 1983, the Tasmanian shipbuilder International Catamarans and the American firm Crowley International announced that they intended to place a 60 metre long catamaran ferry on a fast service between Devonport and Melbourne.

The planned passage time was five hours, and the craft, to be named *Spirit of Tasmania*, would carry 300 passengers and 50 cars. The new craft was to be built in the Hobart yard of International Catamarans, with construction due to commence in January 1984. That, however, was the last heard of this particular project.

In 1982 Australian National Line approached the Finnish shipbuilder, Wartsila, to draw up a suggested design for a suitable vessel. Wartsila was a leading builder of ferries for European operators, and the concept they came up with was very much in keeping with those vessels.

An artist's impression of a possible new building was produced, which depicted a rather stylish vessel of about 15,000 gross tons with the main passenger areas located in the forward section of the superstructure.

It would also have both bow and stern doors opening into the garage decks, in common with the ferries then being built for service in Europe.

Wartsila design for a new Bass Strait ferry to replace *Empress of Australia* (Devonport Maritime Museum)

The twin funnels were depicted with slightly different ANL colours, and the vessel was to revive the name *Princess of Tasmania*. However, nothing further was done, and the project was quietly abandoned.

Instead of proceeding with the Wartsila design, Australian National Line submitted a proposal to the Commonwealth Minister of Transport to provide two ships of about 3,200 gross tons each, with a combined capacity of 600 passengers, 220 passenger vehicles and 360 freight containers. They would replace both *Empress of Australia* and two cargo ships then being used on the Bass Strait trade from Melbourne.

During 1983 the Tasmanian Government requested the Federal Government provide funds for the charter of a passenger ferry to supplement *Empress of Australia* during the 1983/84 peak summer period. There were reports that a coastal permit had been sought for the operation of one of four vessels under consideration.

These vessels were *Scotia Prince*, which usually operated across the Bay of Fundy on the east coast of North America, *St Patrick II*, an Irish Sea ferry, *Stena Baltica*, which was used on a variety of trades in northern Europe, and the Greek inter-island ferry *Odysseus Elytis*. Each of these vessels was somewhat larger than *Empress of Australia* and could carry between 600 and 800 passengers as well as a large number of vehicles.

This proposal was also rejected by the Federal Government. However, the Federal budget for 1983/84 did provide a subsidy of $2.8 million for the operation of *Empress of Australia*.

By 1983 the Federal Government subsidy for the Bass Strait trade was amounting to $2.5 million per year. On 28 November 1983, *Empress of Australia* was bedecked with flags as she departed Melbourne, to mark her 2,500th voyage since being commissioned in 1965, during which time she had carried some 1.3 million passengers.

During 1984 the passenger capacity of *Empress of Australia* was increased to 475 by the installation of extra sleeper chairs, but even this was not sufficient to meet demand in the peak summer period, though adequate for the rest of the year. However, the major problem was the lack of adequate car space, as demand in this area had increased dramatically year round.

On the night of 22 March 1984, while en route from Devonport to Melbourne, *Empress of Australia* was disabled by the seizure of a piston in the port main engine. After drifting for five hours, the engineers were able to raise power again, and the ship limped into Melbourne on one engine, arriving eight hours late, at 3 pm.

Early in 1984 ANL were reported to be considering the purchase of a larger second-hand vessel, which could carry 1,000 passengers and 400 cars, as a replacement for *Empress of Australia*.

However, in June 1984 came the shock announcement that Australian National Line would be pulling out of the Tasmanian passenger trade altogether in mid-1985, at which time *Empress of Australia* would be withdrawn from service and offered for sale.

It was left to the Tasmanian Government to obtain a suitable replacement vessel if the Bass Strait trade was to continue. In September 1984 they were able to purchase the West German ferry *Nils Hogersson*, which was to be renamed *Abel Tasman*, but would not be entering service in Bass Strait for several months.

In the meantime, *Empress of Australia* continued to operate between Melbourne and Devonport.

In September 1984 a meeting of the Australian Shipping Commission approved the introduction of new funnel colours for the ANL vessels. These would be green with two yellow bands separated by a narrow white band, and the ANL senior management decided that all vessels would receive the new colours as soon as possible. Despite her imminent withdrawal, the funnel of *Empress of Australia* was repainted in these colours later in 1984.

In January 1985 *Empress of Australia* passed her twentieth anniversary of operation on the Australian coast, but six months later her service came to an end.

On the evening of 2 June 1985 *Empress of Australia* departed Devonport on her final crossing of Bass Strait, arriving in Melbourne for the last time the next morning.

Once all the passengers, vehicles and cargo had been offloaded, *Empress of Australia* moved to Webb Dock No 1 East berth to be laid up, having been offered for sale. It was reported that at one time ANL was considering operating the ship on a 'no frills' service between Melbourne and Bell Bay during the 1985/86 peak summer months only, on a commercial basis without any Government subsidy, in competition with *Abel Tasman*, but this idea was soon dropped.

At the time *Empress of Australia* was withdrawn the replacement vessel, *Abel Tasman*, was not ready to enter service. The Tasmanian Government tried to charter *Empress of Australia* for several more Bass Strait voyages, but were unable to reach an agreement with ANL. As a result, for four weeks there was no passenger ferry operating between Melbourne and Devonport, until *Abel Tasman* entered service on 30 June.

Meanwhile, after a brief period of idleness, *Empress of Australia* was sold to Phineas Navigation Co, a Cyprus-registered subsidiary of Universal Glow Inc, owned by Antonis Lelakis of Greece. The name of the ship was amended to *Empress*, with Limassol as her port of registry.

On 26 July 1985 the vessel departed Melbourne for the last time, manned by Greek officers and a Polish crew. After a brief stop at Fremantle to top up on fuel and supplies, *Empress* headed off across the Indian Ocean bound for the Mediterranean. On her arrival there the vessel was immediately placed on a regular ferry service between Larnaca in Cyprus and the Lebanese port of Jounieh.

*Empress* served on this route for the next four

*Empress of Australia* in the new funnel colours adopted by ANL in 1984 (Michael Ude photo)

The former *Empress of Australia* was renamed *Empress* (Author's collection)

years, occasionally becoming embroiled in the volatile political situation affecting that part of the world. On 3 January 1987 an Israeli gunboat intercepted *Empress*, which was searched for Palestinian terrorists.

Several times the vessel was also involved in evacuating Lebanese citizens from their war-torn country. Also in 1987 the registered owners of the vessel were listed as Congreve Shipping Corp, Nassau, but in 1989 this was changed again, to Falcon Maritime Co, of Piraeus.

In September 1989 *Empress* was withdrawn from service and sent to the Avlis Shipyard at Khalkis, in Greece, for major rebuilding into a cruise ship. The external appearance of the vessel was considerably altered, the superstructure being extended fore and aft, the bow rebuilt with a sharper rake, the vehicle deck stern door removed and a new stern constructed, and a panel added to the after section of the funnel.

Internally the existing accommodation was all removed, as was the vehicle deck, to be replaced by 301 new cabins, all with private facilities, for a maximum of 623 passengers. A completely new range of public rooms was also constructed on the upper decks. These included a 312-seat dining room, and two large lounges, the forward one having seating for 330, while the two-deck high Starlight Show Lounge right aft could seat 406. Above the bridge was an observation lounge, while another feature was a large casino. Aft on the upper deck an outdoor swimming pool was installed, with a surrounding lido area. When the rebuilding was completed the vessel measured 13,176 gross tons, and the new bow

had increased her length to 142.8 m/468 ft.

During the rebuilding, plans for the future employment of the vessel changed several times. Initially it had been announced that she would be used for cruises in the Caribbean under the name *Empress*. Then a charter was arranged with Starlight Cruises, for a series of weekly departures from San Diego to Mexican ports.

In April 1990 came another change, when it was reported the Swedish company Stena Line had taken *Empress* on a seven-year charter to operate one-day cruises from Gothenburg to Copenhagen, for which she would be renamed *Stena Empress*.

Before the rebuilding was completed early in 1991, the arrangement with Stena Line had been cancelled, and the registered owner of the vessel had changed yet again, to Sun Cruises Maritime, with management by Tony Travel & Agency Ltd, of Piraeus.

Once again it was reported that the vessel would be operated by Starlight Cruises on the west coast of North America. This time, though, the departure point was to be the Mexican port of La Paz, with the first cruise due to commence on 16 June 1991.

Before that happened, however, two American airlines that operated services to La Paz went out of business, leaving the charterers with insufficient seats to carry their passengers to the ship, so that programme was abandoned.

In October 1991 it was then reported the vessel would be renamed *Pacific Empress*, and still chartered to Starlight Cruises, who had resurrected the programme of cruises out of San Diego, but these did not eventuate either.

Throughout this period the vessel had

remained idle in Greece, but early in 1992 she departed the Mediterranean, bound for Singapore, having been renamed *Royal Pacific* , and registered in Nassau.

With poker machines located in most public rooms as well as a fully equipped casino, she began a series of 3-day and 4-day gambling cruises from Singapore to Indonesian ports, which were well patronised. A number of the croupiers on board were Australians, recruited from the Adelaide casino.

In August 1992 the cruise schedule was altered to include a number of weekend cruises to nowhere, the first of which departed Singapore on the evening of Friday, 21 August. The route to be followed was at the discretion of the Greek captain, who decided to go up the Straits of Malacca into the Andaman Sea. *Royal Pacific* was scheduled to return to Singapore on the evening of Sunday, 23 August.

At 3.30 that morning *Royal Pacific* was about 20 miles south-west of Port Dickson, proceeding down the Straits of Malacca in a calm sea with good visibility. On the port side following a parallel course was a Taiwanese fishing boat, *Terfu 51*, which was being overtaken by the cruise ship.

The fishing boat made a turn to starboard, apparently to pass astern of the passenger vessel after it had passed, but instead the bow of *Terfu 51* rammed into the stern of *Royal Pacific*. The impact left a hole later described as 'big enough for two buses to pass through.'

At the time of the collision the watertight doors in the bulkheads were open, and for reasons unknown could not be closed. As water poured through the hole it was able to spread right through the lower decks. *Royal Pacific* listed to port, and began to settle rapidly by the stern. Passengers were hurriedly roused from their cabins and ordered to abandon ship.

Fortunately the Straits of Malacca is a very busy shipping channel, and within minutes of the SOS being sent five ships were converging on the scene. On board *Royal Pacific* the list to port became so severe some lifeboats could not be lowered, while others reached the water vastly overloaded. Reports of the time it took the ship to sink varied, but it seems that it was all over in about ninety minutes.

One survivor spoke of watching the stern of the ship disappear under water as the bow rose straight up into the air, paused there, then slipped rapidly out of sight. Luckily only two persons lost their lives in the incident, and the survivors were brought into Singapore aboard several tankers and bulk carriers that had diverted to assist.

So ended the career of the largest passenger vessel ever built in Australia.

*Royal Pacific* berthed in Singapore (Stephen Berry photo)

# Chapter Sixteen

# Abel Tasman

In June 1984 Australian National Line had announced they would be withdrawing *Empress of Australia* from the Bass Strait trade between Devonport and Melbourne in mid-1985. With the Tasmanian economy very dependent on the provision of a regular passenger shipping connection between the island and the mainland, the Federal Government agreed to fund the setting up of a new Bass Strait ferry service by the Tasmanian state government. This was done as part of a compensation package from the Federal Government for not allowing the Tasmanian Government to build a hydro-electric scheme on the Gordon River.

To run the new ferry service, Transport Tasmania was established as a department of the Tasmanian Department of Transport. It would operate as TT Line, and be controlled by a Board of Management that reported directly to the State Government.

The first task of the new department was to find a suitable second-hand ferry as quickly as possible to take over the service from *Empress of Australia*. Officials were sent to Europe to inspect any available vessels, and select the one that was most suited to the Bass Strait trade.

In August 1984 the Tasmanian Government announced they would be purchasing the West German ferry *Nils Hogersson*, which would be handed over to them the following month.

*Nils Hogersson* was the third ferry to carry that name in recent years, and was operated by Travemunde-Trelleborg Line, usually known as TT Line.

Formed in 1962 as a subsidiary of Trampschiffahrt Gesellschaft MHB, based in

Hamburg, TT Line began operating a service across the Baltic Sea between the north German port of Travemunde and Trelleborg in southern Sweden. Their first vessel was only 3,529 gross tons, and named *Nils Hogersson*.

In 1965 a slightly larger ferry, named *Peter Pan*, was added to the service, being joined in 1967 by a sister ship, which replaced the first *Nils Hogersson* and was given the same name. Over

*Nils Holgersson* (Author's collection)

the next few years both passenger and vehicular traffic on the route grew steadily, and in 1974 TT Line placed orders for two new ferries, much larger than the existing pair, and to carry the same names.

The third *Nils Hogersson* was the second of the new sisters to be completed, being built in West Germany by Werft Nobiskrug GmbH at Rendsburg. Launched on 26 October 1974, the vessel was delivered to its owners on 8 April 1975.

*Nils Hogersson* measured 12,515 gross tons, with a length of 148.9 m/489 feet and a 24 m/79 foot beam. The vessel was powered by a pair of Pielstik-Blohm & Voss 16-cylinder geared diesels driving twin propellers, giving a service speed of 22 knots.

After a shakedown cruise from Travemunde to Gothenburg and Oslo, the vessel entered the trade between Travemunde and Trelleborg. The one-way trip took about seven hours on daylight sailings, while the overnight trip was run at a slower speed and took about eight hours.

*Nils Hogersson* could carry a maximum of 1,600 passengers, of whom 712 were accommodated in cabins, while 888 were unberthed. There was also garage space for 470 cars. *Nils Hogersson* operated in conjunction with an identical sister ship, *Peter Pan*, completed in 1974.

By 1983, *Nils Hogersson* and *Peter Pan* were no longer able to meet the demand for vehicle spaces on the route, so TT Line placed orders for the construction of two much larger ferries to replace them, and be given the same names. In mid-1984 *Nils Hogersson* and *Peter Pan* were offered for sale.

The Tasmanian Government inspected both, selecting *Nils Hogersson* to buy, and also taking out an option on *Peter Pan*, valid until the end of 1987. *Nils Hogersson* was handed over to the Tasmanian Government in September 1984, and renamed *Abel Tasman*.

The total cost was $26 million, though this amount also included $2 million for the upgrading and refurbishment of Station Pier in Melbourne, and the construction of a reinforced concrete ramp for vehicles, as well as the cost of altering the existing terminal at Devonport to handle the larger ship.

Prior to leaving for Australia, *Abel Tasman* had to be refitted. The vessel was sent back to its builders' yard for the work to be done. The most noticeable external change was the addition of an

*Abel Tasman* being refitted in Germany (Polly Woodside Museum)

unsightly box-like structure at the stern, which provided additional facilities for the 114 crew, to meet the demands of the Australian shipping trade unions.

On 21 April 1985 *Abel Tasman* was officially handed over at Rendsburg to the Tasmanian Government's shipping company, Transport Tasmania, also to be known as TT Line.

*Abel Tasman* left Rendsburg on 22 April for Australia, but the next day was forced to abandon the voyage due to an industrial dispute involving the stewards. Initially the vessel docked at Brunsbuttel, but it then proceeded through the Kiel Canal, and was laid up at Kiel on 26 April.

As a result, the Tasmanian Government sent police to West Germany to join the ship until the situation was resolved. On 18 May *Abel Tasman* finally departed Kiel for Australia.

After passing through the Mediterranean and the Suez Canal, then crossing the Indian Ocean, *Abel Tasman* arrived in Fremantle on 15 June. After refuelling, the vessel then continued to Devonport, where it berthed on 20 June.

*Abel Tasman* (TT Line photo - Author's collection)

Owing to the delayed arrival of the ship from Europe, a planned series of promotional visits to Sydney and Brisbane had to be cancelled. After several days of final fitting out and preparation, *Abel Tasman* departed Devonport on the evening of 29 June on a trial trip to Melbourne, arriving there next morning.

Instead of berthing in Webb Dock, the vessel went to the Inner East berth at Station Pier, which now became the Melbourne terminal for the Bass Strait ferry service.

On 1 July, *Abel Tasman* left Melbourne on its first commercial voyage. Initially the passenger numbers were restricted to a maximum of 480, but over the first few weeks of operation the vehicle deck of the vessel was used to full capacity. During this period passenger numbers averaged over 300 per voyage. From 1 October the passenger capacity was increased to 850.

From the start *Abel Tasman* operated three return trips per week, leaving Melbourne at 7.30 pm on Monday, Wednesday and Friday, arriving in Devonport the next morning. Voyages from Devonport departed at 7.30 pm on Tuesday, Thursday and Sunday, with the vessel remaining in Devonport overnight on Saturday.

Passenger facilities on *Abel Tasman* were quite comfortable. There were no aircraft style seats, but a wide range of cabins, located on four of the six passenger decks. These included two suites and ten deluxe cabins, but the majority of the accommodation comprised two, three and four berth cabins, most with private or shared facilities. There was also some male and female hostel accommodation available.

The majority of public rooms were spread along the Restaurant Deck, with the large Heemskirk Lounge right forward, and several smaller lounges, a coffee shop and milk bar. Three restaurants were provided, the à la carte Freycinet Room offering waiter service, while the Carvery and Cafeteria were self-service.

Other facilities included a playroom for young children, shop, saunas and an indoor swimming pool. Outside deck space was rather limited, but there was an enclosed observation deck located above the bridge, which was very popular with passengers when the ship was arriving in port.

There were two vehicle decks, with bow and stern doors providing access. To enable the drive-through system to work efficiently, the

*Abel Tasman* in Hobart (Rex Cox photo)

ship would berth bow in at Melbourne and stern in at Devonport.

In her first year of operation, *Abel Tasman* operated at an average 80 per cent capacity, carrying 188,679 passengers, compared to 124,693 that had been carried by *Empress of Australia* in her final year of service. However, the overall operation of the service lost $2.2 million for the year.

Occasionally *Abel Tasman* would be diverted from her regular run, the first such occasion being on 22 November 1985, when the vessel left Melbourne for Hobart. Proceeding down the east coast of Tasmania, *Abel Tasman* arrived in Hobart on 24 November for the Tasmania Day celebrations.

Leaving the same evening, *Abel Tasman* went around the southern and western coastline to complete a circumnavigation of Tasmania, returning to Melbourne on 26 November.

Through 1986 and into 1987, *Abel Tasman* maintained a regular service across Bass Strait, encountering very few problems or delays. The service was becoming increasingly popular, and passenger loadings remained high throughout the year.

For the financial year 1986/87, *Abel Tasman* carried 186,000 passengers and 49,000 vehicles, earning an operating profit of $3.3 million, compared with a $2.8 million profit the previous year, when 181,000 passengers and 52,400 vehicles were carried.

It was also during 1987 that the Tasmanian Government had to give consideration to whether it was feasible to take up the option to purchase *Peter Pan*, and operate it across Bass Strait alongside *Abel Tasman*. A number of alternatives were also considered, including placing the vessel in service from Hobart, offering regular sailings to Sydney and Brisbane, and also to Adelaide.

Eventually the Tasmanian Government decided against taking up the purchase option, and *Peter Pan* was subsequently sold to operators in Greece. However, TT Line did advise the Government that it would be necessary to replace *Abel Tasman* with a larger and better vessel within the next three years

During 1987 there were reports of two other groups that were intending to commence passenger operations across Bass Strait. One group, calling itself the Bass Strait Ferry Proposal Investigation Committee, was headed by a Launceston businessman, Mr Arthur Hayward, and its members included the founder and principal of International Catamarans, Mr Robert Clifford, and Mr Alan Fogarty, founder of Tamar Steel Boats.

They undertook a feasibility study into the building of a conventional ferry of about 9,000 gross tonnes, which would carry 1,000 passengers in aircraft type seats on a service between Devonport and Hastings or San Remo in Western Port in about 8½ hours. There was also a bid by Burnie to be considered as the Tasmanian terminus for the service.

The second operation was proposed by Tasmanian Ferry Services, another newly formed organisation. They released plans to have a wave-piercing fast catamaran ferry, capable of carrying 350 passengers and 77 cars, built by International Catamarans in Hobart, to be ready to commence service in 1990.

It was claimed that the state-of-the-art vessel would be the largest catamaran in the world. It would be able to cross Bass Strait in a little more than four hours, and thus be able to operate a daily return trip. Although at the time this idea was not taken seriously, as events would turn out it would come to fruition, though a bit later than planned.

On 18 July 1987, *Abel Tasman* departed Devonport for Newcastle, arriving two days later, and entering the floating dock for an overhaul.

Leaving Newcastle on the afternoon of 2 August, *Abel Tasman* made her first visit to Sydney the same evening, entering the harbour and proceeding as far as the Harbour Bridge before turning around and heading back towards the sea.

However, the ship then suffered some serious mechanical problems, and had to anchor in the harbour for several hours while these were rectified. The voyage south then resumed, with *Abel Tasman* arriving back in Devonport on 4 August, and returning to service the next day.

On 21 November 1987, *Abel Tasman* made a special trip from Devonport along the Tasmanian coast to Burnie, narrowly winning a race against a steam train. The vessel stayed in Burnie overnight for the Tasmania Day celebrations, then returned to Devonport.

Meanwhile, *Abel Tasman* remained on the service between Devonport and Melbourne throughout 1988. One voyage during the year was particularly bad, as shortly after leaving Devonport on the night of 24 July, with 636 passengers on board, *Abel Tasman* ran into a severe north-westerly gale.

During the night the wind reached 55 knots (100 kmh), and at times gusts of 70 knots (128 kmh) were recorded. The high winds combined with heavy seas forced the vessel to reduce speed, and it was seven hours late berthing in Melbourne on 25 July.

*Abel Tasman* in the Newcastle floating dock in July 1989 (Peter Plowman photo)

*Abel Tasman* (TT Line photo; Author's collection)

*Abel Tasman* (TT Line photo; Author's collection)

During 1988 TT Line conducted their own feasibility study on a replacement for *Abel Tasman*, which resulted in a submission for a larger vessel being put before the Tasmanian Government.

As a result of this submission, the General Manager of TT Line made a trip to Europe to seek out suitable second-hand tonnage. He was reported to have twice inspected the German-flag ferry *Olau Britannia*, operated by Olau Line,

*Abel Tasman*, in the new funnel colours adopted by TT Line in July 1989 (Lindsay Rex photo)

# Deck Plan

DECKS

OBSERVATION
BRIDGE
A
RESTAURANT
B
VEHICLE
C
D

DECKS

OBSERVATION
BRIDGE
A
RESTAURANT
B
VEHICLE
C
D

**'A' DECK (GREEN)**

For easy identification each cabin deck has a unique colour scheme. And all decks are well sign-posted and accessible by wide stairways or elevators.

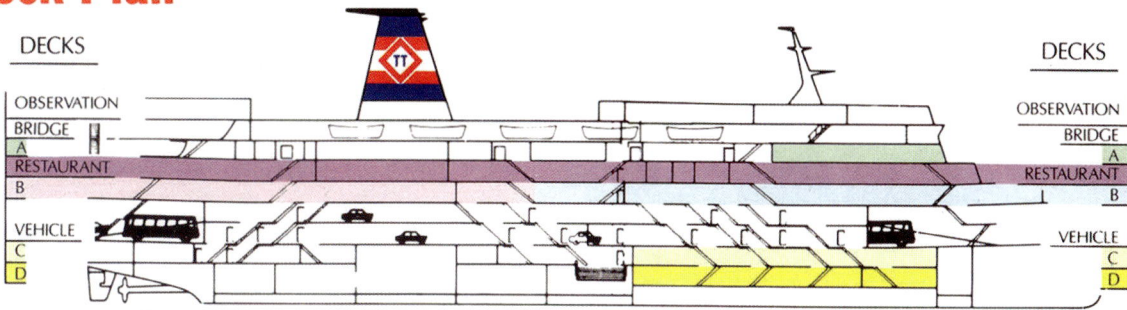

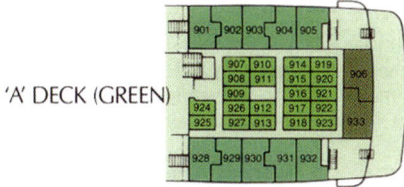

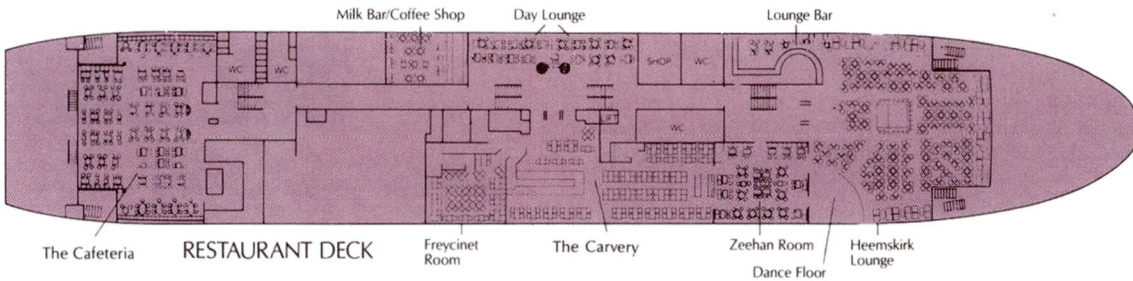

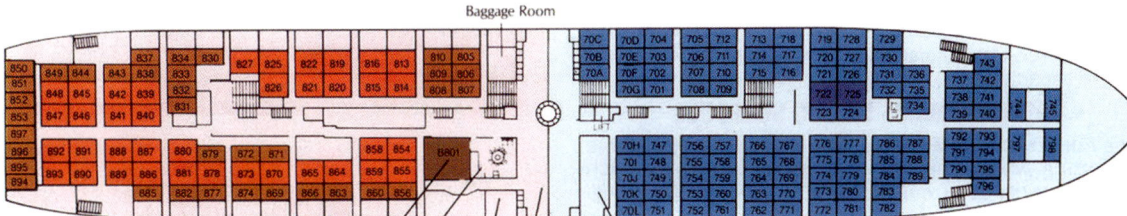

Cabins: Double bedded suites with private facilities
Four berth deluxe with private facilities
Two berth with private facilities

Milk Bar/Coffee Shop    Day Lounge    Lounge Bar

The Cafeteria    RESTAURANT DECK    Freycinet Room    The Carvery    Zeehan Room    Heemskirk Lounge
Dance Floor

Baggage Room

**'B' DECK (RED)**    Cabin for people with disabilities    Sick Bay    Gangways (Entrance Hall)    Reception Purser's Office    **'B' DECK (BLUE)**
Children's Playroom

Cabins: Two berth with private facilities
Four berth with private facilities
Four berth disabled with private facilities    (Two lower berths for disabled, two berths for helpers)

Cabins: two berth with private facilities
Four berth with private facilities

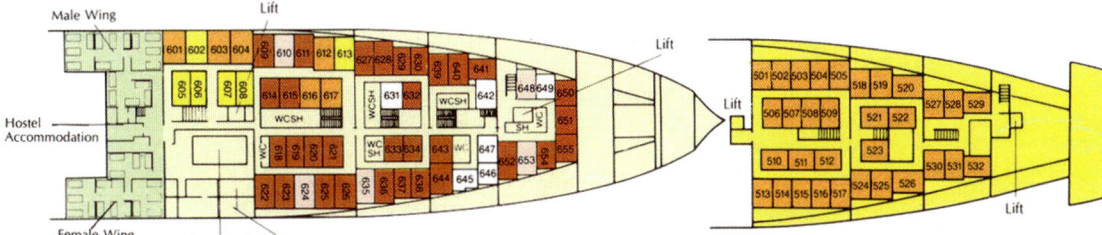

Male Wing    Lift    Lift    Lift

Hostel Accommodation

Female Wing    Swimming Pool Saunas

**'C' DECK (YELLOW)**    **'D' DECK (ORANGE)**

Cabins: Two berth with shared facilities    Three berth with private facilities    Hostel Style with shared facilities    Cabins: Four berth with private facilities
Two berth with private facilities    Four berth with shared facilities
Three berth with shared facilities    Four berth with private facilities

which was due to be replaced in 1990 by a larger new ferry of the same name. It is interesting to note that since 1979 Olau Line had been a subsidiary of the same company that owned to note that since 1979 Olau Line had been a subsidiary of the same company that owned the European TT Line, previous owners of *Abel Tasman*.

the European TT Line, previous owners of *Abel Tasman.*

Built in 1982, the 14,990 gross ton *Olau Britannia* operated a service across the North Sea between Sheerness and Flushing, and could carry 1,800 passengers, though only 938 in berths, and 530 cars.

As this was only a slight increase on the numbers carried by *Abel Tasman*, no further interest was taken in the vessel, and no other suitable ferry able to carry 1,200 or more passengers in berths could be located.

On 24 February 1989 *Abel Tasman* departed Melbourne on her second voyage to Hobart. Bookings for the voyage south and back were extremely good, and some consideration was given to operating regular sailings on the route, but these were eventually shelved.

In July 1989 *Abel Tasman* made a second visit to Newcastle for her biennial drydocking and overhaul. During this time the funnel colours and insignia were changed, becoming very similar to those worn by the ship under its original owners, though the colours used were different.

The dark blue background was retained, but on it was a broad white band edged in red and containing a white diamond, also edged in red, inside which the letters TT were painted in blue.

Departing Newcastle on 30 July, *Abel Tasman* again made a brief visit to Sydney Harbour en route back to Devonport. A number of passengers were carried on this voyage, which encountered some quite rough weather off the south coast of New South Wales, but *Abel Tasman* handled the seas well.

On returning to Melbourne *Abel Tasman* immediately resumed its place on the Devonport service, which had been closed down while the ship was in Newcastle.

Advance bookings across Bass Strait for the rest of 1989 and into 1990 were extremely good, and *Abel Tasman* was fast becoming a victim of its own popularity. The demand for passages on the ship, especially in the peak summer period, was far in excess of the available berths for much of the year.

In late August 1989 the pilots working for all the major Australian domestic airlines went on strike in a dispute over a new salary package. The dispute worsened quickly, and on 24 August all the pilots resigned, leaving Australia without any domestic airline services.

This sudden cessation of services affected Tasmania far more than the mainland states, as it almost brought to a halt the flow of tourists and goods from the mainland.

Demand for passages on *Abel Tasman* soon far outstripped the number of available berths. In October 1989, TT Line began negotiations with the Royal Australian Navy and maritime unions to charter HMAS *Jervis Bay*, the former

*Abel Tasman* arriving in Sydney on the evening of 30 July 1989 (Peter Plowman photo)

*Australian Trader*, to supplement *Abel Tasman* on the Bass Strait service until the pilots' dispute was settled. This plan was defeated by technical difficulties.

The need to obtain a larger vessel was becoming critical. TT Line again began searching for a suitable ship, but at the end of 1989 they announced they had been unable to locate one on the second-hand market.

Instead, the Government was advised that it would be necessary to order a brand new vessel with double the capacity of *Abel Tasman*, at a cost of $100 million, but there was considerable doubt as to the prospects of financing such a replacement.

1990 was not a good year for *Abel Tasman*, as numerous mechanical defects adversely affected her schedule. During February the vessel was delayed several times by engine trouble, and on the night of 24 February the 824 passengers who had boarded in Devonport were informed the vessel would be travelling at reduced speed to Melbourne, with a resultant late arrival.

When the ship was in the middle of Bass Strait, metal fragments from the exhaust system were blown through one of the turbine engines, which had to be stopped. *Abel Tasman* limped into Melbourne on one engine, berthing eight hours late. Emergency repairs were effected, and the vessel was able to sail on schedule the same evening.

In April 1990 the timetable operated by *Abel Tasman* was amended for the first time, in an attempt to provide more berths on the service. Instead of three return trips per week, the vessel began operating to a fortnightly schedule of seven return trips, with no layover in Devonport on Saturday night.

This meant that in the first week *Abel Tasman* would depart Melbourne on Monday, Wednesday, Friday and Sunday, returning from Devonport the following day, while in the second week there would be departures from Melbourne on Tuesday, Thursday and Saturday.

A highlight for *Abel Tasman* occurred on the voyage that departed Melbourne on Friday, 8 June 1990, during which trip the vessel carried its millionth passenger across Bass Strait since entering that service.

The new schedule put extra strain on the vessel, which began suffering rudder problems that caused considerable vibration, especially at the regular service speed. An extra drydocking at Newcastle in August was scheduled, but the problem with the rudder stocks became so serious that immediate repairs were required.

On 13 July *Abel Tasman* arrived in Sydney and entered the Cockatoo Island drydock for temporary repairs. Leaving Sydney on 18 July, the vessel resumed her regular schedule two days later, then on 12 August arrived in Newcastle for the previously scheduled drydocking.

Both rudders were removed for further repairs, and the vessel left Newcastle on 27 August. During both these absences no replacement ship was available, and the Bass Strait service was cancelled.

During 1990 initial plans for a new ship to replace *Abel Tasman* were drawn up, but an order was not placed. Instead, on 30 August the Premier of Tasmania, Mr Field, announced that TT Line would be replacing *Abel Tasman* with a larger vessel, either new or second-hand, within three years. At the same time TT Line reported an operating profit of $8.27 million for the previous financial year.

With a replacement for *Abel Tasman* now desperately needed, TT Line continued to search the world for suitable second hand tonnage. On 24 December 1990 it was announced that an agreement had been reached with the German TT Line, the former owners of *Abel Tasman*, to purchase one of the ships that had replaced her in their service, *Peter Pan*.

Unfortunately, that vessel could not be delivered for at least another two years, which meant *Abel Tasman* would have to remain on the Bass Strait trade until then.

However, the lack of capacity on the service between the mainland and Tasmania had already attracted a rival operator. In December 1990 *Abel Tasman* found itself competing with a much smaller and faster vessel.

## Chapter Seventeen

# SeaCat Tasmania

*SeaCat Tasmania* under construction (Incat)

The changing face of water transport in the latter years of the 20th century is nowhere better illustrated than by the introduction of *SeaCat Tasmania* on the Bass Strait trade in December 1990.

The giant Seacat fast ferries with wave-piercing catamaran hulls, designed and built in Australia, pioneered a new concept in transporting large numbers of people across short stretches of open water at high speed.

These vessels are built in huge, hangar-like buildings by International Catamarans, better known as Incat, at Prince of Wales Bay in Hobart. The company started off building small wooden ferries and fishing boats, and later steel-hulled vessels, then branched out into the construction of aluminium catamaran ferries and excursion vessels.

The concept of a very large, fast catamaran ferry was developed in the late 1980s, and they were dubbed Seacats. A British company, Sea Containers Limited, was the first to place

*SeaCat Tasmania* (Incat)

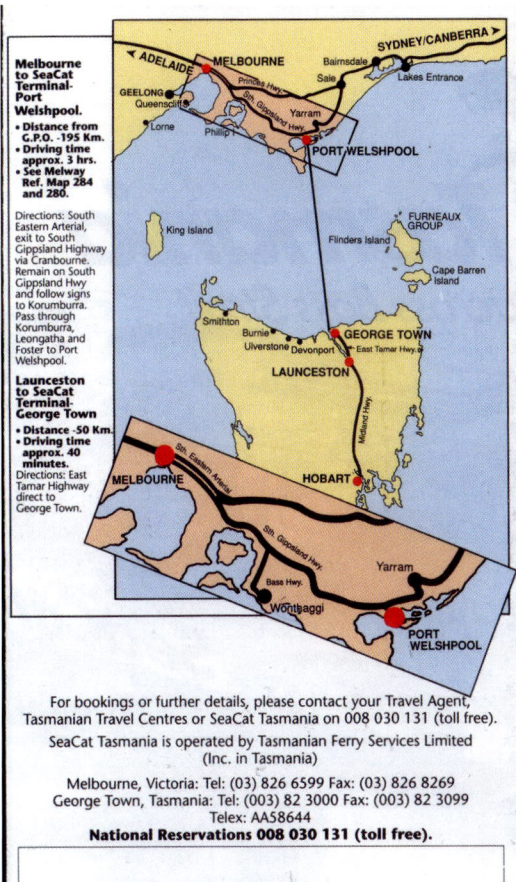

Brochure map depicting the route to be followed by *SeaCat Tasmania* (Author's collection)

orders for several Seacats, which they intended to use on ferry services across the English Channel, though one vessel was also designated for a fast service across Bass Strait.

Construction of this vessel, shipyard number 023, commenced in early 1990, but the work was suspended while various financial problems were overcome. In the meantime work on two more 'Seacats' intended for English Channel service got underway.

The first Seacat to be completed, Incat shipyard number 024, was named *Hoverspeed Great Britain*. On its delivery voyage to Britain, the vessel went across the Pacific and through the Panama Canal to New York.

In June 1990 *Hoverspeed Great Britain* made the fastest crossing yet of the North Atlantic, at an average speed of 36.6 knots, breaking the record held since 1952 by the American liner *United States*, and enabling the owners to claim the 'blue riband' along with the Hales Trophy.

*Hoverspeed Great Britain* went into service across the English Channel between Dover and Calais, on which route it proved highly successful. The second Seacat to be finished, number 025, was named *Hoverspeed France*. It was also built for the English Channel service.

*SeaCat Tasmania* was the third to be completed in the series. A new company had been formed to operate the vessel, Tasmanian Ferry Services

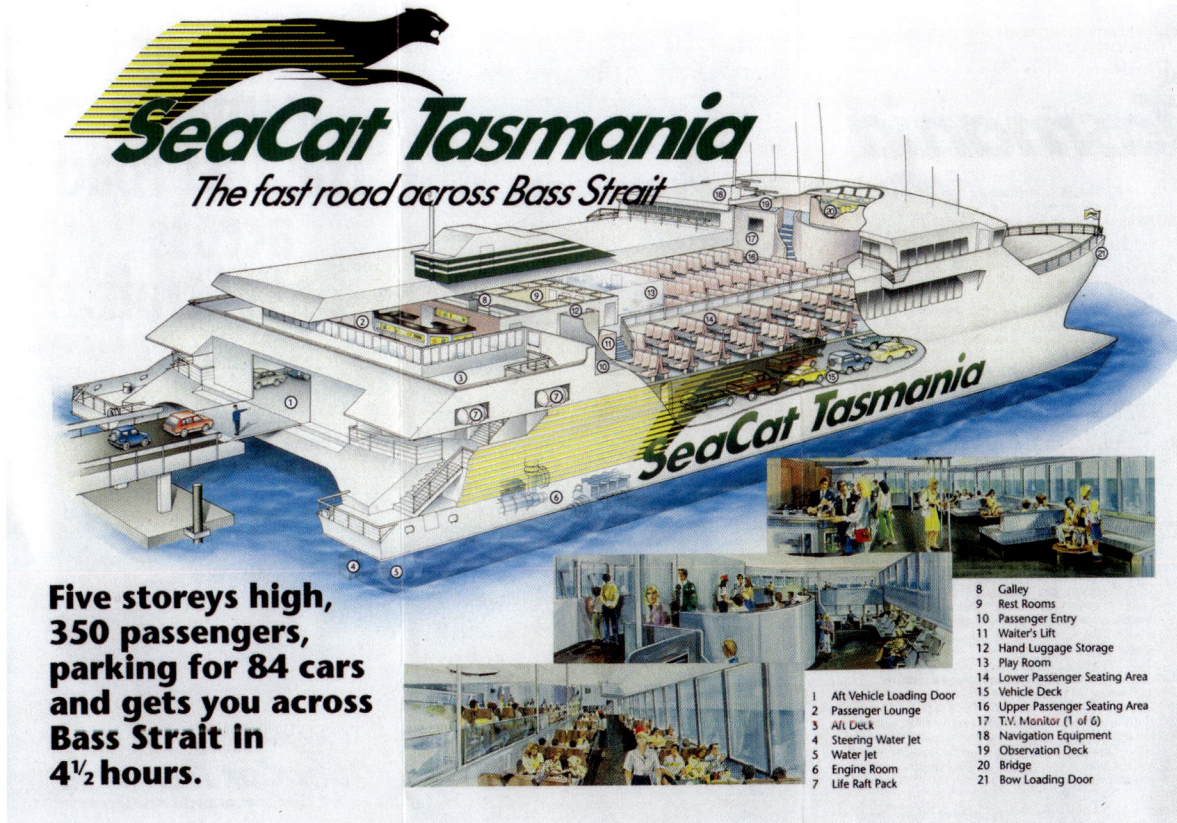

**Five storeys high, 350 passengers, parking for 84 cars and gets you across Bass Strait in 4½ hours.**

| | |
|---|---|
| 1 | Aft Vehicle Loading Door |
| 2 | Passenger Lounge |
| 3 | Aft Deck |
| 4 | Steering Water Jet |
| 5 | Water Jet |
| 6 | Engine Room |
| 7 | Life Raft Pack |
| 8 | Galley |
| 9 | Rest Rooms |
| 10 | Passenger Entry |
| 11 | Waiter's Lift |
| 12 | Hand Luggage Storage |
| 13 | Play Room |
| 14 | Lower Passenger Seating Area |
| 15 | Vehicle Deck |
| 16 | Upper Passenger Seating Area |
| 17 | T.V. Monitor (1 of 6) |
| 18 | Navigation Equipment |
| 19 | Observation Deck |
| 20 | Bridge |
| 21 | Bow Loading Door |

Cutaway drawing of *SeaCat Tasmania* (Author's collection)

Limited, owned 52 per cent by Sea Containers Australia Ltd, a newly formed subsidiary of the British firm, while the remaining 48 per cent was owned by other Australian interests.

*SeaCat Tasmania* was launched on 7 October 1990, but all did not go according to plan, as the vessel moved more slowly than anticipated, and became stuck on the blocks. Following a short delay, while some blocks were removed, *Hoverspeed France* was called in to pull the new vessel into the water.

It was then towed to the fitting out berth, where the engines were installed. Then the prefabricated superstructure was lowered onto the hull in one piece.

When completed *SeaCat Tasmania* measured 3,102 gross tonnes. The catamaran hull was 74.9 m/246 feet in length, with a beam of 26 m/85 feet.

The machinery comprised four Ruston diesels, each driving a Riva Calzoni water jet propulsion unit, which also rotated to act as rudders. The vessel had a fully loaded service speed of 35 knots, with a maximum of about 40 knots in smooth water.

Instead of following the long established services between Melbourne and northern Tasmania, Tasmanian Ferry Services Limited decided to establish a totally new route. The mainland terminal was built at Port Welshpool, on Corner Inlet on the southern Victorian coast, while the Tasmanian terminal was built at George Town, near the mouth of the Tamar River.

This was the shortest sea route across Bass Strait, though it meant that passengers would have a three-hour road journey from Melbourne, and about forty minutes from Launceston. With a proposed passage time of four hours each way, one return trip a day could be regularly operated, with the possibility of a second round trip being made when necessary.

As the regular return trips were to be conducted in daylight, there was no need to provide cabins. Instead, reclining chairs were installed for 350 passengers in a large midships seating area, divided into two levels.

The side lounges were lower than the centre lounge, allowing all passengers a view through the large windows along each side. At the forward end of the lounge, stairs led up to an observation deck, situated behind the bridge, but giving views over the bow through the bridge windows. Aft was a bar with casual seating.

There was also a galley providing meals for passengers, delivered to their seats. A playroom was provided for young children, and six TV monitors were spread around the seating area.

All passenger areas were fully air-conditioned. Below the passenger deck was a full length vehicle deck, with doors at bow and stern, providing space for about 84 cars.

*SeaCat Tasmania* departed Hobart on 20 December, and entered service on Bass Strait from George Town on 22 December 1990.

A rather tight timetable was organised, with the vessel departing George Town at 8.30 am, arriving in Port Welshpool at 1 pm. It was then scheduled to leave Port Welshpool at 2 pm to arrive back in George Town at 6.30 pm.

Fares for the one-way crossing were $99 in peak and shoulder seasons, $89 at other times. This was about half the economy class airfare between Launceston and Melbourne, and considerably less than the fares being charged on *Abel Tasman*. Instead of trying to take passengers away from the airlines and TT Line, the operators stated they were aiming to establish a new market for travel to Tasmania.

The introduction of the vessel into service was not without problems. After only a week, the sailings for 29 December were cancelled due to a technical fault with one of the water jets. The next day *SeaCat Tasmania* made two round trips to clear the backlog of passengers and cars.

In its first four months of service, *SeaCat Tasmania* carried 40,000 passengers and 15,000 cars, but a variety of problems were encountered from time to time.

As the vessel was built entirely of lightweight aluminium, and had a shallow draft of just over 2 m/7 feet, it tended to be quite lively in anything more than a moderate sea. This resulted in a rather uncomfortable combination of pitching, rolling and yawing motions, which resulted in seasickness amongst both passengers and crew. Also, when the waves did get up the vessel was forced to reduce speed, which adversely affected the timetable.

Steering and manoeuvring capabilities were found to be poor when the vessel was proceeding at slow speed, as there were no rudders, and difficulties were encountered when docking, especially at Port Welshpool when a wind was blowing.

On Saturday, 20 April 1991, *SeaCat Tasmania* was suddenly withdrawn from service for an indefinite period, after a routine warranty inspection found a crack in the bedplate of one of the four engines. The vessel had to return to the builder's yard in Hobart for repairs.

So extensive were the mechanical problems with *SeaCat Tasmania* that all four engines had to be removed for repairs, with the engine manufacturers accepting responsibility for the faults. For three months *SeaCat Tasmania* remained in Hobart, then when the repairs were completed ran a series of trials. On 14 July the craft operated four 90-minute excursions from Hobart to Bruny Island, then departed Hobart on 16 July for George Town.

*SeaCat Tasmania* resumed her service across Bass Strait on 20 July 1991. Instead of operating regular return trips every day, as had been planned, a revised schedule was adopted, which was not as arduous on the vessel.

Meanwhile, on 25 March 1991 *Abel Tasman* had suffered minor damage when a fire broke out while work was being done on the vehicle deck when the ship was berthed in Melbourne. Fortunately the fire was quickly put out, and the ship sailed on schedule.

In April 1991 *Abel Tasman* reverted to its original sailing schedule of three round trips per week, with an overnight layover in Devonport on Saturday.

In order to attract more business during the quieter winter months, TT Line introduced a three-night 'weekender bargain season package'. Costing as little as $197 per person in twin-share accommodation, passengers joined the ship in Melbourne on a Friday night for the overnight trip to Devonport.

They stayed on board for Saturday night while the vessel remained alongside in Devonport, leaving there on Sunday night and returning to Melbourne early on Monday morning, in time to get to work. This package deal proved so successful that instead of being terminated in October as planned, it was extended until 23 April 1992, except for the peak summer period.

During the winter months, when demand for travel was lower, *SeaCat Tasmania* would make only four round trips per week, increasing to five in spring and autumn, and six in early December. From 23 December to the end of February, a daily return service was provided.

TT Line also introduced an extended sailing schedule for the peak 1991/92 summer period. From the end of November to early February, *Abel Tasman* again made seven round trips every two weeks, which meant the Saturday night layover in Devonport was abolished.

During this period the vessel sailed full on almost every voyage in both directions. On 22 November 1991, *Abel Tasman* completed its two-thousandth crossing of Bass Strait, by which time it had carried about 1.3 million passengers.

Meanwhile, in late October 1991 yet another proposal for an alternative Bass Strait service was put before the Tasmanian Government. This one came from Van Diemen Line, a company based in Ulverstone, who proposed to replace *Abel Tasman* with two faster 12,000 gross tonne vessels.

They would each be able to carry 480 passengers, 180 in two-berth cabins, 300 in seats, with space for 120 cars, and cost about $60 million to build in Tasmania. They would each operate a daily round trip between Devonport and Hastings, departing either port at 9 am, arriving at 6 pm, then leaving again three hours later for an overnight crossing.

Van Diemen Line claimed its scheme would be far more economic than the plan to replace *Abel Tasman* with a larger vessel. As with other similar proposals, this one disappeared without a trace quite quickly.

The number of passengers utilising the *SeaCat Tasmania* service in the winter and autumn months was far below expectations, and even in early summer passenger loadings remained uneconomic.

In November 1991 Sea Containers Ltd, the British parent company of Tasmanian Ferry Services, caused uproar on the island state when they announced that *SeaCat Tasmania* was to be taken off the Bass Strait trade from April to October 1992.

Originally it was announced that the vessel would be chartered out and transferred to the west coast of North America to operate a service between Seattle and Victoria, on Vancouver Island. This plan was abandoned, due to the imposition of Canadian import duties.

A second charter arrangement with a French company to operate the vessel across the Mediterranean also fell through.

At the end of April *SeaCat Tasmania* went back to Hobart for maintenance, and was originally expected to be laid up there for the winter. Instead it was arranged that *SeaCat Tasmania* would go to Britain for a period of six months to operate under bareboat charter for the Sea Containers Group.

Having loaded a cargo of medical supplies donated by the Pharmacy Guild of Tasmania to the people of Latvia, *SeaCat Tasmania* left Hobart in May and made the long voyage to Britain via the Panama Canal.

On arrival there she replaced *Hoverspeed France*, which had been chartered to Italian operators, and spent the northern summer running across the English Channel between Dover and Calais, though still bearing her Australian name and colours.

The withdrawal of *SeaCat Tasmania* once again left *Abel Tasman* as the sole ferry crossing Bass Strait, but on 25 July she left Melbourne bound for Newcastle, arriving there on 27 July and entering the dry dock to undergo routine maintenance. *Abel Tasman* departed Newcastle on the afternoon of 5 August, and again made a brief appearance on Sydney Harbour before heading back to Melbourne, and resuming the service to Devonport on the night of 7 August. During the time *Abel Tasman* was away there was no passenger service at all across Bass Strait.

In October 1992, *SeaCat Tasmania* made the long trip from Britain back to Hobart, returning to her builders' yard for overhaul. Whilst undergoing trials in November on the Derwent River, *SeaCat Tasmania* hit a rock, causing considerable hull damage.

Repairs delayed the re-entry of the vessel into the Bass Strait trade by a week, from 27 November to 4 December. By this time the vessel was being promoted as '*Seacat the Starship*', though its official name remained *SeaCat Tasmania*.

Unfortunately the service continued to be uneconomic, so it was decided to terminate the service again at the end of the summer season. *SeaCat Tasmania* made what would turn out to be its last run across Bass Strait on 19 April 1993. The vessel then went to Hobart to undergo further modifications prior to returning to the northern hemisphere again for the summer service across the English Channel, operating between either Dover and Calais or Folkestone and Boulogne.

Throughout 1991 and 1992 and into 1993, *Abel Tasman* had continued to operate across Bass Strait, though by now quite unable to meet the growing demand for passages, especially in the peak summer holiday period. The vessel was also faced with competition for part of that time from *SeaCat Tasmania*.

At times throughout her career *Abel Tasman* was affected by very severe weather when crossing Bass Strait, but one of her worst voyages was on the night of August 15-16 1993. Having left Devonport on schedule, the vessel ran into five metre high waves churned up by 70 knot winds.

*SeaCat Tasmania* (Incat)

After a most uncomfortable trip, the vessel finally arrived off Station Pier at 1.30 pm, four and a half hours late. However, there were still strong winds blowing, and when *Abel Tasman* was attempting to berth the stern lines broke, and the vessel was blown at a right angle to the pier. Fortunately the bow lines held firm, but the stern swung so far round it finally ran aground on a sandy bottom off the beach.

The tug *Marimba* was called in to pull *Abel Tasman* free, which took about thirty minutes, after which the vessel was finally able to berth. However, in doing so the bow door suffered some damage, and the departure from Melbourne on the evening of 16 August was delayed four hours while repairs were completed.

*Abel Tasman* was now coming to the end of her career in Australian waters, and was due to be replaced on the Bass Strait trade in November 1993 by a larger vessel, *Spirit of Tasmania*.

Initially it had been thought that *SeaCat Tasmania* would be returning to Australia in October 1993, and operate across Bass Strait during the 1993/94 summer. However, on 14 July 1993 an administrator was appointed to take over Tasmanian Ferry Services Pty Ltd, whose offices closed later the same month.

Ownership of the vessel was then transferred to Sea Containers Australia No. 2 Ltd. *SeaCat Tasmania* was repainted in Hoverspeed colours, and renamed *SeaCat Calais*.

At the end of the 1993 English Channel summer season, *SeaCat Calais* was chartered to a Uruguayan firm, Navegacion Atlantida SA, and renamed *Atlantic II* for service across the estuary of the River Plate.

In 2000 the vessel was chartered to Societa Navigazone Alta Velocita (SNAV) of Naples, Italy. Renamed Croazia Jet, it operated a summer service across the Adriatic Sea between Ancona and Split in Croatia

In 2002 the vessel returned to Britain, was renamed SeaCat France, and resumed operating a regular service across the English Channel until the end of the 2002 summer season. The vessel was then taken out of service, and moved

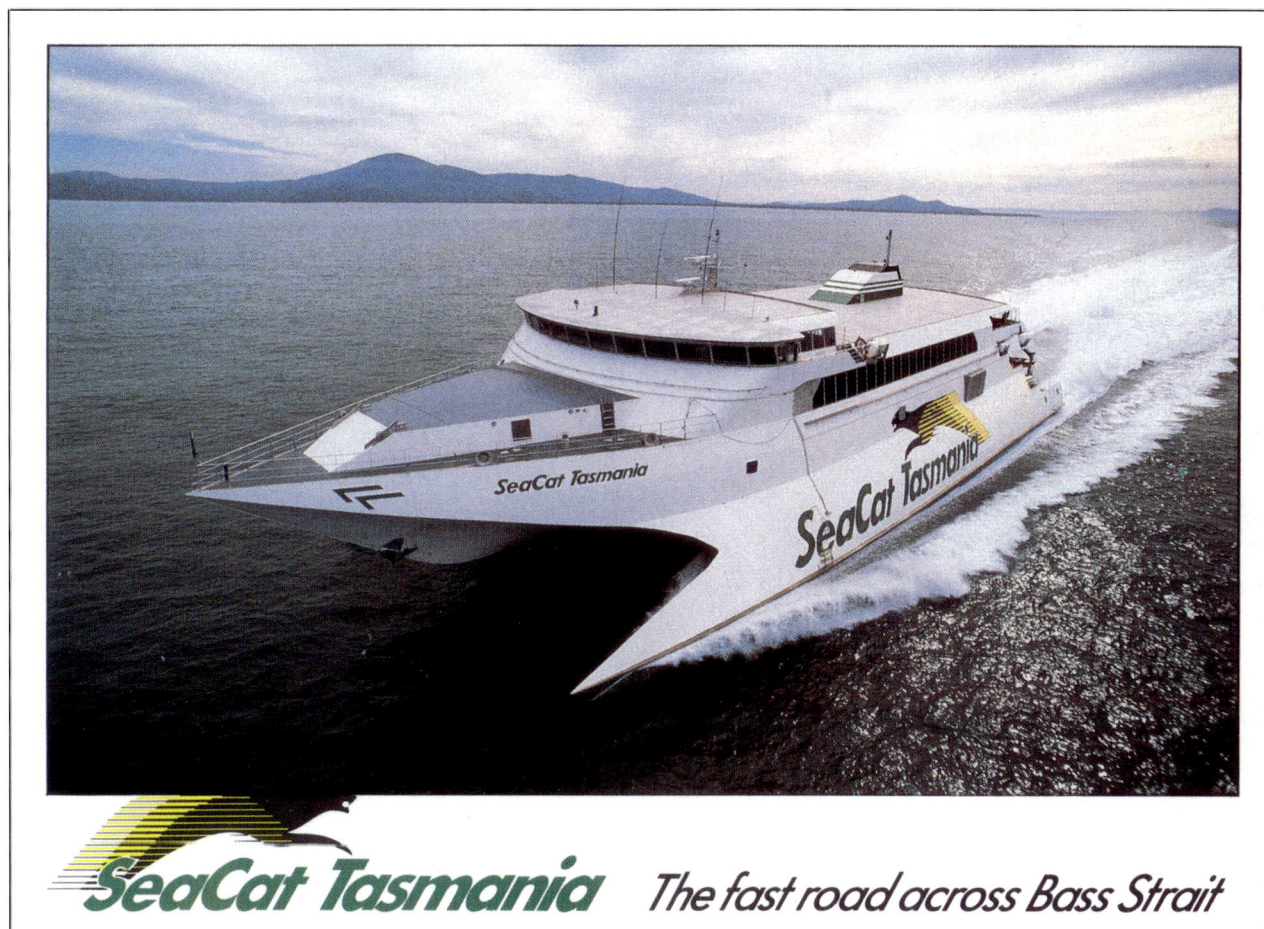

This postcard of *SeaCat Tasmania* was sold on the vessel (Author's collection)

# Chapter Eighteen

# Spirit of Tasmania

In December 1990 TT Line arranged to purchase a large second-hand ferry, *Peter Pan*, to replace *Abel Tasman* on the service between Melbourne and Devonport, but it would not be available for at least two years. As events panned out, it would be another three years before the ship would enter the service as *Spirit of Tasmania*.

*Peter Pan* had been built in 1986 by Seebeckwerft AG at Bremerhaven in West Germany for Travemunde-Trelleborg Line, who also traded as TT Line. At 31,356 gross tons, the new vessel had a length of 161.5 m/530 feet and a beam of 27.6 m/92 feet.

She was powered by four non-reversible four-stroke MAK diesels, one pair acting clockwise, the other anti-clockwise through reduction gears, attached to twin propellers. On trials *Peter Pan* attained a top speed of 21.5 knots.

Prior to the ship being built, extensive tank testing with models at the Shipbuilding Research Institute in Vienna had been conducted to come up with the best hull design. This resulted in an extremely bulbous bow being fitted, which greatly reduced the amount of pitching, and fin stabilisers being installed to dampen rolling. A bow thruster was fitted to assist in manoeuvring, and the ship could be turned around in its own length by the use of the bow thruster, full rudder and counter-rotating propellers.

Launched on 30 November 1985, *Peter Pan* was delivered to Travemunde-Trelleborg Line on 30 May 1986. The vessel was registered in Hamburg, and paid a quick visit to that port prior to entering service. On 2 June the vessel departed Travemunde on its first voyage to Trelleborg, in Sweden, which lasted eight hours

*Peter Pan* (Author's collection)

as an overnight trip, but was reduced to seven hours in daytime.

In 1987 *Peter Pan* was joined by a sister vessel, *Nils Hogersson*, which was registered under the Swedish flag, and actually owned by Wallenius Lines, but bareboat chartered to TT Line for twenty years.

*Peter Pan* could carry a maximum of 1,600 passengers, of whom 1,324 were accommodated in 489 two and four berth cabins, all with private facilities, located on six decks in the forward part of the superstructure.

A further 145 passengers travelled in aircraft style reclining seats, while the remainder were not allocated specific quarters, and were only carried on daytime trips.

Public rooms and other amenities were spread over three decks at the stern of the ship. These included several lounges, children's playroom, TV room, fitness centre, gymnasium, two saunas, solarium, indoor swimming pool, and a supermarket. Later a casino was added.

For meals there was a 330-seat à la carte restaurant, a 300-seat buffet restaurant and a cafeteria with seating for 336. Garage space for 550 cars was spread over three decks, with access through bow and stern doors.

The continuing enormous growth in passenger and vehicular traffic between Germany and Sweden meant that within a few years of entering service *Nils Hogersson* and *Peter Pan* were unable to cope with the demand for space for both passengers and vehicles, especially in the summer months, and two even larger vessels would have to be built.

It was under these circumstances that Transport Tasmania was able to arrange the purchase of *Peter Pan* in December 1990, with a forward delivery date of about two years, to take over the Bass Strait trade from *Abel Tasman*.

The sister ship to *Peter Pan*, *Nils Hogersson*, was sold under a similar arrangement to Brittany Ferries, being renamed *Val de Loire* in 1993, and has since operated services from the British ports of Plymouth and Portsmouth to either France or Spain.

It was not until the end of August 1993 that Travemunde-Trelleborg Line was able to withdraw *Peter Pan* from their service, when it was replaced by a larger vessel of the same name. The vessel was delivered to TT Line at Bremerhaven on 2 September, then went to the Lloyd Werft shipyard to undergo a $5 million refit, which included twelve days in dry dock.

Very few structural changes were made to the ship, with all the public rooms, including the casino, being retained, but the aircraft-style seats and the supermarket were removed, leaving spaces for the creation of extra lounges for passengers.

Having been renamed *Spirit of Tasmania*, the vessel left Bremerhaven on 5 October on the long voyage to Australia, via the Suez Canal, arriving in Devonport on 12 November. It then underwent two weeks of intensive final preparations and refurbishment for entering the Bass Strait trade.

Surprisingly, the funnel colours of the new vessel were not changed to those that had been carried by *Abel Tasman* for the last few years, but remained the same as when the ship was operating in the Baltic.

Meanwhile, on 1 November 1993 the original TT Line, which had operated as a department of the Tasmanian Department of Transport and was run by a Board of Management, was replaced by TT Line Company Pty Ltd. This was established as an incorporated business enterprise wholly

owned by its single shareholder, the State of Tasmania.

The Head Office and central reservations department remained in the terminal complex at East Devonport. The company became responsible for the operation of the Bass Strait trade as well as the passenger and freight terminals at both Devonport and Station Pier in Melbourne.

On 25 November *Spirit of Tasmania* departed Devonport on a quick promotional trip to Hobart, arriving there on the morning of 26 November. The vessel berthed for several hours at Princes Wharf, then proceeded up the Derwent to anchor off the Bellerive Oval, where an international cricket match was being played.

In the late afternoon of 26 November *Spirit of Tasmania* left Hobart for the return voyage to Devonport, arriving there the following

*Spirit of Tasmania* in the Derwent River on 26 November 1993 (Rex Cox photo)

morning. *Abel Tasman* continued in service until the evening of Saturday, 27 November, when both *Spirit of Tasmania* and *Abel Tasman* departed Devonport for Melbourne. Only *Abel Tasman* was carrying passengers, and berthed at Station Pier Inner East just after 8am.

As soon as *Abel Tasman* had disembarked her final passengers and vehicles, a group of TT Line guests boarded the vessel, which left the dock at 9.30am and steamed out into Port Phillip Bay to meet the incoming *Spirit of Tasmania*, making its maiden arrival in Melbourne.

The two vessels steamed towards Port Melbourne together, and *Spirit of Tasmania* berthed alongside Station Pier Inner East at 10.50 am. At the same time *Abel Tasman* went alongside Station Pier Inner West. Having been withdrawn from service, the vessel was laid up and offered for sale.

*Spirit of Tasmania* made her first commercial

*Abel Tasman* and *Spirit of Tasmania* together in Devonport on 27 November (Dale Crisp photo)

*Abel Tasman* (above) going out to greet the arriving *Spirit of Tasmania* (below) (Lindsay Rex photos)

*Abel Tasman* and *Spirit of Tasmania* in Port Phillip Bay (Lindsay Rex photo)

departure from Melbourne on the night of Monday, 29 November. Next day *Abel Tasman* was moved back to the Inner East pier for several hours to be destored, then returned to the Inner West berth.

*Spirit of Tasmania* initially operated to the same schedule as had *Abel Tasman*, with 6pm departures from each terminal, completing the crossing in fourteen hours. Departures from Melbourne were on Monday, Wednesday and Friday, the return trip from Devonport leaving on Tuesday, Thursday and Sunday.

In Melbourne *Spirit of Tasmania* always berthed bow in, while in Devonport it berthed stern first, enabling a drive-through system to be operated for vehicles. The vessel would stay overnight in Devonport on Saturday.

However, from 5 February 1994 a new schedule was introduced, under which *Spirit of Tasmania* would leave Devonport on the Saturday night, berthing in Melbourne on Sunday morning, and remaining there overnight.

With the introduction of the new ship came a number of innovations, including improved boarding procedures. Instead of needing keys, cabin doors were opened by plastic cards, which were handed over to passengers when they checked in at the terminal, and no cash deposit was required, as had been the case with keys on *Abel Tasman*.

Passengers were handed a small guide to the layout of the ship, which also listed the opening hours of the various facilities on board. Although the ship did not depart until 6 pm, boarding could be made any time after 3 pm, and many of

A fireboat welcome for *Spirit of Tasmania* on 28 November 1993 (Lindsay Rex photo)

the on-board facilities, including the shop and casino, would open at 3.30 pm.

The accommodation provided was of a very high standard, equal to that offered on many modern cruise liners, comprising 1,323 berths in 489 cabins plus the hostel quarters. All cabins except the hostel accommodation had private facilities.

There were 16 suites on C deck, and 45 deluxe cabins, all fitted with a double bed, on C, D and E decks. A further 424 cabins with either two or four berths were spread over six decks, of which 198 had a porthole. For passengers in the suites and deluxe cabins there was a special lounge, the 1642 Club, reserved for their use, with access only by use of their cabin entry card.

The public rooms were all renamed with a Tasmanian theme, such as the Huon Room, Leatherwood Lounge, Freycinet Room and Devil's Kitchen. The *Taroona*, Nairana and Princess of Tasmania meeting rooms were all named after former Bass Strait ferries.

The former supermarket was converted into a large Visitor Centre, with displays and information about Tasmania. The only drawback was a lack of seating on the open decks, and limited open areas offering a forward view, apart from the deck above the bridge, which was always crowded with passengers at departures and arrivals.

In April 1994 *Abel Tasman* was sold to Ventouris Group Enterprises, for $24.7 million (US$17.4 million). The price was the subject of much criticism, as many experts believed it was far less than the vessel was worth.

Placed under the nominal ownership of Delba Maritime SA, and registered in Greece, the vessel was renamed *Pollux*, under which name it departed Melbourne on 30 April 1994 for a new career in the Mediterranean.

*Pollux* departing Melbourne (Dale Crisp photo)

In late May 1994, *Pollux* was placed on a regular ferry service between Igoumenitsa in Greece and the Italian port of Bari. However, in March 1995 the vessel changed hands again, being purchased by another Greek operator, Lesvos Shipping Co. Handed over to them in May, the vessel was renamed *Theofilos*, and began operating from Piraeus to the islands of Lesvos and Chios.

As with her predecessors, *Spirit of Tasmania* was occasionally affected by bad weather while crossing Bass Strait. On the night of 25 May 1994 the vessel ran into very rough seas after leaving Port Phillip Bay, and on arriving off Devonport next morning was forced to steam in circles off the coast awaiting a break in the weather.

During the day three attempts to enter the

mouth of the River Mersey were aborted, and it was only at the fourth attempt that the vessel finally was able to enter the river, not tying up at the Devonport Terminal until 6 pm.

This late arrival delayed the departure of the return trip, and the vessel did not berth in Melbourne until 2.45 pm on 27 May. Her departure from Melbourne that evening was two hours behind schedule, but then she was able to return to her regular schedule.

With *Spirit of Tasmania* remaining in Melbourne on Sunday evening, it was decided to experiment with occasional Sunday evening cruises around Port Phillip Bay. The first of these operated on 22 May 1994, departing Station Pier shortly after 6 pm, returning at 10 pm.

From January 1995 the departure time for these excursions was brought forward to 5.30 pm, with the vessel returning to Station Pier at 9.30pm, though the bars on board remained open until 10 pm.

Advertised as 'Sunset Bay Cruises', these excursions proved quite popular, and the fare included a meal on board. Three dining options were offered, the most expensive being a three course set meal in the Huon Room, which cost $75 per person. For $63 per person, there was a buffet provided in both the Promenade and Nauticals restaurants, which offered a choice of roasts, pasta, seafood, fresh salads and a variety of desserts.

The various bars on the vessel were also open throughout the cruise, and live entertainment provided as well as dancing. After leaving Station Pier, *Spirit of Tasmania* would follow the regular Port Melbourne shipping channel as far as the Fawkner Beacon off Brighton Beach, then proceed much closer to the eastern shore of Port Phillip Bay than large ships usually did. This provided interesting viewing from the ship, and also of the ship from the shore.

On Sunday, 24 July 1994 *Spirit of Tasmania* operated her first afternoon excursion around Port Phillip Bay, departing Station Pier at noon, returning at 4 pm. These daytime trips, which were operated occasionally during the latter part of 1994 and early 1995, included lunch on board, but did not prove as popular as the evening excursions.

The annual report of TT Line for the financial year from July 1993 to June 1994 showed that the company achieved a trading profit of $6.3 million, but sustained an overall loss of $573,000. This was primarily caused by a deduction of $4.4 million for depreciation of *Spirit of Tasmania* and $2.6 million for interest on borrowings to purchase the ship.

All in all this was an excellent result, as it was noted that on a month by month basis compared to *Abel Tasman*, since entering service *Spirit of Tasmania* was carrying 42 per cent more passengers, 41 per cent more vehicles and 36% more freight. It was expected that during 1994 the vessel would carry over 250,000 passengers, and contribute $45–50 million to the economy of Tasmania.

Despite the failure of the *SeaCat Tasmania* operation, and the growing success of *Spirit of Tasmania*, during the latter months of 1994 a new consortium was formed whose stated aim was to develop a faster, cheaper and more efficient service across Bass Strait.

The consortium spokesman was Mr Arthur Hayward, who had previously been involved in the Bass Strait Ferry Proposal Investigation Committee. He said that the Tasmanian Government should scrap the TT Line service to make way for two 95 m long vessels capable of 30 knots operating daily return trips between Burnie and Hastings, in Western Port.

These monohull vessels would carry passengers, cars and light freight only, and the crews would not live on board, reducing overheads. In comparison to *Spirit of Tasmania*, which had a capacity of about 300,000 passengers annually, the proposed service would be able to carry 520,000 passengers. As had happened with so many other similar proposals, nothing further was heard of this project.

Early in 1995 a delegation from a group called the Committee for Bass Strait Transport Equality met with Federal Government officials requesting the provision of a $29 million subsidy to enable a second passenger ship to be placed in service between the mainland and northern Tasmania.

One member of the delegation, TT Line's General Manager Finance, Mr Brian McGuire, stated that his company was interested in adding a second ship provided they could secure the subsidy, as they already had all the necessary infrastructure in place. However, it was possible that the subsidy could be offered to a new company, but the proposal was not accepted by the Federal Government.

Despite this, there were reports that TT Line was actively seeking a second ferry. They were reported to be looking at the P & O Ferries sister vessels *Pride of Portsmouth* and *Pride of Le Havre*, both of 33,336 gross tons and built in 1990, which were operating across the English Channel between Portsmouth and Le Havre. It was even stated that if a suitable vessel were found and purchased it would be renamed Spirit of Bass Strait, and could operate at least once a week from Melbourne to Hobart in addition to a service to northern Tasmania.

*Spirit of Tasmania* continued to ply across Bass Strait through 1995, with the regularity of the service suffering only an occasional disruption, usually caused by bad weather. On Friday, 26 May 1995 *Spirit of Tasmania* arrived in Port Phillip Bay and was met by gale force winds, which caused major problems when the ship reached Station Pier.

By coincidence this happened exactly a year after a similar problem was encountered at Devonport. Three times the captain tried to bring his vessel alongside Station Pier, twice striking the berth hard, and on the third attempt almost being blown ashore on the nearby beach. *Spirit of Tasmania* then had to pull back into the bay and steam around for two hours until a tug was available, which assisted the vessel to berth shortly after 10 am.

On 23 July 1995 *Spirit of Tasmania* arrived in Melbourne on a regular trip from Devonport, but then left the same afternoon on a voyage to Newcastle, where it arrived on 25 July for drydocking and overhaul.

For the previous three weeks some contractors had been doing work on the ship in preparation for the overhaul, during which several major alterations were made to the interior. The cafeteria on E deck was enlarged and upgraded to become a 350-seat buffet restaurant, while the entrance foyers were also upgraded and refurbished. The Galactica teenagers centre was moved from its original position on E deck to the former Admiral's poker machine area on C deck, these machines being repositioned next to the Tiger Bar.

*Spirit of Tasmania* was refloated on 11 August, leaving Newcastle the same day and returning to Melbourne on 13 August. The vessel resumed its schedule on the Bass Strait trade on the night of 14 August.

Unlike previous drydocking trips by *Abel Tasman*, *Spirit of Tasmania* did not carry passengers on either of these voyages. During the period *Spirit of Tasmania* was away there were no passenger services across Bass Strait.

For some years there had been a vocal group of Devonport residents who wanted to have the Bass Strait ferry terminal moved from the east side of the River Mersey to the western side, where the city was located. This was raised again late in 1995, and brought the same response from the port authorities. The proposal had been examined several times in the past, and abandoned due to the lack of a suitable site.

Over the summer months of 1995/96 *Spirit of Tasmania* was able to provide accommodation for almost all the people wishing to travel across Bass Strait. During December 1995 *Spirit of Tasmania* carried its 500,000th paying passenger since being introduced on the Bass Strait trade.

As usual there were several weeks around the Christmas/New Year period and at the end of the January school holidays when the ship was full on every departure, and also had a lengthy waiting list for any last minute cancellations. Those unable to secure a booking voiced the usual complaints about the lack of a second vessel on the run, but from an economic standpoint it was simply not practical to have a second ship on anything more than a temporary basis.

This did not deter other groups from coming up with proposals for new services between the mainland and Tasmania. In April 1996 a Melbourne consortium announced plans to place a 24-knot 'Superflyte' type catamaran ferry on the Bass Strait trade.

The consortium claimed it was already negotiating with the Western Australia shipbuilder, Wavemaster, to build the vessel they required, which would carry 296 passengers and make the crossing from Melbourne to Devonport in 9½ hours.

A short while later the same group announced they had changed their plans, and now intended to have Wavemaster build them a fast, 55 m long monohull vessel, which would be ready to enter service in January 1997. This vessel would be able to carry 340 passengers, but no cars.

*Spirit of Tasmania* in the Newcastle Floating Dock (Peter Plowman photo)

However, their attempts to obtain the use of the TT Line terminal at Devonport were thwarted, so they would have to operate to another port, with Burnie the most likely choice. After this, all further reference to the service and the vessel ceased.

In August 1996 there were reports that another company, calling itself Oceania Cruise Line, had been registered in Victoria, and announced plans to operate a regular passenger and cargo service between Sydney and Bell Bay. The company was said to be negotiating the charter of an unnamed 20,000 gross ton ferry built in 1990, that would become available at the end of September, and could commence service from Sydney by the end of the year.

It would be able to carry up to 1,500 passengers, and be scheduled to operate two return trips a week, with an extra trip in the peak summer period. It was claimed the vessel would use a berth at Darling Harbour in Sydney, and the No 2 berth at Bell Bay, which was previously used by the now defunct Coastal Express Line. Yet again, this service did not eventuate.

In the 1995/96 financial year *Spirit of Tasmania* carried 216,919 passengers and 62,851 cars, but the overall operation recorded a loss of $5.2 million, again largely due to depreciation expenses on *Spirit of Tasmania*.

In September 1996, after considerable lobbying by the Tasmanian State Government, the Federal Government introduced the Bass Strait Passenger Vehicle subsidy scheme. Under the scheme, passenger-accompanied vehicles would attract a Commonwealth Government rebate. This enabled TT Line to reduce the charge for carrying passenger's vehicles to as little as $25 per voyage, depending on the size of the vehicle and the time of year.

This change resulted in an increase in demand for vehicle spaces, the effect of which wrought quite a startling change in the financial returns for TT Line. Their results for the 1996/97 financial year showed a profit of $2.5 million. During the year, *Spirit of Tasmania* crossed Bass Strait 313

*Spirit of Tasmania* departing Devonport (Rex Cox photo)

*Stern*     *Bow*

| | A Deck |
|---|---|
| | B Deck |
| 'Tiger Lounge' Conference Centre | 'Admiral's Casino' | Foyer | Cabins | C Deck |
| 'Nauticals' '1642 Club' 'Huon Room' 'Leatherwood Lounge' | Foyer | Cabins | D Deck |
| 'Galactica' 'Bass Strait Diner' 'The Ship's Photographer' 'Allders On Board' 'Visitor Centre' | Reception | Foyer | Cabins | E Deck |
| | Cabins | Entrance | Cabins | Car Deck | F Deck |
| Cabins | Cabins | G Deck |
| | Level Vehicle Deck | H Deck |
| Cabins | J Deck |
| Pool | Gym | Saunas | Hostels | K Deck |

## C Deck (Cabin number C100 – C180)

Conference Centre

Foyer

Tiger Lounge     Admiral's Casino

## D Deck (Cabin number D200 – D296)

Nauticals     1642 Club     Leatherwood Lounge

Kitchen

Foyer

Huon Room

▢ **Suites**    ▢ **Deluxe**    ▢ **Porthole**    ▢ **Family**    ▢ **Hostel**

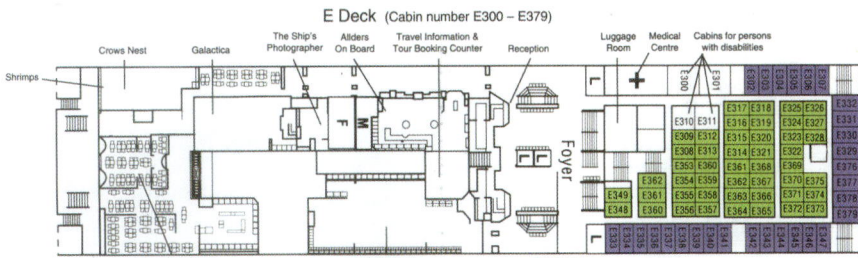

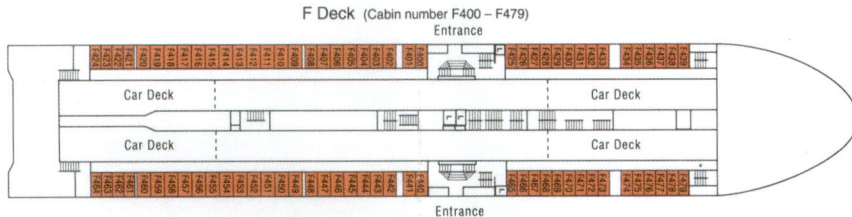

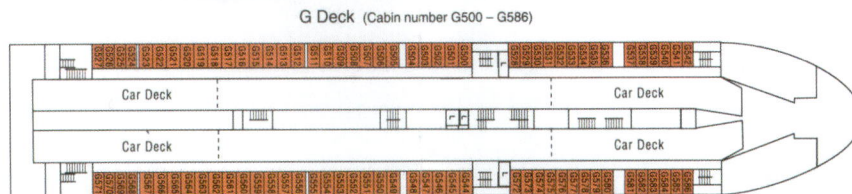

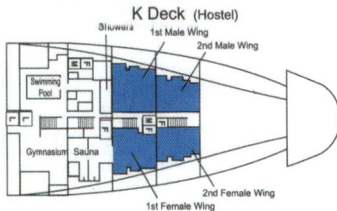

## E Deck (Cabin number E300 – E379)

Crows Nest    Galactica    The Ship's Photographer    Allders On Board    Travel Information & Tour Booking Counter    Reception    Luggage Room    Medical Centre    Cabins for persons with disabilities

Shrimps

Foyer

Bass Strait Diner    Visitor Centre    Telephones

## F Deck (Cabin number F400 – F479)

Entrance

Car Deck     Car Deck

Car Deck     Car Deck

Entrance

## G Deck (Cabin number G500 – G586)

Car Deck     Car Deck

Car Deck     Car Deck

## J Deck (Cabin number J600 – J666)

## K Deck (Hostel)

Showers    1st Male Wing    2nd Male Wing

Swimming Pool

Gymnasium    Sauna

2nd Female Wing

1st Female Wing

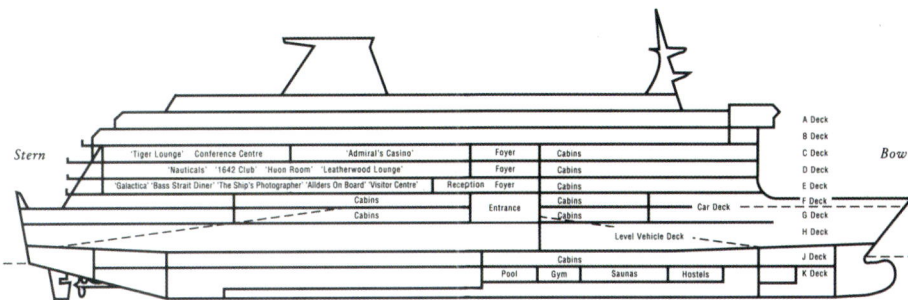

times, with passenger numbers increasing by 20 per cent, to 259,169, while the number of cars carried, 80,462, was an increase of 28% over the previous year.

On Saturday, 12 July 1997, *Spirit of Tasmania* arrived in Devonport as usual, but once all the passengers, cars and freight had been unloaded, was taken off the Bass Strait service for two weeks. The vessel departed Devonport on 13 July for Sydney, to undergo her biannual drydocking and overhaul in the Captain Cook Dry Dock at the Australian Defence Industries facility at Garden Island.

This was to be the first time the vessel visited Sydney, where she was due to arrive on the morning of 15 July, and go straight into the drydock. However, the cruise liner *Fair Princess* had been placed in the Captain Cook Dry Dock on 9 July for urgent repair work, and was due to be refloated on the afternoon of 14 July.

At the last moment this was changed to early in the morning of Tuesday, 15 July. On that day *Spirit of Tasmania* arrived in Sydney Harbour on schedule on a very foggy morning, but had to wait off Fort Denison until *Fair Princess* had been refloated.

When the time came for *Fair Princess* to be

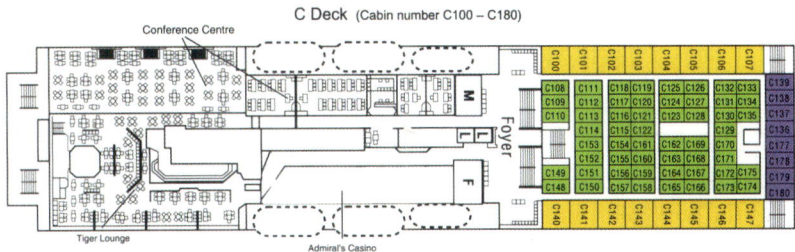

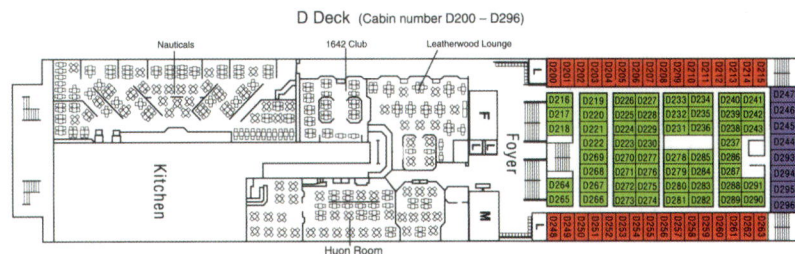

*Spirit of Tasmania* arriving in Sydney to enter the Captain Cook Dock (Ian Edwards photo)

removed from the dock, the liner suffered a total loss of power, and could not use its winches to pull in the lines attached to the shore. Eventually these were hauled in by hand, and two tugs were called upon to move the ship out of the Captain Cook Dock to the east wall berth. With *Fair Princess* safely berthed, *Spirit of Tasmania* was finally able to enter the Captain Cook Dock.

However, while *Spirit of Tasmania* was out of service, TT Line took the opportunity to operate a series of experimental voyages across Bass Strait using a fast catamaran ferry. This would enable TT Line to conduct their own feasibility study on the use of such a vessel on the trade.

Officially named *Incat 045*, but advertised as *Tascat*, the vessel was built to a new and larger design. This made it much more stable than *SeaCat Tasmania*, the fast catamaran that had previously operated across Bass Strait between 1990 and 1993. *Incat 045* was launched on 3 July 1997 in an almost complete state, ran trials a few days later, and was ready for service within a week.

*Incat 045* measured 5,007 gross tonnes, and was 86.6 m/285 feet long and 26 m/85 feet wide. It was powered by four Ruston diesel engines driving water jets on each hull, providing a top speed of 48 knots, though the usual service speed was about 43 knots. It could carry 900 passengers, all in non-reclining seats, and had garage space for up to 136 vehicles.

When operating as *Tascat* it was scheduled to make a single one-way trip each day during daylight only, departing at 10.30 am, and making the crossing in 5½ hours. The inaugural crossing was from Devonport to Melbourne on 13 July, with the first trip from Melbourne operating the following day.

Both these trips went well, but two hours after departing Devonport on 15 July, *Tascat* encountered such rough seas that the vessel was unable to make any headway. The captain decided to abandon the trip, and turned back to Devonport. Most passengers and even some of the crew were laid low by severe bouts of seasickness, and thirty cars on the vehicle deck suffered minor damage during the storm.

Later in the day the weather calmed down, and *Tascat* was able to depart again, though without 20 per cent of the passengers who had been booked to travel that day. They were not prepared to remain on the vessel and brave the vagaries of Bass Strait again.

The next day, 16 July, the departure of *Tascat* from Melbourne was delayed for two hours by engine trouble, and on 23 July the craft had to abort its voyage and return to Melbourne due to more engine trouble. *Tascat* made its final crossing of Bass Strait on Sunday 27 July, from Devonport to Melbourne, and subsequently returned to Hobart.

*Incat 045,* was operated across Bass Strait by TT Line as *Tascat* for two weeks in July 1995 (Lindsay Rex photo)

Despite special discounted fares being offered during the fast ferry trial period, bad publicity as a result of the abandoned trip from Devonport caused passengers to stay away, and loadings were far less than had been anticipated.

On its fourteen crossings of Bass Strait, when 12,600 seats were available, *Tascat* carried only 3,365 passengers, an average of 240 per trip. The best loading was 307 passengers, while only 151 were carried on the final trip. With an overall capacity for about 1,900 vehicles over the two weeks, on several northbound trips the full capacity of 136 was achieved, and altogether 1,601 vehicles were carried.

*Tascat* was returned to her builders, and remained in Hobart until June 1999, when the vessel was chartered to the Royal Australian Navy for two years. Repainted in naval grey, it was commissioned on 10 June as HMAS Jervis Bay, pennant number 45. This was the same

*Incat 045* as HMAS *Jervis Bay* (Ian Edwards photo)

name given to the former Bass Strait ferry *Australian Trader* when it was purchased by the Royal Australian Navy in 1977.

The vessel was used extensively to support Australian troops stationed in East Timor, operating a regular service between Darwin and Dili, a passage time of eleven hours. In all Jervis Bay made 107 trips, carrying over 20,000 passengers and 430 military vehicles.

When the navy charter ended in 2001, the craft was sent to Italy, and began operating a ferry service from Genoa to Sardinia under the name *Winner*, showing the enormous versatility of these vessels. In 2003 the craft was sent to Britain, but did not enter service until 19 May 2004, when it began operating across the English Channel as *SpeedOne*, operating five round trips

daily between Dover and Boulogne for a new company, SpeedFerries.

*Spirit of Tasmania* came out of the Captain Cook Dock in Sydney as scheduled on Friday 25 July. The vessel headed straight back to Melbourne, to resume her regular service with a departure on Monday, 28 July.

The vessel also continued to operate occasional cruises on Port Phillip Bay on Sunday evenings. Some of these were advertised as a 'Themed Cruise Night', which included an AFL Grand Final Cruise on 28 September, Legends Cruise on 19 October and a Melbourne Cup Eve Cruise on 2 November.

*Spirit of Tasmania* was adequate to meet the needs of the route for much of the year, but the peak summer months still presented the problem of insufficient accommodation. To try and alleviate this during the summer of 1997/98, TT Line decided to introduce an extra return trip across Bass Strait at the weekend from 14 December 1997 to 24 January 1998, instead of the ship remaining in Melbourne from Sunday morning to Monday night.

This involved a number of changes to the existing schedule. *Spirit of Tasmania* would leave Devonport at 4 pm on Saturday afternoons, carrying passengers and their cars only, but no freight, arriving in Melbourne at 5 am Sunday. It would then have a very quick turnaround, leaving Melbourne at 9 am on the return trip, again with just passengers and cars, arriving in Devonport at 10 pm.

This offered the first daylight crossing of Bass Strait by a large passenger ferry for many years, and it proved very popular with passengers. The vessel would then depart Devonport at 2am on the Monday morning, arriving in Melbourne at 3 pm that afternoon, with the ship then departing at 8 pm, arriving in Devonport at 9am on Tuesday, and resuming its regular schedule for the rest of the week.

At the same time, TT Line caused quite a surprise when they announced that they would also be operating a fast catamaran ferry service across Bass Strait during the 1997/98 summer season, which would be commencing in mid-December 1997.

# Chapter Nineteen

# The Devil Cats

Considering the apparent lack of success enjoyed by TT Line when they operated *Incat 045* under the name *Tascat* between Melbourne and Devonport for two weeks during the winter of 1997, it came as quite a surprise that the company was prepared to again operate a fast catamaran service across Bass Strait during the summer of 1997/98.

Despite strong lobbying from Port Welshpool to be the mainland terminal, it was decided the summer service would operate from Station Pier at Melbourne. However, instead of going to Devonport, the service would use the former *SeaCat Tasmania* terminal at George Town, near the mouth of the River Tamar. At 227 nautical miles, this would be the longest non-stop open sea fast ferry route then being operated in the world.

The service was to be maintained by *Incat 046*, another vessel chartered from International Catamarans at Hobart. Built as their 22nd high speed fast catamaran ferry, it was the first of a new series of larger vessels, being 5,617 gross tonnes and 91.3 m/300 feet long, though still 26 m/85 feet wide.

The design of these fast catamaran ferries had been increasingly refined and improved by Incat over fifteen years of experience. The latest craft had a restyled steel hull form that maximised speed and efficiency while providing increased ride comfort for the passengers. The superstructure was constructed of aluminium.

The new design was characterised by long, slender waterborne hulls, each subdivided into eight watertight compartments, with very little buoyancy at the bow. To enable the hulls to pierce through the waves rather than ride over them, at the bow they were only 10 per cent immersed and contained 10 per cent reserve buoyancy.

*Incat 046* in Devil Cat colours shortly after being launched (Incat)

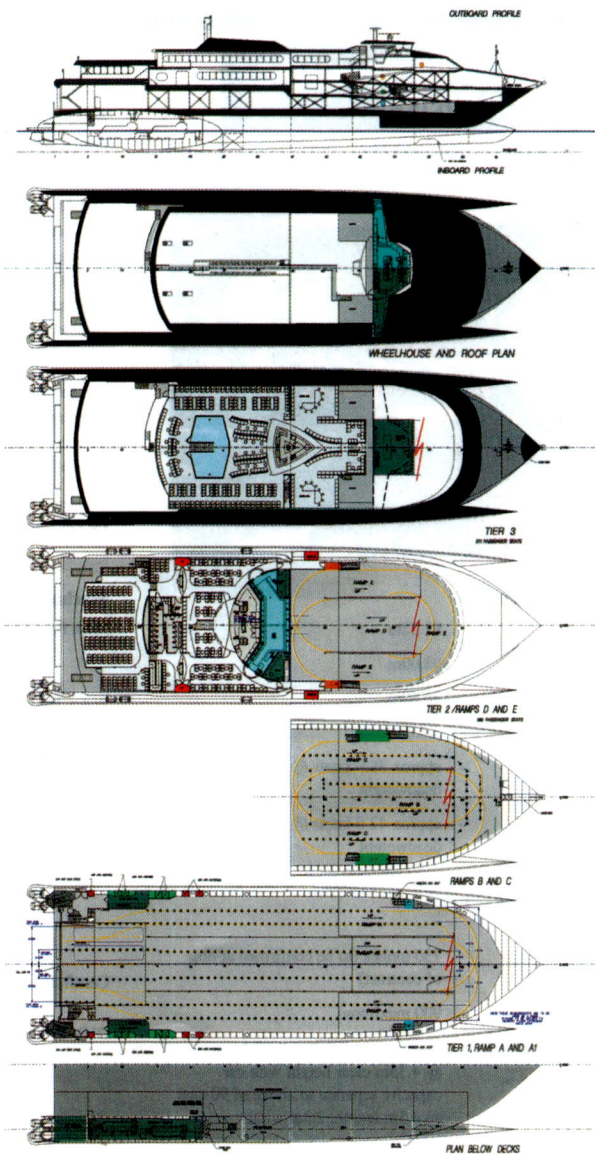

Deck plan of *Incat 046*

*Incat 046* at Hobart (Nancy Jacobs photo - Dale Crisp collection)

Interior view of *Incat 046* at Hobart (Dale Crisp photo)

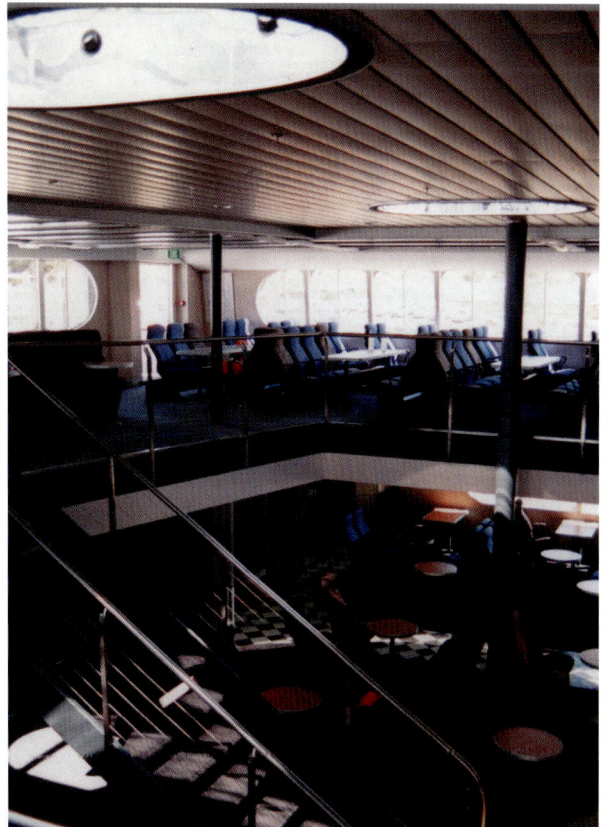

Interior view of *Incat 046* at Hobart (Dale Crisp photo)

The remaining 80 per cent reserve buoyancy was held in the forward central hull, located above the loaded smooth water line. This resulted in a very versatile hull form which was sympathetic to a safe, smooth ride in all weather and sea conditions.

*Incat 046* had the same power plant as previous vessels, four Ruston 20 RK270 conventional medium speed diesel engines, which each could develop 9,500 hp, or 7,080 kW. Each engine drove a transom mounted waterjet through a Renk reduction gearbox. The vessel had a maximum speed of about 48 knots with a service speed of 41 knots.

Non-reclining seating was provided for 877 passengers, and there was garage space for 240 vehicles.

Launched on 20 September 1997, *Incat 046* began running trials on the weekend of 11/12 October. The appearance of the vessel was quite startling, as it was painted black, with the eyes, ears, whiskers and paws of a cat at the bow, and was advertised as the *Devil Cat*.

The vessel was scheduled to make a single one-way crossing of Bass Strait on alternate days to the departures from either end by *Spirit of Tasmania*, being scheduled to complete the trip in about six hours.

*Devil Cat* would depart Melbourne at 1pm on Tuesday, Thursday and Saturday, returning from George Town at 1pm on Wednesday, Friday, and Sunday, with Monday spent alongside in Melbourne.

*Devil Cat* was handed over to TT Line in Hobart on 15 December, and made its first crossing from George Town to Melbourne on 17 December.

To keep passengers occupied during the trip, a variety of movies was shown on television monitors located in all the accommodation areas. Children's videos were screened in the designated children's area, on the lower deck, which also had a limited range of toys and cots.

A selection of snacks, beverages, magazines and newspapers was available for purchase from a canteen, and there were also several vending machines. The *Devil Cat* Bar, located on the upper deck, was a comfortable place to enjoy a quiet drink and watch the world rush by. However, there was no access to an outside deck.

During the summer period the waters of Bass Strait tend to be smoother, and *Devil Cat* was usually able to arrive either on time or close to the scheduled time. On some trips the sea was quite rough and speed had to be reduced, causing a late arrival, and occasionally the problem of passengers becoming very seasick.

The Maritime Safety Authority decided they would not allow *Devil Cat* to carry passengers when wave heights exceeded four metres in Bass Strait, and during late March 1998 several crossings were cancelled because waves were in excess of that height.

This created a buildup of passengers and vehicles, so *Spirit of Tasmania* made a special trip from Melbourne to Devonport during daylight on Sunday, 29 March, returning overnight from Devonport, berthing in Melbourne at 1.55pm on 30 March.

On the whole TT Line considered the fast ferry service operated with reasonable success during the summer period, though at a financial loss. The extra vessel greatly alleviated the shortage of accommodation on Bass Strait during the peak weeks around Christmas and the New Year.

*Devil Cat* completed its final trip for the season, from Melbourne to George Town, on Saturday, 18 April 1998. However, advance bookings were so high for the start of the off-peak season, that *Spirit of Tasmania* was scheduled to operate extra sailings for the next three weekends, following the same schedule as in December/January.

The first of these extra weekend trips was operated from Devonport on 25 April, with the last being operated on 10 May. The vessel then reverted to three return trips a week, with a Sunday night layover in Melbourne.

From the first weekend in February 1998, *Spirit of Tasmania* had operated a series of Sunday Bay Cruises, departing Station Pier at 5.30pm, returning at 9.30pm. These proved so popular that all nine cruises operated in February, March and April were fully booked.

During May two more Sunday cruises were operated, with three in June and two each in July and August, but only one in September. During both October and November there were a further three Sunday cruises, but after the trip on 6 December the programme of Sunday cruises was terminated until February 1999.

Meanwhile, having finished its charter to TT Line, *Devil Cat* had returned to Hobart on 19 April 1998 for an overhaul, before embarking on a long ocean voyage.

The vessel had been chartered to a Canadian firm, Bay Ferries, and it was originally stated it would be used on a service between St Johns, Newfoundland, and Prince Edward Island.

Bay Ferries had the option to extend the original six-month charter if they wished, or purchase the vessel outright at the end of the charter. Departing Hobart on 25 April, the delivery voyage to Canada was made via New Zealand, Tahiti and the Panama Canal.

A two-day stopover was also included at Fort Eustace, a United States military base near Washington, DC. The vessel was inspected by representatives from the United States Army, Navy and Air Force, as well as the Marines and Coast Guard. This gave them an opportunity to assess the potential of these Australian-built craft to operate as fast carriers of military equipment and troops.

When the vessel, still officially named *Incat 046*, did enter service in Canada, it retained its black and grey colour scheme, and was advertised as *The Cat*. It was placed on a route across the Bay of Fundy, operating a summer service between Yarmouth, Nova Scotia and Bar Harbor, in Maine, reducing the crossing time to 2 hours 45 minutes, compared to 6 hours by a conventional ferry.

Shortly after commencing this service, *The Cat* encountered some unusual problems. Local boat owners lodged complaints about the speed at which the craft was operating when close to Bar Harbor. This followed an incident in which two persons were injured when the wake of *The Cat* hit their small boat so hard they were flung into the air and had to be hospitalised.

Bay Ferries were sufficiently impressed by the vessel they decided to purchase it outright when the six-month charter period ended.

Having completed its season of operation across the Bay of Fundy, *The Cat* was moved south for the winter, to operate a new service from Miami to the Bahamas. The vessel made two round trips a day, the destination on four days each week being Nassau, which took five hours each way. On the other three days of the week the destination was Freeport, for which the crossing time was only 2 hours 30 minutes. *The Cat* remained on this service until April 1999, then returned to the Bay of Fundy route.

During 1998 International Catamarans in Hobart had commenced construction as a speculative venture of the first of an even larger design of fast catamaran. However, this craft would have a smaller passenger capacity than previous catamarans, enabling an increase in vehicle and cargo capacity.

In June 1998 two of the companies involved in the freight trade between the mainland and Tasmania were reported to have expressed interest in the craft. At the same time a consortium that included Burnie City Council was also said to be looking at the project.

Ultimately neither of these groups took the matter any further, but TT Line decided they would take the new craft on charter for the coming summer season of 1998/99. Built as hull number 050, it was 96 m/315 feet long, and measured 5,029 gross tons.

Unlike previous vessels built by Incat, it was powered by four Caterpillar 3618 marine diesels driving four Lips 150D waterjets, giving a service speed of about 45 knots. Launched on 7 November 1998, the vessel was completed on 21 November, then underwent sea trials, following which some minor modifications were made.

Meanwhile, prior to the start of the summer holiday season, some modifications were also made to the vehicle decks of *Spirit of Tasmania*, at a cost of $300,000. This resulted in space being provided for an additional 50 cars, bringing the vessel's capacity up to 355 cars and 35 trucks.

As the vehicle deck capacity was usually filled before the passenger accommodation, the increased vehicle space brought about a general increase in revenue for TT Line, and soon offset the cost of the modifications.

The new fast catamaran was handed over to TT Line on 10 December, and although officially named *Incat 50*, was also given the trading name *Devil Cat*. This second *Devil Cat* was not as brightly painted as its predecessor, being mostly grey, with *The Cat* face at the bow.

This vessel could only carry a maximum of 570 passengers, but had space for 220 cars and a number of large trucks on the vehicle decks.

The new *Devil Cat* commenced service across Bass Strait on 12 December 1998, from George Town to Melbourne. However, the schedule organised for the summer was different to that of the previous year.

During the peak holiday season, *Devil Cat* made a daily return trip between George Town and Melbourne from Tuesday to Sunday, double that of the previous summer.

At other times the return trips were operated on Saturday and Sunday only, with one way trips from Tuesday to Friday. The craft would layover in George Town on Mondays for maintenance.

The fares charged were the same as for the standard cabin accommodation on *Spirit of Tasmania*. *Devil Cat* was able to operate most trips on schedule, though again the occasional days of rough seas caused problems, but no trips were cancelled.

*Incat 050* operating as *Devil Cat* (Richard Bennett photo—courtesy Incat)

With *Devil Cat* operating an increased number of voyages, it was not necessary for *Spirit of Tasmania* to make an extra return trip at the weekends, apart from Sunday, 27 December, when *Spirit of Tasmania* departed Melbourne at noon, returning next day at 4.30pm. On most other weekends the vessel operated Sunday evening excursions on Port Phillip Bay during the summer months.

Incat 050 completed its final trip for TT Line on 18 April 1999, then returned to the International Catamarans facility in Hobart the following day.

After the second *Devil Cat* completed its charter to TT Line in April 1999, advance bookings for the start of the off-peak period were so heavy, *Spirit of Tasmania* was scheduled to operate an extra weekend round trip from 25

The unusual stern arrangement of *Devil Cat* (Lindsay Rex photo)

April for the next seven weekends, to 13 June. The vessel then reverted to three round trips per week.

By the time Incat 050 was returned to International Catamarans, they had arranged another charter for the vessel. This was with a New Zealand firm called Fast Cat Ferries Ltd, previously known as Sea Shuttles New Zealand Ltd.

*Devil Cat* passes inbound *Spirit of Tasmania* in Port Phillip Bay, with cruise ship *Silver Cloud* in the background (Andrew Mackinnon photo)

*Spirit of Tasmania* passing through the Rip on 27 December 1998 (Andrew Mackinnon photo)

After an overhaul in Hobart, Incat 050 was renamed *Top Cat*, and crossed the Tasman Sea, calling at Dunedin and Lyttelton prior to arriving in Wellington on 30 April 1999. It began operating under the banner of Fast Cat Ferries on 12 May from Waterloo Quay in Wellington to Picton, in direct competition with the service operated by TranzRail.

This comprised two conventional ferries and the fast catamaran *Condor 10*, built by Incat in Hobart as hull number 030, which was trading as *The Lynx*. At first *Top Cat* carried rather plain grey colours, but in December 1999 the forward sections of each hull had Maori *taniwha*, or 'water guardians', painted on them in symbolic form.

On 20 July 2000 *Top Cat* arrived at Newcastle for an overhaul, leaving on 2 August to return to New Zealand, where it remained in service until 3 November, when the service ended for financial reasons.

*Top Cat* departed Wellington on 4 November 2000 to return to Hobart, where it was again offered for charter or sale. On 24 July 2001 the craft was chartered to the United States military for extensive evaluation and testing, being renamed *HSV-X1 Joint Venture*.

A large section of the original passenger accommodation area towards the stern was removed to make way for the installation of a helo-deck, capable of accommodating large military helicopters. Internal alterations and modifications were also made to suit the transportation of up to 500 combat troops with all their equipment.

The vessel departed Hobart on 11 September 2001 for the United States, but after a brief period of testing was called upon to join the fight against terrorism. Crewed by US Navy personnel, the vessel was deployed to the Persian Gulf early in 2003.

Just hours after Operation Iraqi Freedom began, *Joint Venture* sped into the shallow waters near the southern Iraqi port of Umm Qasr, acting as an afloat forward staging base for Marine Fleet Anti-Terrorism Security Teams and US Navy SEAL commandos.

*Joint Venture* returned to the International Catamarans shipyard at Hobart on 14 August 2003 for a period of scheduled maintenance, then was handed over to the US Army for further evaluation testing. The craft returned again to Hobart in January 2004 for further maintenance, then went back to the United States.

On Saturday, 17 July 1999, *Spirit of Tasmania* departed Devonport on its second trip to Sydney, arriving there on 19 July and entering the Captain Cook Dock for her biannual overhaul. The vessel was refloated on 2 August, and left immediately for Melbourne, resuming service on 4 August from Melbourne.

During the period *Spirit of Tasmania* was off the run there was no passenger service between the mainland and Tasmania.

In September 1999 there was another period of heavy advance bookings, so once again *Spirit of Tasmania* was scheduled to operate the extra weekend round trip, for five weeks commencing on 4 September.

On the evening of Friday, 3 September, *Spirit of Tasmania* departed Melbourne as usual, but experienced some engine problems on the crossing to Devonport, though they were not considered serious at the time.

On the afternoon of 4 September, *Spirit of Tasmania* departed Devonport on schedule for the first of the extra weekend sailings, but soon after leaving port three of her four engines seized, and had to be shut down.

The vessel turned around and limped back on one engine to Devonport, where all passengers and vehicles had to be offloaded. An inspection by engineers revealed that massive damage had been caused to the machinery by a batch of contaminated fuel.

The supplier of the fuel insisted that samples taken when the fuel was delivered to the ship did not show any sign of contamination, and other customers supplied from the same batch of fuel had not reported any problems.

An intensive independent inquiry began into how the fuel had become contaminated, but produced no conclusive finding. While sabotage could not be ruled out, there was no reason to suspect the breakdown was the result of a deliberate act to delay the vessel.

The sudden withdrawal from service of *Spirit of Tasmania* disrupted the travel plans of about 10,000 booked passengers. TT Line assisted passengers who were most drastically immediately affected, such as those requiring essential and emergency travel, by transferring them to commercial or chartered flights.

Other passengers, including those travelling without vehicles, were given a full refund of their passage fare and flown to their destinations, when seats were available. Qantas assisted by offering discounts of more than 30 per cent to passengers who were booked on the vessel. Passengers booked to take their vehicle with them had to have their passages cancelled.

An arrangement was quickly finalised by TT Line to charter the fast catamaran ferry *Condor 10*, which had been operating across Cook Strait in New Zealand and was laid up in Wellington, but it could not begin the service until the morning of 12 September.

To assist passengers who had been booked to take their cars with them on *Spirit of Tasmania*, TT Line chartered the car carrier *Turandot* to make a special return trip across Bass Strait, carrying vehicles only, while the passengers would have to fly.

Owned by Wallenius Lines of Sweden, the 55,598 gross ton *Turandot* was built in South Korea in 1995, and could carry up to 5,850 cars in its capacious vehicle decks, with access through ramps at the stern and along the side of the vessel. *Turandot* was engaged in a regular service bringing new cars to Australia from European countries, and arrived in Melbourne on 8 September, berthing at Appleton Dock.

When it had completed discharging cars destined for Melbourne, *Turandot* moved on 9 September to the Station Pier Outer East berth, where the cars to be carried to Tasmania were driven on board. *Turandot* departed Melbourne on 11 September for Devonport.

Car carrier *Turandot* was chartered for a return trip to Tasmania (Alan Travers collection)

*Condor 10* at Station Pier on 11 September, with *Turandot* berthed ahead (Dale Crisp photo)

After the cars from Melbourne had been discharged, *Turandot* took on board another consignment of cars to be carried back to the mainland. *Turandot* arrived back in Melbourne on 12 September, again berthing at Station Pier Outer East, remaining there overnight.

As soon as the last cars from Tasmania were driven off on the morning of 13 September, *Turandot* departed to continue its regular voyage to Sydney, though now running four days behind its original schedule.

As *Turandot* carried no passengers, the owners of the cars had to fly across Bass Strait, and collect their cars once they had been off-loaded. The Bass Strait service was then temporarily taken over by *Condor 10*.

Built by International Catamarans in Hobart, *Condor 10* was hull number 030, one of their early series of fast catamaran ferries, and a sister vessel of *SeaCat Tasmania*. *Condor 10* was 74.9 m/246 feet in length, with a beam of 26 m/85 feet, measuring 3,241 gross tons.

It was launched on 30 September 1992 and completed on 11 December 1992, and could accommodate 600 passengers and 84 vehicles. Fitted with four Ruston diesel engines driving waterjets, *Condor 10* had a top speed of 42 knots, but usually operated at 37 knots.

It was originally placed in service across the English Channel from Weymouth to the Channel Islands in March 1993 by Condor Line.

At the end of its 1994 English Channel season, *Condor 10* was chartered by the New Zealand operator Interisland Line, later renamed TranzRail. The vessel left Weymouth on 20 November 1994, voyaging by way of Valetta, Suez, Djibouti, Colombo, Cilacap, Darwin and Cairns to arrive in Wellington on 15 December.

On 21 December it began operating four trips a day between Wellington and Picton. Whilst engaged on this trade the craft was advertised under the name *The Lynx*, though it still carried *Condor 10* on the bow and stern.

*Condor 10* remained in New Zealand until April 1995, then returned to Britain for another season of service on the English Channel. In November 1995, *Condor 10* once again made the long trip back to New Zealand, but then remained on the Cook Strait service trading as *The Lynx* for the next four years.

During 1999 TranzRail suspended their fast catamaran service across Cook Strait, and *Condor 10* was laid up in Wellington. When the opportunity arose to use the vessel on Bass Strait, it was given a quick overhaul, then left Wellington on 9 September.

Arriving in Melbourne on 11 September, *Condor 10* went alongside Station Pier Inner East. *Condor 10* departed Melbourne on 12 September on its first trip to Devonport, then on 13 September made a morning trip back to Melbourne, leaving the same afternoon for Devonport. No trip was made on 14 September, but the next day *Condor 10* again made a trip to Melbourne and back to Devonport.

The vessel arrived back in Melbourne on

*Condor 10* at Station Pier (Dale Crisp photo)

16 September, but rough seas in Bass Strait prevented it returning to Devonport. The bad weather continued for several days, so it was not until 19 September that *Condor 10* again left Melbourne for Devonport.

On 20 September *Condor 10* was able to complete a trip from Devonport to Melbourne and return, and a return trip was operated on the following day. By then repairs to the engines on *Spirit of Tasmania* had been completed, so *Condor 10* was no longer required.

*Spirit of Tasmania* resumed service with a departure from Devonport on the evening of Tuesday, 21 September. The overall cost of the breakdown, including repairs to the machinery, lost revenue from cancelled trips, and charter costs for *Turandot* and *Condor 10*, amounted to $8.2 million, but after insurance had been claimed this was reduced to about $5.5 million.

*Condor 10* remained in Devonport for several days, then left for Hobart, arriving there on 25 September. With the charter arrangement in New Zealand ended, the vessel was given an overhaul at the International Catamarans facility, then laid up pending future employment, being offered either for sale or charter.

In the end the vessel remained idle in Hobart for several years before again being chartered for service in the English Channel, commencing in 2002. Since then the vessel has been operating between the Channel Islands and St Malo, in France.

The sudden withdrawal of *Spirit of Tasmania* for three weeks once more raised the question of whether the trade would be better serviced by having two smaller ferries, able to operate a daily service in each direction.

It was probably not surprising that at this time yet another potential competitor to TT Line on the Bass Strait trade resurfaced, reviving a proposal for a fast ferry service from Stony Point in Victoria to Burnie.

This was a much shorter route than that operated by the *Devil Cat* during the summer, and would enable a daily return trip to be operated on a regular basis. At the same time, it was reported that the Tasmanian Government was reconsidering the use of a fast ferry across Bass Strait during the summer months, following substantial losses incurred again in 1998/99 by the second *Devil Cat*, which had amounted to about $3 million.

However, the proposed abolition of the diesel fuel excise for ships as part of the Federal Government's tax reforms would result in a saving of roughly the same amount.

With this in mind, it was announced in September 1999 that TT Line would again be operating a fast catamaran service across Bass Strait for the summer of 1999/2000, and for the next two summers as well.

To operate the service, TT Line had signed a three-year agreement with Canadian operator Bay Ferries to charter their fast catamaran, *The Cat*, from December to April each year up to 2002.

This particular craft was originally named *Incat 045*, which had operated for TT Line across Bass Strait in the summer of 1997/98 as the first *Devil Cat*, and it would be advertised under that name while operating the service again.

Since leaving Australia the vessel had been engaged in a seasonal ferry service across the Bay of Fundy, which operated from May to October, and been laid up for the rest of the year, so it was an advantageous arrangement to both parties.

The one major problem encountered by the fast ferries crossing Bass Strait was the rough seas that could be experienced, sometimes without prior warning. To overcome this, TT Line considered placing a weather reporting buoy in the centre of Bass Strait to provide accurate and up-to-the-minute details of sea conditions. This would alleviate the number of times a fast ferry would have to slow down, or even return to port because of bad weather, or excessive wave heights.

Meanwhile, demand for passages across Bass Strait in the early spring of 1999 was so strong that *Spirit of Tasmania* was again scheduled to operate a number of extra return trips at the weekend. The first of these departed Melbourne on 26 September, with further trips being operated over the next two weekends, and again on 14 November. On other Sundays in November *Spirit of Tasmania* operated evening excursions on Port Phillip Bay.

On 18 November 1999 *The Cat* left Bar Harbor, Maine, carrying only a crew of 15, and arrived back in Hobart in early December. After an overhaul the vessel voyaged to George Town to commence its new service on 14 December, being scheduled to operate 126 trips during the summer season.

With its passenger capacity reduced to 740 passengers, *The Cat* operated between George Town and Melbourne throughout the summer. Unlike the previous year, the fast ferry made only three round trips per week, departing Melbourne at 8.30 am on Tuesday, Thursday and Saturday, returning from George Town at 2pm on Wednesday, Friday and Sunday, with a layover day in Melbourne on Mondays.

To meet the extra demand for passages, *Spirit of Tasmania* was scheduled to run extra weekend round trips on 5, 19 and 26 December, the first four Sundays in January 2000, and throughout February, March and April.

*The Cat* completed its final trip in the Bass Strait service on 24 April 2000, then after an overhaul in Hobart returned to North America, and its regular seasonal service across the Bay of Fundy.

However, demand for passages was still so strong that *Spirit of Tasmania* continued making extra weekend trips through May, the last extra trip being completed on 29 May.

The only unusual event for *Spirit of Tasmania* during 2000 occurred on the morning of 11 July, when the vessel arrived off the mouth of the River Mersey. Instead of proceeding up the river, *Spirit of Tasmania* turned in a large circle, then made her entry into the river mouth. This was done when the local port authority requested the vessel delay its entry so traffic within the port could be re-arranged.

During the year the vessel continued to operate occasional Sunday evening excursions on Port Phillip Bay. Passenger and vehicle loadings increased steadily, and from 3 September until 8

*The Cat* carried these colours while operating for TT Line in 1999/2000 (Lindsay Rex photos)   1917

October the extra weekend return trips were reintroduced, and again from 3 December, being operated every weekend to 27 May 2001.

For the 2000/01 summer season, *The Cat* returned again from Canada in early December. The vessel operated between George Town and Melbourne from 21 December to 16 April 2001, the return fare being reduced to $290 for passengers and $80 for cars.

During the peak period around Christmas and the New Year *The Cat* was scheduled to operate a return trip six days a week, reducing to a one-way trip six days a week at other times.

As in previous summer seasons the service was disrupted occasionally by bad weather, which delayed some trips, and in the 2000/01 season trips on five days had to be cancelled due to extreme weather conditions. However, a major mechanical problem resulted in considerable disruption to the service.

Early in January 2001 *The Cat* suffered a broken crankshaft in one of her four diesel engines, and until spare parts arrived from England, tried to continue operating on three engines, though this added up to ninety minutes to the crossing time. However, on 7 January, when the vessel was making a crossing from George Town to Melbourne, another engine had to be shut down.

Fortunately the sea was exceptionally calm, and the vessel completed the voyage on only two engines, travelling at less than half its usual speed. The 400 passengers did not reach their destination until 12.30am, three hours behind the already extended schedule. The latest problem was quickly rectified, and the vessel resumed service with three engines.

When the replacement parts for the fourth engine did arrive, the vessel was taken out of service from 29 January to 13 February while repairs were effected. This withdrawal affected the travel plans of several thousand booked passengers, but most of them were able to be transferred to *Spirit of Tasmania.*

On the evening of Friday, 23 February 2001, *Spirit of Tasmania* left Melbourne for Devonport at 6pm, carrying 967 passengers, 112 crew and 10 staff from licensed businesses. During the night, while the vessel was in the middle of Bass Strait, a fire broke out in the photographic shop on board.

The outbreak was detected about 1.30 am, and soon after all passengers were roused from their cabins and directed to emergency gathering stations in case it became necessary to abandon ship. Fortunately the fire was extinguished by crew members within half an hour, and passengers were then allowed to return to their cabins.

As inevitably happens in such instances, the media blew the entire episode out of all proportion, with television news showing interviews with passengers who likened the experience to the sinking of the Titanic. One man said he would fly back to the mainland and never travel by ship again. Comments by a TT Line spokesperson were barely referred to, though on one TV station the comments were played in full, and put the entire incident in proper context.

The vessel's schedule was not disrupted by the incident, as repairs were completed between voyages.

An inquiry into the fire was conducted by the Australian Maritime Safety Authority, whose report illustrated how well the crew coped with the situation. The report concluded that the crew had taken appropriate precautions, and the passengers had never been in any danger.

In August 2001 there were reports of another potential new service across Bass Strait. The Chairman of International Catamarans, Robert Clifford, announced that talks had taken place with an operator regarding the establishment of a year-round fast catamaran service between Victoria and Tasmania.

The proposed service would see a newly constructed Incat catamaran vessel operate a service with freight customers in mind, but also offering passenger accommodation. As with previous proposals, the use of George Town as the Tasmanian terminal was put forward, while the mainland terminal would be at either Port Welshpool or Stoney Point.

At the same time, the Tasmanian Government announced that, as the charter of *Devil Cat* would be terminating at the end of its 2001/02 summer season, TT Line had been asked to make a submission to government by the end of the year, listing their proposals and options for the 2002/03 summer season.

As subsequent events would pan out, the

service offered by TT Line in the summer of 2002/03 would be totally different to anything they had provided before, and effectively put a stop to any attempt to establish a rival passenger service across Bass Strait.

As planned, *The Cat* returned to Australia in early December 2001, making the passage from Canada to Tasmania in record time. *The Cat* set out on her 10,294 nautical miles passage to Hobart from Nova Scotia at 0630 hrs GMT on 13 November. Just 15 days, 2 hours and 30 minutes later the craft berthed alongside Incat's Hobart facility.

The first leg of the voyage, a distance of 2,238 nautical miles, was completed on 15 November when *The Cat* arrived at the Panama Canal, averaging an impressive 37.5 knots. The next stage of the voyage, 4,500 nautical miles to Tahiti, was made at an average speed of 26.47 knots, and was accomplished when the craft arrived at Papeete on 23 November.

The third and final leg from Tahiti to Hobart, a distance of 3,556 nautical miles, placed *The Cat* in Hobart at 0900hrs GMT (8 pm local time) on 28 November, beating all previous passage times between Canada and Tasmania, which were usually about twenty days.

After an overhaul in Hobart, *The Cat* resumed the TT Line service between George Town and Melbourne shortly before Christmas. As happened the previous year, during the peak period around Christmas and New Year *The Cat* was scheduled to operate a return trip six days a week, reducing to a one-way trip six days a week at other times.

Meanwhile, on 25 November *Spirit of Tasmania* had begun operating an extra return trip from Melbourne at weekends, which operated every weekend until the end of May 2002.

By the time *The Cat* was about to finish its charter in April 2002, TT Line had announced their impending purchase of two second-hand ferries then operating in the Mediterranean. They would take over the Bass Strait trade in September 2002, replacing both *Spirit of Tasmania* and the *The Cat*.

*The Cat* completed its last Bass Strait crossing for TT Line in April 2002, and then returned to the International Catamarans facility at Hobart, but this time it would not be making the long trip back to Canada as in previous years.

Bay Ferries had come to an arrangement with Incat that saw them take delivery of a brand new, larger, fast catamaran, built as hull number 059, while the older vessel, hull number 046, was handed back to the builders as a trade-in. As *Incat 046* once again, it was laid up in Hobart and offered for sale or charter.

Through the winter of 2002 *Spirit of Tasmania* continued to operate her regular schedule of three return trips per week, with a layover in Melbourne on Sunday night. The vessel also operated occasional Sunday evening excursions around Port Phillip Bay, the last being on 25 August.

On the evening of Friday, 30 August, *Spirit of*

*The Cat* departing Melbourne (Lindsay Rex photo)

*Spirit of Tasmania* in Port Phillip Bay (Lindsay Rex photo)

*Tasmania* departed Station Pier in Melbourne for her final crossing to Devonport, arriving there the next morning on schedule. *Spirit of Tasmania* departed Devonport for the last time on the evening of Saturday, 31 August 2002. The vessel entered Port Phillip Bay for the final time on the morning of Sunday 1 September, berthing at Station Pier Inner East at 5.25 am.

At noon on 1 September, *Spirit of Tasmania* left the wharf, and moved around to the other side of Station Pier, to go alongside the Inner West berth, and be laid up.

*Spirit of Tasmania* had completed 2,849 crossings of Bass Strait. Since her inaugural crossing in November 1993, *Spirit of Tasmania* had carried 2.3 million passengers, 807,000 vehicles and 185,000 containers safely across Bass Strait and covered close to 680,000 nautical miles in the process.

It was estimated that during her Bass Strait career the vessel directly and indirectly contributed $160 million annually to the Tasmanian economy and $50 million annually to the economy of Victoria.

After being withdrawn from service, *Spirit of Tasmania* remained alongside Station Pier Inner West until the late evening of 5 September, when it moved back to the Inner East berth. *Spirit of Tasmania* remained there for two hours, then

departed Melbourne for the last time just before midnight on 5 September.

*Spirit of Tasmania* headed up the east coast to Sydney, where she arrived on 7 September, berthing alongside the Oil Wharf at Garden Island. At the time it was stated the vessel was being offered for sale, and her eventual destination was Singapore.

Instead, *Spirit of Tasmania* remained laid up in Sydney at Garden Island, being moved from the Oil Wharf to the Cruiser Wharf in mid-October. On 7 November the vessel was moved again, this time passing under the Sydney Harbour Bridge to berth at 2 White Bay.

On 16 December *Spirit of Tasmania* left her berth at White Bay and headed down Sydney Harbour and out to sea. It was later discovered that this was to demonstrate the vessel to potential buyers, as the next day *Spirit of Tasmania* returned to Sydney.

This time the vessel berthed at 3 White Bay. A

*Spirit of Tasmania* laid up at Garden Island in Sydney Harbour (Peter Plowman photo)

*Spir* passing the Sydney Opera House as it leaves on 24 December 2002 (Ian Edwards photo)

deal was then finalised for the sale of the vessel, for a reported $61 million, to Fjord Line/Colour Line, a Norwegian ferry operator.

The ship was renamed *Spir* at 3 White Bay on 22 December, and her port of registry changed from Devonport to Bergen. The only other visible alteration was changing the name along the hull of the ship, but the map of Tasmania remained, as did the funnel colours.

Shortly after noon on Tuesday, 24 December, *Spir* left its berth at White Bay, and headed off down the harbour, blowing three blasts as

it passed under the Sydney Harbour Bridge. Turning south after passing through Sydney Heads, *Spir* passed through the familiar waters of Bass Strait without stopping at either Melbourne or Devonport.

Instead the vessel went non-stop to Fremantle, where it arrived on 30 December, berthing at No 9 North Quay. Remaining in port only a few hours to take on bunkers, the vessel was soon heading off across the Indian Ocean.

After passing through the Suez Canal and Mediterranean, *Spir* arrived in the Danish

*Fjord Norway* at Bergen on 5 April 2003 (Jim Freeman photo)

port of Frederikshavn on 28 January 2003, and shortly after entered the Orskov Staalskibsvaerft shipyard for a refit. During this time the hull of the vessel was repainted black, with the owner's name in white on each side, and new funnel colours were also applied.

In March 2003 the vessel was renamed *Fjord Norway*, though the official naming ceremony did not take place until 3 April in Bergen, after the vessel had arrived from its refit. On 8 April *Fjord Norway* entered her new service, operating for Fjord Line from Bergen on the southern coastline of Norway to Egersund and on to Hantsholm in northern Denmark.

Unfortunately the entry of *Fjord Norway* into this service was not as smooth as had been hoped. On 25 June the vessel was due to depart Bergen, but suffered serious engine trouble, and the departure had to be cancelled.

All passengers had to disembark, then the vessel made a slow passage under partial power to Denmark to undergo repairs, causing the cancellation of the return trip from Hanstholm due to depart on 26 June. *Fjord Norway* resumed service the next day.

Also in June 2003 it was announced that *Incat 046* had been chartered to TranzRail Holdings Limited, to replace *The Lynx*, a larger fast catamaran built by Incat as hull number 057. *Incat 046* would operate on the ferry service across Cook Strait between Wellington and Picton.

*The Lynx* left Wellington on 14 July for Hobart, while *Incat 046* left Hobart on 21 July, arriving in Wellington on 24 July. Although the vessel was advertised as *The Lynx*, it was not officially renamed, and remained registered in Nassau. It was also not repainted, instead having a darkish grey hull while the top deck and upper sides were black.

Entering the Cook Strait trade on 4 August, *Incat 046* was initially scheduled to make only one round trip each day, departing at 1100 from Wellington and returning at 1415 from Picton, while the conventional ferry *Aratare* was drydocked in Auckland.

When *Aratare* returned to service, *Incat 046* still only operated a single daily return trip. This was primarily due to the fact that the craft was in need of some major engine work, but repairs were delayed while necessary parts were manufactured.

Early in October, *Incat 046* was taken out of service for major repairs after cracks were discovered in two of the four engines. On 8 October parts from engines 2 and 4 were scattered over the vehicle deck, while a small barge was sitting alongside ready to lift No 2 engine out through a hole cut in the port side of the hull.

When this was done the vessel was turned around so that No 4 engine could be removed through a hole cut in the starboard side of the hull. Both these engines were replaced by new machinery, and *Incat 046* was due to resume service in early November.

However, it was then discovered that No 1 engine would also have to be replaced, as the entablature was cracked through to the bedplate. This kept the vessel out of service a further four weeks, with engine trials being conducted on 28 November.

During this time the vessel was also adorned with *The Lynx* logo, but still not officially renamed. From 5 December *Incat 046* began operating two return trips daily between Wellington and Picton through the peak summer period, reducing to one return trip for the rest of the year.

# Chapter Twenty

# Two New Spirits

On 8 March 2002, the Tasmanian Government announced that an agreement had been reached to purchase a pair of ferries then operating in the Mediterranean, *Superfast III* and *Superfast IV*. They would enter the Bass Strait trade for TT Line on 1 September 2002, replacing *Spirit of Tasmania* and the summer *Devil Cat* catamaran on the service.

*Superfast III* and *Superfast IV* were built in 1998 for Superfast Ferries, which was only formed in 1993 as a subsidiary of the Greek firm Attica Enterprises, a company with thirty years experience in shipping. Superfast planned to operate a fast service between Ancona in Italy and the Greek port of Patras, one of the busiest international ferry routes in Western Europe.

Rather than buying second-hand vessels to commence their operation, Superfast ordered two 23,663 gross ton ships to be built by Schichau Seebeckwerft, Bremerhaven. These would be a revolutionary new type of high-speed ferry, capable of carrying a large number of trucks and other vehicles as well as offering comfortable passenger accommodation.

The first was delivered in March 1995 as *Superfast I*, being followed a few months later by sister *Superfast II*. With a service speed of 27 knots the pair were faster than any other vessels on the trade, cutting up to eight hours off the schedules of their competitors.

The Superfast operation proved an instant success, with the company quickly becoming the major carrier of passengers and vehicles on the route. With room for more growth on the trade between Italy and Greece, Superfast decided to order two more ferries of similar design, but larger.

This time the order was placed in Finland, with the Kvaerner Masa shipyard at Turku, which had a long-standing reputation for building large cruise liners and ferries for a number of operators around the world.

At Turku the ships were built in a dry dock by a modular system. Under this arrangement, sections of the ship were constructed in various parts of the yard, then transported to the building dock when required, and lifted into place by cranes.

Even the cabins were built in modular blocks, then placed in position as complete units, with all furniture and fittings installed. The wiring and plumbing was also already in place, ready to be joined up to the main systems.

When each vessel was in an advanced state of construction, the dry dock was flooded so it could be floated out, and the internal fitting out completed while the vessel was berthed alongside a wharf. Meanwhile, construction of another vessel could begin immediately in the vacated dry dock.

The first of the new pair, named *Superfast III*, was floated out in December 1997, and completed early in February 1998. The vessel passed through the Kiel Canal on 17 February on its way from the builder's yard and the cold waters of the Baltic Sea to the warmth of the Mediterranean.

The second vessel, *Superfast IV*, was floated out in March 1998, and completed two months later, following her sister to the Mediterranean to enter service in time for the 1998 summer peak season.

As completed each of the ships measured

*Superfast III* off Patras on 18 May 2000 (Mel Gatehouse collection)

29,067 gross tons, and was 194 m/636 feet long with a maximum beam of 25m/82 feet.

They were powered by four 4-stroke single acting turbo-charged Sulzer diesels, each producing 10,560 kw of power. These were connected through 510/147 rpm reduction gearboxes to twin variable pitch propellers, giving a service speed of 27.5 knots, or about 50 kph, with several knots in reserve when needed.

Each ship provided accommodation for a maximum of 1,400 passengers, of whom 810 were provided with berths in cabins. The large vehicle decks could hold up to 830 vehicles, including large trucks.

With the arrival of *Superfast III* and *Superfast IV*, the first pair was transferred to the route between Patras and the Italian port of Bari. The two new ships soon dominated the trade between Ancona and Patras, and maintained their service with great regularity.

However, on 1 November 1999 a fire broke out in the garage space of *Superfast III* when it was about 15 miles out of Patras on a voyage to Ancona. The 307 passengers on board were safely evacuated and picked up by nearby ships, but the fire was not fully extinguished by crew members until the following day. *Superfast III* was then towed back to Patras, where it was found that the vehicle spaces had suffered heavy damage.

A grisly clue to the cause of the fire was the discovery of the bodies of 14 illegal immigrants in the garage area. It was thought they had been smuggled on board, and may have been trying to cook themselves a meal over an open fire which got out of control. *Superfast III* was repaired and returned to service in December.

With four ships in service, Superfast ferries

*Spirit of Tasmania I* at Devonport on 16 February 2004 (Peter Plowman photo)

*Spirit of Tasmania II* leads *Spirit of Tasmania I* into Melbourne (Dale Crisp photo)

*Spirit of Tasmania I* at Station Pier Outer West with *Spirit of Tasmania II* nearest the camera at Outer East (Lindsay Rex photo)

*Spirit of Tasmania* at Station Pier Inner East joins her two replacements on 18 August 2000 (Lindsay Rex photo)

dominated the route between Ancona and Patras, but the company was not content to rest on their laurels. They sought out other routes around Europe on which to place more ships of the same type. Over the next few years a further eight similar ferries were built. The first four of these vessels were placed on various services in the North Sea and Irish Sea.

The last four to be built were placed on a route in the Baltic Sea between Rostock in Germany and the Swedish port of Sodertalje, south of Stockholm. Unlike their other ventures, this route produced very poor results for Superfast Ferries, and early in 2002 Superfast decided to withdraw from the service.

Two of the vessels were transferred to open a new service across the North Sea between Rosyth and Zeebrugge, while *Superfast XI* and *Superfast XII*, the newest and largest vessels in the Superfast fleet, replaced *Superfast III* and *Superfast IV* on the original Superfast route between Ancona and Patras, which was still growing steadily.

*Superfast III* and *Superfast IV* were then offered for charter or sale, and soon snapped up by TT Line, at a cost of $290 million for the pair. *Superfast III* was renamed *Spirit of Tasmania* II, while *Superfast IV* was renamed *Spirit of Tasmania* I.

The two vessels voyaged to Australia at the same time, their departure point from Greece being the island of Syros. *Spirit of Tasmania* II left on 6 July, while *Spirit of Tasmania* I departed on 7 July.

The vessels passed through the Suez Canal, then down the Red Sea and across the Indian Ocean to Colombo, where they refuelled. The next leg of their delivery voyage was to Fremantle, where *Spirit of Tasmania* II arrived on 24 July, closely followed the next day by *Spirit of Tasmania* I. After refuelling again, the pair continued their voyage to Tasmania, their first destination being Hobart.

The two vessels arrived together off the Iron Pot at the entrance to the River Derwent at 9.30am on Monday 29 July. They cruised slowly up the river together, arriving in the Port of Hobart at approximately 10.30am. *Spirit of Tasmania* II berthed at Princes Wharf while *Spirit of Tasmania* I docked at Macquarie 2/3.

The Premier of Tasmania and the Deputy Premier were at the berths to welcome the vessels and their crews after the journey from the Mediterranean. While in Hobart the vessels received their final fit-out and were provisioned in preparation for commencing their new service.

Prior to their introduction into regular service, both ships were opened for several days of public inspection at three ports, the first being held in Hobart on 11 August. The pair departed Hobart on 12 August, and arrived in Melbourne together on Wednesday, 14 August, receiving a gala welcome and creating a great deal of interest.

As *Spirit of Tasmania* was still operating the service to Devonport, neither of the new vessels could berth at the TT Line dock, so *Spirit of Tasmania II* went alongside Station Pier Outer East, while *Spirit of Tasmania I* berthed on the opposite side at Station Pier Outer West.

The two vessels remained alongside for the next six days, and on several days *Spirit of Tasmania* was also in port at Station Pier Inner East. Open days were held in Melbourne on 17 and 18 August, with over 10,000 persons taking advantage of this opportunity to inspect the two new ships.

*Spirit of Tasmania I* departed Station Pier on the evening of 23 August, while her sister remained in Melbourne until the new service commenced. After crossing Bass Strait overnight, *Spirit of Tasmania I* detoured to the west to enable residents of the north west coast of Tasmania to see the new vessel as it sailed by close to shore.

From 12 noon on Saturday, 24 August 2002 the vessel was visible to Smithton residents, and it made a magnificent sight as it slowly made its way along the north-west coast, regularly sounding its siren to let residents know that it was passing nearby. *Spirit of Tasmania I* was visible from the fishing and tourist village of Stanley at 1pm and from Rocky Cape at 1.30pm.

Residents of Wynyard and Burnie saw the vessel for the first time at 2pm and 3pm respectively, before the ship finally entered the Mersey River at 3.45pm, docking at the TT Line Devonport Terminal at 4.30pm. In Devonport another highly successful public inspection day was held on 25 August.

*Spirit of Tasmania* departed Devonport for the

last time on the evening of Saturday, 31 August 2002, berthing at Station Pier Inner East at 5.25 on the morning of Sunday, 1 September. At noon *Spirit of Tasmania* left the wharf, and moved to the other side of Station Pier, to go alongside the Inner West berth, having been withdrawn from service.

*Spirit of Tasmania II* then berthed at Station Pier Inner East, to prepare for its first commercial voyage across Bass Strait. The two new ships began their Bass Strait careers on the evening of Sunday, 1 September 2002. *Spirit of Tasmania* I departed from Devonport at 9 pm while at the same time *Spirit of Tasmania II* left Melbourne.

Subsequently the pair provided daily departures from both Melbourne and Devonport at 9 pm, arriving at their destination at 7 am next day. It was planned that this would be their regular schedule for eight months of the year.

From just before Christmas to late April, they would each provide one return trip a day, taking full advantage of their high speed capability. These trips would depart each terminal at 9 am, arriving at 6 pm, then depart again at 9 pm, with a 6 am arrival.

Thus during the prime Tasmanian tourist months there would be two voyages a day from Melbourne to Devonport and return, compared to the four trips a week previously operated.

With the introduction of these two ships, TT Line adopted new funnel markings, and retained the red hulls the ships had when operated by Superfast ferries. They also had their names emblazoned in large letters along each side of the hull.

The passenger accommodation was reduced slightly from what it had been in the Mediterranean, with a maximum of 876 passengers being carried on overnight sailings, and up to 1,400 passengers on daylight crossings.

Accommodation for 750 passengers is provided in 222 cabins, spread over the forward section of deck 7 and all of deck 8. All cabins have private facilities and contain two or four berths. Top of the range are eight deluxe cabins with queen-size beds.

There are 59 outside cabins with two lower berths, as well as 72 outside four-berth cabins, plus 81 four-berth inside cabins, while two cabins are specially fitted out for use by people with physical disabilities.

There are also 126 reclining seats located in a large lounge midships, which are used on overnight sailings only. On daylight sailings, up to 650 additional deck passengers can be carried, and the lounge in which the reclining seats are located becomes a movie theatre, with two or three films being shown during the crossing.

The major public rooms are all located on deck 7, including lounges, bars and eating areas. Meals are not included in the passage fare, but there is a choice of locations in which passengers can obtain a meal, both dinner and breakfast on a night crossing or lunch on a daylight trip.

The Les Amis dining room, which is very attractively fitted out on the port side of deck 7 near the stern, has waiter service and offers an extensive quality menu and fine Tasmanian wines.

On the opposite side of the ship is The Eatery, a buffet style cafeteria, where passengers can choose from a wide selection of hot and cold dishes including seafood, roasts and fresh salads, and a range of desserts, at a very reasonable price.

The main bar and lounge is located right aft on deck 7, providing comfortable seating with views through large windows over the stern.

Opposite the reception desk is a shop, selling a wide variety of goods from food and essential items to clothing and souvenirs. There is also a fully equipped travel office, providing information on Tasmania and able to arrange bookings on the island for passengers.

Several smaller lounges are located around the ship, and all are fitted with television screens, showing programmes beamed in by satellite. Also on deck 7 is a children's play area, and a gaming room.

On the upper decks there are several bars, and numerous machines providing tea and coffee. A number of vending machines dispensing soft drinks in cans and various types of chocolate bars and other fast foods are also spread through the passenger decks.

When the ships first entered service there was a small swimming pool midships on the top deck, but this saw little use. In the winter of 2003 the swimming pools were covered over to provide additional deck space. At the same time additional windbreaks were installed at the after end of deck 9, following passenger complaints

Les Amis Restaurant

and the main bar on *Spirit of Tasmania II* (Peter Plowman photos)

The reception desk and gift shop on *Spirit of Tasmania II* (Peter Plowman photo)

that the area was too windy when crossing Bass Strait.

Below the passenger accommodation are the vehicle decks, providing 2,470 metres of vehicle lanes. This provides space for up to 650 cars, or a mixture of cars and commercial trucks.

Deck G3, at lower ramp level, is full height for the full length of the ship, and usually used by trucks and caravans. The deck above, G5, is full height to midships, then half height to the bow, enabling extra cars to be carried.

In the peak season cars can also be carried on the two lower vehicle decks, G1 and G2. Passengers travelling with their cars drive on board the ship, and after parking their vehicle ascend to passenger deck 7 via stairs or one of the two lifts provided. Foot passengers board the ships near the stern, and are conveyed by escalators to deck 7.

The two ships each have a bunker capacity of 1,260 tonnes of fuel for their four diesel engines, and burn seven tonnes of fuel per hour during each voyage. When they are only operating night sailings bunkering is carried out once a week, when a fuel barge comes alongside in Melbourne. During peak periods when daylight trips are also being made, bunkering is required twice a week.

The ships are also fitted with stabilisers, located on either side of the hull just forward of midships. These fins are each eight metres long and 600 millimetres wide, and can be brought into action when sea conditions on Bass Strait are rough, greatly smoothing the ride for passengers.

For assistance when manoeuvring in confined areas, especially in the River Mersey at Devonport, both bow and stern thrusters are

*Spirit of Tasmania I* arriving in Melbourne (Lindsay Rex photo)

*Spirit of Tasmania II* makes an early morning arrival in Devonport on 19 February 2004 (Peter Plowman photo)

fitted. These enable the ships to turn around in their own length, and they can also move sideways without outside assistance.

Such was the interest generated by the arrival of the two new ships that even before they entered service, bookings across Bass Strait were up by 66 per cent for September and 47 per cent for October compared to the previous year.

As a result, TT Line decided to operate six extra daylight voyages on the last two weekends in September and the first weekend in October. These provided capacity for an additional 6000 passengers to travel during this school holiday peak demand period.

The first daylight voyages were operated on Friday, 20 September and Saturday, 21 September, but on the next two weekends the daylight services operated on Saturday and Sunday.

*Spirit of Tasmania I* and *Spirit of Tasmania II* are substantial vessels capable of operating in severe weather. However, there will always be the odd occasion when the captain will decide that sea conditions on Bass Strait are too rough for the comfort of the passengers, which is always the first consideration.

On Friday, 19 September, strong winds gusting up to 90 kph swept across Victoria, especially

*Spirit of Tasmania II* alongside Station Pier in the early morning sunlight of 20 February 2004 (Peter Plowman photo)

*Spirit of Tasmania I* passes her sister in the middle of Bass Strait on 25 April 2003. (John Beckhaus photo)

along the southern coastline, inflicting major damage in many areas. *Spirit of Tasmania I* left Station Pier at 6 pm as scheduled and made her way across Port Phillip Bay and through The Rip into Bass Strait.

However, the seas in the Strait were so rough the captain decided it was best for the ship to turn around and return to Station Pier, where it tied up safely at 1 am. During the early hours of the morning the winds calmed, and at 6 am *Spirit of Tasmania I* left Station Pier again. This time it made the crossing to Devonport in much more pleasant conditions. Meanwhile *Spirit of Tasmania II* had been able to make its crossing from Devonport on schedule, as the winds had died down by the time the vessel neared the Victorian coastline.

On the afternoon of Sunday, 13 October, *Spirit of Tasmania II* was berthed at Station Pier in Melbourne, and the loading of vehicles was proceeding as normal when, at 6.50pm a violent squall swept through the Port Melbourne area.

The sudden gusts of wind tore *Spirit of Tasmania* II from the wharf, but the captain and crew immediately activated the emergency procedures to meet such an occurrence.

The vessel was safely returned to its berth with the assistance of a tug. A vehicle that was about to drive onto the ferry at the time suffered some minor damage to its bonnet, but no injuries were caused to any passengers or crew.

Following an inspection by the Australian Maritime Safety Authority, *Spirit of Tasmania II*

was cleared to sail, though departure was delayed until 10.30 pm.

*Spirit of Tasmania I* and *Spirit of Tasmania II* continued to carry capacity loadings across Bass Strait through October and into November. To meet demand, additional daylight sailings were scheduled for the weekends of 16/17 and 23/24 November, and 30 November/1 December, as well as 18/19 December. These extra sailings provided space for an additional 12,000 passengers to travel across Bass Strait.

When *Spirit of Tasmania I* and *Spirit of Tasmania II* first entered service most of the public rooms were designated smoke-free zones, as had been the case on *Spirit of Tasmania*.

However, there were several interior areas in which passengers were allowed to smoke. Following complaints by passengers, in December all interior areas of both vessels were designated smoke-free. Passengers who wished to smoke could now only do so at the two outside bars located on decks 9 and 10.

Beginning on 21 December 2002, *Spirit of Tasmania* I and *Spirit of Tasmania II* began operating return services every Saturday and Sunday across Bass Strait until 27 April 2003. In addition, during the last week of December and up to 26 January 2003 the vessels operated a return trip every day.

With fourteen departures each week from both Melbourne and Devonport, the trade had never been so frequent, and the perennial problem of insufficient accommodation to meet demand around Christmas and the New Year was finally overcome. Advance reservations remained well in excess of previous years, and at 20 January 2003, bookings were already up by 43 per cent, representing an additional 113,000 passengers compared to the previous year.

In order to meet all the advance bookings, TT Line scheduled 20 additional daylight sailings. The first of these operated on Fridays 14, 21 and 28 February, then Monday 10 March and Fridays 14, 21 and 28 March, and 4 April, as well as Mondays 14 and 21 April.

These additional sailings provided accommodation for an extra 28,000 passengers, and brought to 50 the number of crossings that had to be added to the original sailing schedule since the vessels entered service on 1 September 2002.

In the six months to March 2003, about 116,700 people arrived in Tasmania by sea, representing a 65 per cent increase on the 70,800 visitors arriving by sea in the six months from September 2001 to March 2002.

In June 2003, nine months after the two ships entered service, Tasmanian Premier Jim Bacon summed up his Government's appreciation of their success. He said that when the State Government bought *Spirit of Tasmania I* and *Spirit of Tasmania II* it was looking to the future, as they were considered to be ships of greater capacity than was then needed on the Bass Strait run.

Referring to the number of passengers already carried, and advance booking figures, Mr Bacon said passenger demand for the two Spirits had exceeded all expectations. It had taken the pair just one year to reach passenger loadings the Government had thought would take at least five years to achieve.

In August 2003 it was reported that bookings on the Bass Strait service for June, July and August, which was the shoulder season, were up by 25 per cent on the same period the previous year.

The demand for passages across Bass Strait showed no sign of slowing as the year progressed. With an increasing number of passengers booking their travel dates up to a year in advance, on 30 November 2003 it was announced that the two ships had already been scheduled to operate 12 additional daylight sailings on the last two weekends of September 2004, as well as the first weekend and last weekend of October, due to the heavy demand.

In the last weeks of 2003 refurbishment work was carried out on each vessel during the daily layover in port between trips. The changes were the result of passenger feedback over the first year the ships had been operating.

*Spirit of Tasmania II* approaching Station Pier in Melbourne (Lindsay Rex photo)

**DECK 10**
- Bar (Outside)
  Toilets (Ladies, Gents)

**DECK 9**
- Bar (Outside)
  Toilets (Ladies, Gents)

**DECK 8**
- Cabins (8000-8256)

**DECK 7**
- Cabins (7000 -7225)
  Restaurant
  Main Bar
  Tourism on Board
  Admirals Gaming lounge
  **Cruise Seats**
  Lounge Bar
  Children's Playroom
  Reception
  Eatery
  Tasmania at Sea, Gift Shop
  Toilets (Ladies, Gents
  and Disabled)

DELUXE    TWO BERTH CABINS    FOUR BERTH CABINS    DISABLED CABINS    MUSTER STATIONS

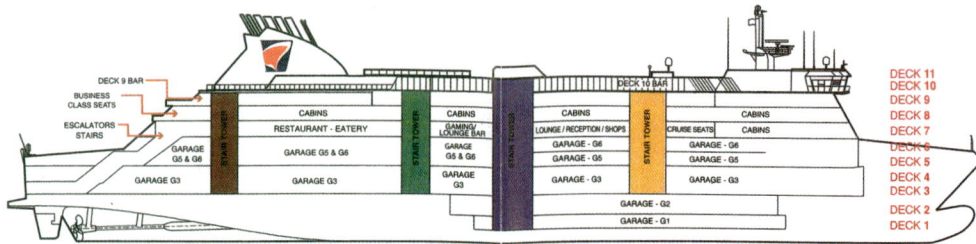

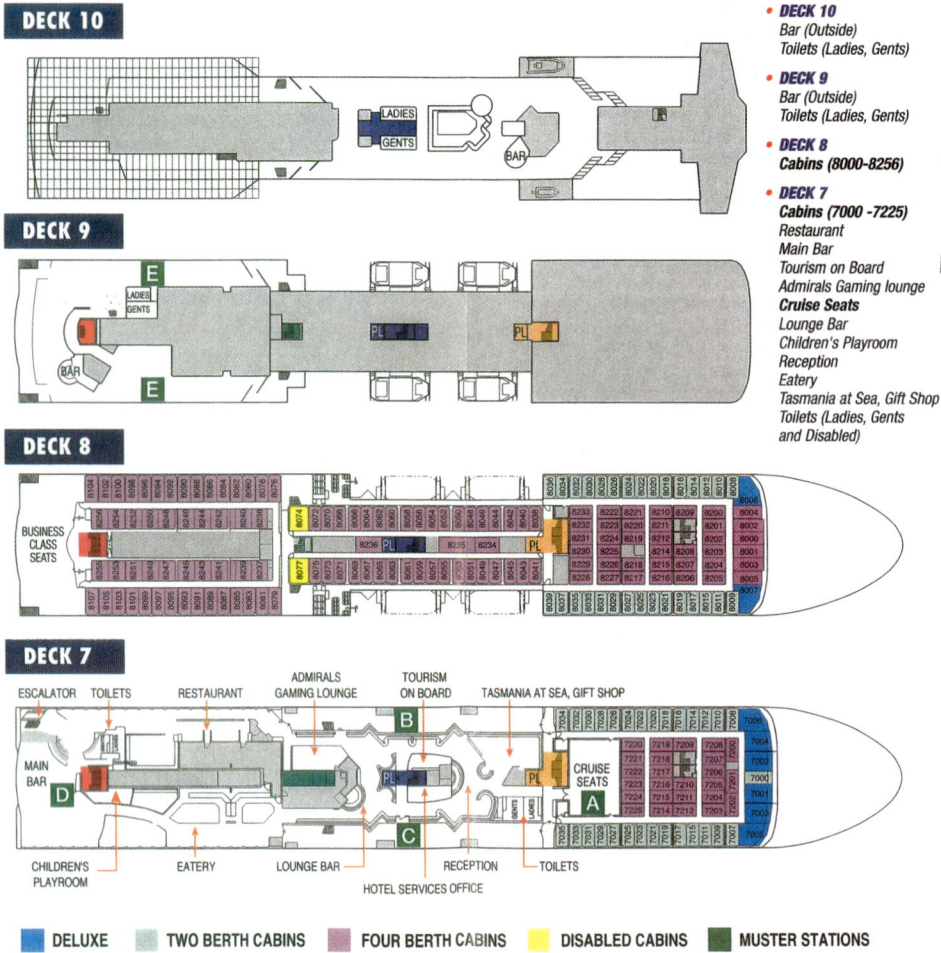

Deck plan of Spirit of Tasmania I and II from 1 February 2004

Inparticular the outdoor bar area on deck 9 was considerably altered and improved. This included enclosing the outdoor area, the laying of improved floor coverings and the provision of more modern and comfortable chairs and tables. The new layout also featured a new video amusement centre, which was of particular interest to young people.

The refurbished areas on both ships were made available to passengers for the first time on the voyages departing on the night of Wednesday, 17 December.

The two vessels had been scheduled to begin their additional peak season daylight crossings on a daily basis from 20 December 2003. However, to meet the huge extra demand of the Christmas holidays, eight extra daylight sailings were added, commencing on Tuesday, 16 December, and continuing on the following Wednesday, Thursday and Friday.

The vessels then operated two sailings every day until 18 January 2004, after which there were only daylight departures on weekends up to 25 April.

During January 2004 a number of changes were effected on both *Spirit of Tasmania I* and *Spirit of Tasmania II* which resulted in the introduction of a new type of travel from 1 February, advertised as business class seating.

A new lounge was created at the stern on deck 8 containing 146 reclining seats with individual reading lights. The seats are more comfortable than those provided in the ordinary seating lounge. Six of the seats were specially designed for the use of disabled passengers. Storage space for passengers' belongings is also provided.

The business class lounge can only be accessed by a swipe card that unlocks the door. This is handed to passengers travelling in the lounge as they board. Fares for these seats come at a slightly higher cost, being $145 in the off-peak season, and $155 in the shoulder season, rising to $180 in peak season.

By the time these changes became effective, TT Line had added a third vessel to their fleet, and reopened the long-dormant passenger trade between Sydney and Tasmania.

A bow view of *Spirit of Tasmania II* berthed at Station Pier on 20 February 2004 (Peter Plowman photo)

# Chapter Twenty-One

# Reviving the Sydney Service

At the time TT Line withdrew *Spirit of Tasmania* from the Bass Strait trade in September 2002, they had given considerable thought to transferring the vessel to reopen the service between Sydney and Tasmania, which had been dormant for twenty-five years.

A tourist survey conducted in New South Wales and Queensland for TT Line in February 2002 had revealed that an extra 50,000 tourists a year would support such a service, and contribute an extra $100 million to Tasmania's economy each year.

However, the research also indicated that whilst this substantial potential market existed, the voyage time of 30 hours between Sydney and Tasmania that would be required by *Spirit of Tasmania* was too long. The service was not considered feasible unless it could be operated by a faster and more suitable vessel.

Subsequent research in March 2003 found that, for this type of service a market existed immediately for 103,000 passengers a year in both directions, representing a potential 51,500 holiday visitors to Tasmania. It was estimated that once a new Sydney service was actually operating it could trigger further growth to 71,000 holiday visitors from New South Wales and Queensland to Tasmania each year.

The research also showed visitors travelling on the Sydney-Tasmania service would spend more and stay longer than those coming from Melbourne. Records indicated holiday visitors from Queensland spent $2370 on a visit to Tasmania, compared to $2100 for those from New South Wales and $1530 for Victorians.

The historic shipping connection between Sydney and Tasmania was with Hobart, and it was reported that by using a fast ferry the passage time between Sydney and Hobart would be about 20 hours, while the time to Bell Bay in the north of the state would be 22 hours.

However, the passage time to Devonport was only slightly longer than Bell Bay, and suitable facilities were already in place there, whereas new terminals and berths would have to be constructed at either Hobart or Bell Bay. It was for this reason that Devonport was selected as the Tasmanian port for the service.

During May and June 2003, representatives of both TT Line and the Tasmanian Government travelled to Europe to inspect several vessels of suitable size and speed that were available for purchase. It was no surprise when it was announced in early July that the vessel selected for purchase was *Superfast II*, a near sister to the two vessels already being operated by TT Line between Melbourne and Devonport.

Although slightly older and smaller than *Spirit of Tasmania I* and *Spirit of Tasmania II*, the chosen vessel would require identical docking facilities, and could carry a similar number of both passengers and cars. Tasmanian premier Jim Bacon estimated the overall cost of acquiring the ship, delivering it to Australia, refitting it to suit the Sydney service and constructing suitable wharf facilities in Sydney, would be in the region of $105 million.

At the time the announcement of the new service was made, *Superfast II* was operating on the busy Adriatic route between Patras and Igoumenitsa in Greece and the southern Italian port of Bari. It was stated that the vessel would continue to operate on this service until September, at which time it would be withdrawn and handed over to TT Line.

*Superfast II* was the second of a pair of ferries completed in 1995 for Superfast Ferries, to operate a fast service between the Greek port of Patras and Ancona in Italy, which is one of the busiest ferry routes in Europe.

Superfast Ferries was formed in 1993 as a subsidiary of the Greek firm Attica Enterprises, whose owner, Pericles Panagopulos, founded Royal Cruise Line in 1972. The order for the two vessels was placed in November 1993 with Schichau Seebeckwerft, at Bremerhaven in Germany.

This shipyard had a reputation for building superior quality large ferries for a number of European operators, including *Peter Pan*, which later became *Spirit of Tasmania*. However, they had not previously constructed a fast ferry, which required a specially designed hull to enable a greater speed to be attained.

The two ships were each built in the remarkably fast time of eighteen months, with the first, appropriately named *Superfast I*, being launched on 30 July 1994. The second vessel, the 50th ferry to be built by the Seebeckwerft yard, was launched, but not named, on 12 January 1995, though at that time the bow was not completed.

In a double ceremony held at the Seebeckwerft shipyard on 25 March 1995, *Superfast I* was officially handed over to Superfast ferries, then *Superfast II* was christened. At that time the second vessel was at the fitting out berth, still in the final stages of construction, and not yet painted.

*Superfast I* made her delivery voyage to Patras, where final touches were completed to the interior, and on 30 April 1995 commenced the new ferry service. Work on completing *Superfast*

*Superfast I* (Author's collection)

*II* proceeded on schedule, and the vessel was handed over to Superfast Ferries in early May. On 31 May, *Superfast II* joined her sister on the trade between Ancona and Patras, enabling the company to operate six trips in each direction every week.

*Superfast I* and *Superfast II* were built to the highest standards of quality and safety. Following several disasters in recent years involving ferries sinking following failures of the bow doors, the pair were the first ferries to be fitted with an advanced monitoring system as well as triple bow doors and an extra forward bulkhead to ensure additional sealing. The bow door was designed to open forward and upward, and would be held in place by water pressure during a voyage even if there were a fastening failure.

On sea trials both *Superfast I* and *Superfast II* achieved in excess of 30 knots, but what was most pleasing to both builder and owner was the minimal vibration caused by the high speed. At the regular service speed of 27 knots there was no noticable vibration at all.

As completed both these vessels measured 23,663 gross tons, with an overall length of 173.7 m/570 feet and a beam of 24 m/79 feet. The hull was painted Ferrari racing car red, to emphasise the concept of speed. A particularly noticeable distinguishing feature was the wings fitted to either side of the funnel.

The Superfast ships could each carry a maximum of 1,397 passengers, though not all were provided with cabin accommodation. There were berths for 626 passengers in 200 cabins, all located on two decks in the forward section of the superstructure, and also 140 reclining aircraft style seats in a large, sound-insulated room in the centre of the ship. Hostel type quarters were provided for an additional 40 passengers.

Public rooms were spread along the after section of a single deck, and included several lounges, two dining areas, a casino, children's playroom, and a special lounge for truck drivers. The interior designers were a Norwegian firm, Yran & Storbraaten, who had previously done similar work for cruise liners, and they gave the public areas a decidedly continental touch.

One feature not normally found on European ferries was an outdoor swimming pool aft on A deck, surrounded by an open deck with tables and chairs, and serviced by a Pool Bar.

The ships were fitted with three particularly large vehicle decks, providing space for up to 830 cars. In addition, an area of open deck space at the stern was provided for large trucks, which were an important part of the operating strategy. This space could also accommodate large campervans, with the occupants being able to stay in these vehicles during the voyage.

*Superfast I* and *Superfast II* were faster than any other vessels on the trade between Ancona and Patras, with a service speed of 27 knots, which reduced passage time to twenty hours, cutting up to eight hours off the schedules of their competitors.

*Superfast I* and *Superfast II* proved an instant success, with the company quickly becoming the major carrier of passengers and vehicles on the route. They departed both Ancona and Patras every night of the week during the peak travel periods, but at other times reduced the schedule to six departures a week, with a layover day in the middle of the week, when cargo loadings were lowest.

Although the vessels were fitted with doors at both the bow and stern, the port facilities in both Ancona and Patras were not adequate to enable both doors to be used. Because of a lack of wharf space, ferries using these ports have to berth stern-in, and the bow doors were never used. This lack of adequate shore facilities meant neither vessel was able to operate to its maximum vehicular capabilities.

Eventually *Superfast I* and *Superfast II* became victims of their own success, as in 1997 Superfast ordered two larger ferries of similar design for the service between Patras and Ancona. When they entered service in April 1998 as *Superfast III* and *Superfast IV*, the original pair was transferred to a new service, from Patras and Igoumenitsa to Bari, in southern Italy.

While this was not as busy a route as the one from Ancona, *Superfast I* and *Superfast II* soon became the major vessels on their new service, which began to show a steady increase in patronage over the next few years. By 2003 the two original Superfast ships were again unable to cope with the demand for passages on the route.

*Superfast I* and *Superfast II* were replaced by larger and newer vessels, and both vessels were offered for sale. In July 2003 TT Line signed an agreement to purchase *Superfast II*. Several months later sister ship *Superfast I* was sold to an Italian company.

*Superfast II* was handed over to TT Line on 30 September, and first sent to the Nerion Dockyard on the island of Syros to undergo a refit and be prepared for the delivery voyage to Australia.

Having been renamed *Spirit of Tasmania III*, and under the command of Captain Glen Cole, the vessel departed Syros on the evening of Friday, 10 October. After passing through the Suez Canal, *Spirit of Tasmania III* crossed the Indian Ocean to Fremantle, berthing there on the morning of Monday, 27 October to refuel.

Two views of *Spirit of Tasmania III* departing Fremantle (Rhod Jones photos)

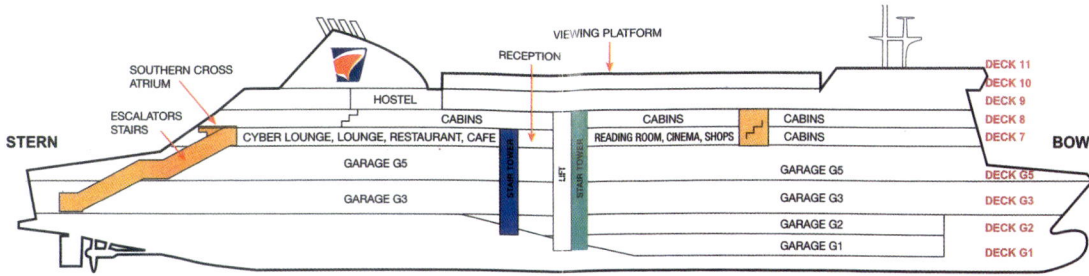

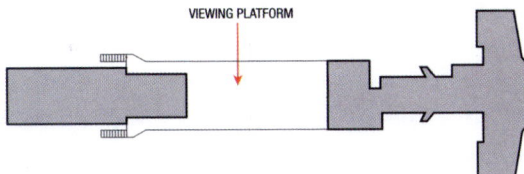

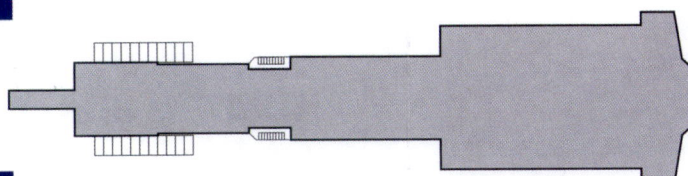

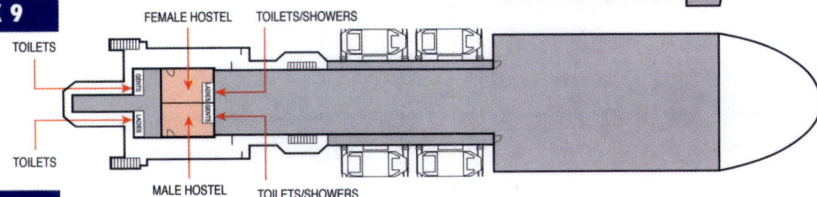

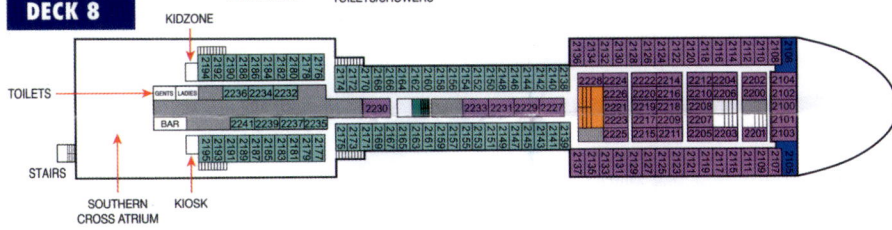

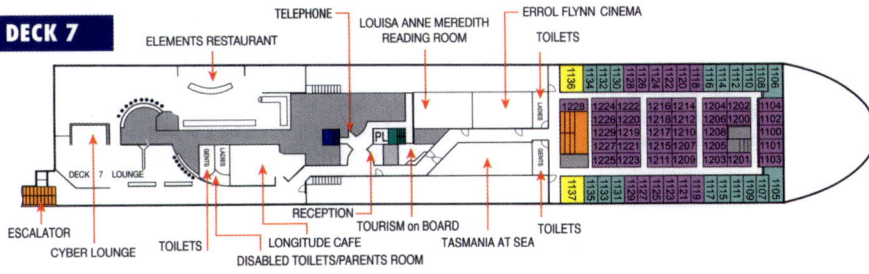

Deck plan of Spirit of Tasmania III

The vessel then continued on its way to Tasmania, and early on the morning of Thursday, 30 October, *Spirit of Tasmania III* arrived in Hobart, berthing at No 6 Macquarie Wharf. Captain Cole, who had previously been in command on both *Spirit of Tasmania I* and *Spirit of Tasmania II*, said the ship had handled excellently on the delivery voyage.

While in Hobart *Spirit of Tasmania III* underwent a major overhaul and some alterations prior to entering service. The contract for this work had been awarded to Taylor Brothers, who did a similar job on the two ferries delivered the previous year. Among the changes to the ship were the addition of 32 staff cabins, refurbishment of the restaurant and bar areas, and upgrading

The refurbished area aft on Deck 8 (Peter Plowman photo)

some of the passenger accommodation.

There was also a major modification to the after end of deck 8. This was originally an open air space, which included a small swimming pool and surrounding lido area. For the Tasmanian trade the swimming pool was removed, and the whole area was enclosed with a metal roof and windows on three sides. The original bar and fast food outlets were retained, while tables and chairs were placed around the deck.

On Thursday, 3 July, an official announcement of the new service had been made in Sydney at a press conference held by Mr Bacon. Also attending the press conference was the New South Wales Premier, Mr Bob Carr, who expressed his strong support for the new service, and even made the first reservation for the maiden voyage from Sydney.

Bookings for *Spirit of Tasmania* III had opened on 4 July, and the TT Line reservation centre in Devonport was immediately inundated with people calling to book on the new service.

Although in the future peak fare rates will apply in January, as a special introductory offer, from January 15 to April 26, 2004, passengers would only have to pay shoulder fare rates. These ranged from $495 one-way for a double berth porthole cabin to as low as $255 for an adult in hostel accommodation.

Because the voyage from Sydney is longer than that between Melbourne and Devonport, and requires a full night and morning at sea, dinner and brunch were included in the fare.

The Federal Government's $150 Bass Strait equalisation rebate would also apply to the Sydney service, meaning accompanied cars travel free for 45 weeks of the year, and cost $55 one-way during the summer peak season.

In August 2003, Tasmanian Premier Jim Bacon said that preparations for the commencement of the *Spirit of Tasmania III* service were progressing extremely well. Mr Bacon also said that so far more than 4000 bookings had been received, and that was without any form of advertising.

In Sydney work had commenced on 22 September on the construction of a vehicle ramp for the vessel next to the cruise liner terminal at 8 Darling Harbour. The project started off with three weeks of pile driving, and the entire job was completed in sixteen weeks. The new ramp juts out from the existing wharf, and can be utilised on either the northern or southern side.

On 19 December in Hobart, there was an official naming and blessing ceremony for *Spirit of Tasmania III* held at Macquarie Wharf. It was a very cold, windy day, but several hundred spectators watched naval chaplain Father Michael Delaney bless the vessel.

Then Associate Professor Jennifer Butler, the wife of Tasmanian Governor Richard Butler, formally named the ferry, with the breaking of a traditional bottle of champagne against the bow.

Later Tasmanian Premier Jim Bacon announced that the movie theatre on board *Spirit of Tasmania III* would be named after Tasmanian-born Hollywood legend Errol Flynn.

It was also announced that the vessel would be entering service slightly earlier than originally planned. Instead of making its first commercial voyage from Devonport on 15 January, the vessel would depart Sydney on 13 January on a voyage to Devonport.

When operating in the Mediterranean as *Superfast II*, this vessel had been able to carry up to 1,400 passengers, but as *Spirit of Tasmania III* the number of passengers was reduced to 626, all of whom had cabin or hostel accommodation for the overnight voyage.

At 8 am on Friday, 2 January 2004, *Spirit of Tasmania III*, under the command of Captain Jim Lewis, departed Hobart for Devonport. For some members of the 80-strong crew this was also their first voyage. On board were invited guests and 500 passengers who had paid $170 for adults and $125 for children, which included two meals.

As *Spirit of Tasmania III* steamed up the east coast of Tasmania it kept as close to the shore as possible, giving those on land a good view of the passing ferry.

*Spirit of Tasmania II* and *Spirit of Tasmania III* together at Station Pier on 5 January 2004 (Dale Crisp photo)

*Spirit of Tasmania III* alongside 8 Darling Harbour (Peter Plowman photo)

At Devonport hundreds of spectators turned out to watch the vessel enter the port for the first time, berthing at the TT Line terminal just after 9pm.

On 3 January the vessel was inspected by local travel agents and invited guests, then at noon on 4 January *Spirit of Tasmania III* headed out into Bass Strait on a voyage to Melbourne, this time carrying no passengers.

Berthing in Melbourne at Station Pier Inner East at 10pm, the vessel moved to the Outer East berth at 5.30 am on 5 January, to allow *Spirit of Tasmania II* to use the Inner East berth when it arrived from Devonport. During the day, *Spirit of Tasmania III* was inspected by local travel agents and invited guests.

At 8 am on Tuesday 6 January *Spirit of Tasmania III* departed Melbourne for Sydney, where it arrived at 11 am the next day, berthing alongside the Overseas Passenger Terminal in Sydney Cove, usually used by cruise liners.

*Spirit of Tasmania III* berthing at the Overseas Passenger Terminal in Sydney on 7 January 2004 (Peter Plowman photo)

On the morning of Friday, 9 January, *Spirit of Tasmania III* moved from the Overseas Passenger Terminal to Darling Harbour, for a test docking at the loading ramp there.

On most visits to Sydney, *Spirit of Tasmania III* would berth at 8 Darling Harbour, but when its schedule coincided with a cruise ship using 8 Darling Harbour the ferry would berth at 5 Darling Harbour, on the northern side of the ramp.

*Spirit of Tasmania III* made test dockings on both sides of the new ramp, then returned to Sydney Cove, remaining there until 10.30 am on Tuesday, 13 January, when the vessel moved again to 8 Darling Harbour, berthing bow-in at the southern side of the new loading ramp.

During the early afternoon the first passengers and vehicles were taken on board, and as sailing time approached the ship quickly filled. Among those joining the ship for the maiden commercial voyage was the Premier of Tasmania, Mr Bacon, and a number of invited guests.

Precisely at 3 pm, *Spirit of Tasmania III* moved away from the wharf and headed slowly down Darling Harbour, being preceded by the Sydney Ports firetug making a fine show with all its equipment spraying water in the air.

Also accompanying the ferry for a short distance was the vintage steam tug *Waratah*, operated by the Sydney Heritage Fleet, which was bedecked with flags for the occasion. Above hovered a helicopter carrying a television news team, while a number of private craft also sailed and motored along with the vessel.

Shortly after *Spirit of Tasmania III* rounded Millers Point and headed towards the Sydney Harbour Bridge, a group of four environmental protesters suddenly unveiled a large banner along the port side of the ship, and then swung themselves over the side in chairs attached to ropes. Apparently the four had paid for their passages, but their protest was brought to a quick end, and the four were removed from the vessel by Sydney Water Police.

The departure from Sydney then proceeded as planned, and soon *Spirit of Tasmania III* was passing through Sydney Heads, then turned

*Spirit of Tasmania III* alongside 8 Darling Harbour (Peter Plowman photo)

Loading a large semi-trailer on *Spirit of Tasmania III* (Peter Plowman photo)

south for Tasmania. When the ferry entered Bass Strait on the Wednesday morning a strong head wind was whipping up the waves, forcing the ship to slow down, and it did not arrive in Devonport until 2 pm.

On Thursday, 15 January, *Spirit of Tasmania III* left Devonport on its first voyage to Sydney, but again encountered bad weather and was two hours late arriving in Sydney in pouring rain. Due to this the ship did not depart for the return trip until 4.30 pm. Bad weather continued to upset the timetable over the next week, but then things settled down, and most voyages departed and arrived close to schedule.

Apart from the usual amenities found on board a large ferry, for the first four weeks *Spirit of Tasmania III* was operating there was an added attraction – 'Buttons the Burnie Burrowing Crayfish', also known as interpretation ranger Chris Mead. He was joined by fellow interpretation ranger Peter Tonelli, to provide on-board information about Tasmania's national parks and the wildlife to be found in them. The pair ran children's activities, slide shows and DVD presentations during each voyage.

The introduction of *Spirit of Tasmania III* caused some alterations to the berthing arrangements in Devonport. The TT Line ferries always arrive and depart from Berth 1 in East Devonport, while Berth 2 is occupied by the ro-ro cargo vessels *Searoad Tamar* or *Searoad Mersey* most days of the week. As a result a third berth has been added, at which one of the TT Line ferries can dock bow-in when Berth 1 is needed by another vessel.

*Spirit of Tasmania III* passing the Sydney Opera House (Peter Plowman photo)

*Spirit of Tasmania III* arriving in Devonport (Peter Plowman photo)

On Saturday and Monday, the ferry arriving in Devonport from Melbourne about 7 am will dock at Berth 1 as usual, but several hours later will move down to Berth 3. *Spirit of Tasmania III* arrives in Devonport about 11.30am on those days, docking at Berth 1.

At 3pm on Saturday and Monday, *Spirit of Tasmania III* departs for Sydney, following which the Melbourne ferry at Berth 3 moves stern first back up the river and into Berth 1, to prepare for its departure at 9pm.

The Devonport Port Authority will not allow two ships to be moving at the same time within the dock area, and this causes a series of movements to be made when it becomes necessary to have two of the TT Line ferries swap their berths during the day.

As the TT Line vessels always berth stern-in at Devonport, with their bows pointing away from the river entrance, it is necessary for them to execute a 180 degree turn in the river so they can depart.

This is completed in a wide section of the river, known as Port Frederick, and is quite an interesting manoeuvre to observe. With little space to spare, the huge ferries turn in their own

*Spirit of Tasmania III* alongside Berth 1 in Devonport, with *Spirit of Tasmania II* at Berth 3 (Peter Plowman photo)

Wednesday afternoon in Devonport, with *Spirit of Tasmania I* at Berth 1 and *Spirit of Tasmania III* at Berth 3 (Peter Plowman photo)

On Thursday morning *Spirit of Tasmania III* passes *Spirit of Tasmania II* as it heads out to sea to enable the two ferries to exchange berths (Peter Plowman photo)

*Spirit of Tasmania II* at Berth 3 in Devonport (Peter Plowman photo)

*Spirit of Tasmania II* moving astern from Berth 3 to Berth 1 (Peter Plowman photo)

length using their bow and stern side thrusters.

On Wednesday mornings the ferry that has arrived in Devonport from Melbourne again has to move to Berth 3 before *Spirit of Tasmania III* comes in from Sydney about 11.30 am. However, as *Spirit of Tasmania III* remains in Devonport overnight, it has to vacate Berth 1 later in the day, and move to Berth 3.

Once all the passengers, cars and cargo have been disembarked, *Spirit of Tasmania III* undocks, moves down river to the turning basin to turn around, and then heads out to sea.

Once *Spirit of Tasmania III* is clear of the Devonport docks, the Melbourne ferry at Berth 3 moves astern to go alongside Berth 1. Meanwhile *Spirit of Tasmania III* completes a slow 180 degree turn outside the entrance to the Mersey River, then re-enters the port, docking at Berth 3, where it remains overnight.

On Thursday morning about 10 am, *Spirit of Tasmania III* undocks from Berth 3, turns around and heads out to sea again, to allow the ferry that has arrived that morning from Melbourne to move from Berth 1 to Berth 3.

Once this has been completed, *Spirit of Tasmania III* comes back up the river to dock at Berth 1, departing the same afternoon at 3 pm. Soon after, the Melbourne ferry moves astern back to Berth 1, and departs that night at 9 pm.

On the night of Thursday, 18 March 2004, *Spirit of Tasmania II* departed Devonport on time, and soon was heading at speed across Bass Strait towards Melbourne. It was a cool night, with a 25 knot south-westerly wind blowing, and a 2.5 metre swell running, but not uncomfortable conditions for the passengers.

Suddenly, shortly after 10.30pm, came the cry that all seamen dread – 'Man Overboard!' It soon transpired that a passenger, who had clearly been in an agitated state when the ship left port, had jumped overboard when the ship was 40 nautical miles, about 75 kilometres, out from Devonport.

The alarm was raised by members of the crew who saw the man go overboard, and a life belt dropped into the water, which was a very cool 17°C. The captain responded by immediately turning the ship around, but by then it had travelled some distance from the spot where the man was last seen in the water, and took some time to locate the life belt.

A search began as *Spirit of Tasmania II* moved slowly, shining a searchlight on the dark water, but there was no sign of the missing man. The incident was immediately reported to the Australian Maritime Safety Authority, which resulted in three more ships, two night vision-equipped helicopters and a fixed-wing aircraft arriving on the search scene over the next few hours.

From first light the next morning three helicopters, a fixed-wing aircraft and the Royal Australian Navy survey vessel, HMAS *Melville*,

*Spirit of Tasmania II* berthed at Station Pier in Melbourne (Peter Plowman photo)

joined the search. *Spirit of Tasmania II* was released to continue its journey to Melbourne, where it berthed ten hours late, at 3.30 pm.

Disembarking passengers described the man, who jumped from the ship, said to be in his late 40s, as 'obviously disturbed' and 'strange'. One said she had noticed the man just after she boarded the ferry. 'He was acting rather strange and abusing passengers –swearing at them'. An English backpacker said the man had 'made a real impact on the ship. He was disruptive. Everyone said he was drunk'.

Another passenger said he saw the man push a 'little Canadian girl out of the way when trying to board'. A Devonport man had talked to the man he knew as Matthew some time before he jumped. "He was all right but he was going crook because he wanted a smoke and he reckoned he shouldn't have to go outside."

A TT Line spokesman said the man was being attended by a nurse and security staff when he broke free and jumped overboard. A security guard had left to get handcuffs for the man but he was not told he would be handcuffed or detained in a cell on board.

When the man had first become agitated, security staff had managed to calm him down, but he became agitated again and a nurse was called. The man calmed down again, and the nurse was going to provide him with medication when he became agitated for a third time. He appeared to calm down once more and everyone

relaxed, then he suddenly said, 'I'm going', ran to the railing and jumped.

The search for the missing man by aircraft and naval vessels continued through Friday and into Saturday before it was called off. Experts believe he would probably have died within an hour of jumping into the water because he appeared to be drunk, was wearing heavy clothing, the sea was choppy, and he had fallen about 15 metres when jumping from the ship. This was the first such incident since TT Line took over the Bass Strait service almost twenty years earlier.

The 2004 Easter holiday was another busy period for the TT Line ships. From Thursday, 8 April to Monday, 12 April, the three vessels made a total of 23 voyages to and from Tasmania.

On Easter Sunday, *Spirit of Tasmania I* and *Spirit of Tasmania II* each made two trips across Bass Strait, while *Spirit of Tasmania III* arrived in Sydney in the morning and left again the same afternoon for Devonport.

Between them the three ships had over 8,000 passengers on board during the day, and as a special treat every one received a chocolate Easter egg, while all children travelling on other days over the long weekend also were given a chocolate egg.

On the afternoon of Sunday, 2 May, *Spirit of Tasmania III* departed Sydney for Devonport, with about 150 passengers on board. All went well at first as the vessel passed down the New South Wales coastline, but towards midnight,

The viewing deck is a popular spot on *Spirit of Tasmania III* (Peter Plowman photo)

Leaving a straight wake, *Spirit of Tasmania III* crosses a very placid Bass Strait on 11 February 2004 (Peter Plowman photo)

*Spirit of Tasmania III* arriving in Devonport on 11 February 2004, with *Searoad Tamar* at Berth 2 and *Spirit of Tasmania II* at Berth 3 (Peter Plowman photo)

when *Spirit of Tasmania III* was approaching Gabo Island, sea conditions worsened, and a reduction in speed was required.

That night a major storm was sweeping across Bass Strait from the west, with 50 knot winds churning up heavy seas, raising waves up to ten metres high. Heading straight into the huge waves, the vessel was pitching heavily, with a loud bang each time a wave hit the bow. Many of the passengers became seasick, and were treated

quickly by medical staff on board. Any moveable objects in the public rooms and cabins were thrown about, and some passengers were almost tossed out of their beds at times.

At about 3 o'clock on Monday morning, when the vessel was six nautical miles south-south-east of Gabo Island and entering Bass Strait, a freak wave crashed over the bow and slammed into the freight door on deck 5. The impact snapped the weld at the bottom of the door, which was pushed in almost a metre, and hit nine cars. The damage to the cars was minor, ranging from a broken number plate to a dented side panel.

Although the damaged door did not affect the structural integrity or safety of the ship, the captain prudently reduced speed further to prevent spray entering the upper garage deck through the open door. As an extra safety precaution, passengers were advised on evacuation procedures should they become necessary. Despite the frightening conditions, passengers did not show any signs of panic, and after the voyage were universal in their praise of the crew of the ship.

With the reduction in speed, *Spirit of Tasmania III* did not reach Devonport until 7.30 on Monday night, eight hours late. With *Spirit*

A bow view of *Spirit of Tasmania III* (Dale Crisp photo)

*Spirit of Tasmania III* entering Devonport on 19 February 2004 while transferring from Berth 3 to Berth 1 (Peter Plowman photo)

*Spirit of Tasmania III* departing Devonport, with *Spirit of Tasmania II* in the background (Peter Plowman photo)

*Spirit of Tasmania III* passing the Sydney Opera House as it arrives in Sydney Harbour (Mel Gatehouse photo)

*Spirit of Tasmania III* at berth 3 in Devonport (Peter Plowman photo)

*of Tasmania II* docked at Berth 1 and loading passengers and vehicles for its 9 pm departure for Melbourne, *Spirit of Tasmania III* was forced to go to Berth 3, where it docked bow-in.

This caused some complications for passengers without vehicles, who had to be transported on buses from the ship to the main terminal, while the cars had to be re-organised for a bow door landing.

*Spirit of Tasmania III* had been scheduled to depart Devonport at 3 pm on Monday afternoon for Sydney, but the late arrival combined with the necessity to repair the damaged door resulted in that voyage being cancelled. This also affected the planned return trip from Sydney on Tuesday, disrupting the travel plans of 420 booked passengers,

for whom alternative arrangements were made.

Instead *Spirit of Tasmania III* remained in Devonport at Berth 3. It was decided that rather than repair the damaged door, it would be removed completely, as it was never used, and the opening was sealed up permanently with a steel sheet. The vessel returned to service with a scheduled departure from Devonport on Thursday, 6 May.

On the night of Tuesday 11 May, *Spirit of Tasmania III* again encountered gale force winds and high seas on its voyage to Devonport. For the comfort of passengers the captain slowed the ship, with the result that it was more than nine

*Spirit of Tasmania III* berthing in Darling Harbour, Sydney (Peter Plowman photo)

hours late arriving in Devonport.

*Spirit of Tasmania III* continued to operate three return trips a week between Sydney and Devonport until 31 May 2004. The schedule was then reduced to just two return trips a week for the winter, with the Monday departure from Devonport and Tuesday return trip from Sydney being dropped.

From 17 July to 8 August 2004 there was no service between Sydney and Devonport at all. During this period *Spirit of Tasmania III* was transferred to the overnight run between Melbourne and Devonport while each of the ferries regularly operating that service to be withdrawn in turn for an overhaul.

This enabled TT Line to maintain a regular nightly departure from both Melbourne and Devonport, though it did create some booking problems, as the layout of *Spirit of Tasmania III* is quite different from the other ships.

*Spirit of Tasmania I* was the first of the Melbourne ships to be withdrawn, arriving in Sydney on the morning of Sunday, 18 July, and and going straight into the Captain Cook Graving Dock in the ADFI facility at GArden Island.

*Spirit of Tasmania I* was refloated on 28 July, and left Sydney immediately, resuming service on the night of 29 July. *Spirit of Tasmania II* arrived in Sydney on 30 July, also going straight into the dry dock. It was refloated on 9 August,

and also went straight back to Melbourne to resume service on 10 August.

On Thursday, 12 August, *Spirit of Tasmania III* returned to the Sydney service, still operating only two trips a week. The regular schedule of three trips a week resumed from Monday, 30 August, when the shoulder season fares commenced on both routes.

Peak season fares became effective from 10 December until 30 January 2005, and it was also during this period that a fare of $55 each way was charged for accompanied vehicles.

It is quite amazing how much the ferry service from the mainland to Tasmania has developed in a very short time.

As recently as 2002 there was but one ferry making three return trips a week between Melbourne and Devonport, capable of transporting some 8,500 passenger a week.

Today there is a nightly departure from both these terminals, providing up to 2,000 passages a day. During peak periods, when both night and day trips are being operated, almost 20,000 passengers can be carried in each direction in a week.

In addition, the service between Sydney and Devonport has the capacity to transport about 150,000 passengers in each direction during the year.

There is no doubt that Tasmania is now enjoying the best ferry service ever provided between the mainland and the island state.

*Spirit of Tasmania I* in Devonport (Peter Plowman photo)

# Bibliography

**Books**

Bach, John, *A Maritime History of Australia*, Thomas Nelson (Australia) Limited, Melbourne, 1976

Bateson, Charles, *Dire Strait*, A H & A W Reed, Sydney, 1973)

Cox, G W, *Bass Strait Crossing*, Melanie Publications, Hobart, 1986

*Ships in Tasmanian Waters*, Fuller's Bookshop Publishing Division, Hobart, 1971

Diamond, Marion, Ben *Boyd of Boydtown*, Melbourne University Press, 1995)

Fitchett, T K, *The Vanished Fleet* (Rigby Limited, Adelaide, 1976

Jeremy, John, *Cockatoo Island*, UNSW Press, Sydney, 1998

Pemberton, Barry, *Australian Coastal Shipping*, Melbourne University Press, 1979

Plowman, Peter, *Passenger Ships of Australia & New Zealand*, Vol 1 & Vol 2, Doubleday Australia, Sydney, 1980

*The Wheels Still Turn*, Kangaroo Press, Sydney, 1992

Plummer, Russell, *Super-Ferries of Britain, Scandinavia, and Europe*, Patrick Stephens Ltd, Wellingborough, 1988

Robson, Lloyd, *A History of Tasmania*, Oxford University Press, Melbourne, 1991

**Newspapers, Periodicals & Magazines**

*The Age*

*The Argus*

*Australian Sea Heritage*

*Daily Commercial News & Shipping List*

*The Log*

*Marine News*

*Sydney Morning Herald*

World Ship Society NSW Branch Newsletter

World Ship Society Victoria Branch Newsletter

A stern view of *Spirit of Tasmania I* at Devonport (Peter Plowman photo)

# Index